KB035689

북한 핵 문제

IAEA 핵안전조치 협정 체결 6

북한 핵 문제

IAEA 핵안전조치 협정 체결 6

한국학술정보

| 머리말

1985년 북한은 소련의 요구로 핵확산금지조약(NPT)에 가입한다. 그러나 그로부터 4년 뒤, 60년대 소련이 영변에 조성한 북한의 비밀 핵 연구단지 사진이 공개된다. 냉전이 종속되어 가던 당시 북한은 이로 인한 여러 국제사회의 경고 및 외교 압력을 받았으며, 1990년 국제원자력기구(IAEA)는 북핵 문제에 대해 강력한 사찰을 추진한다. 북한은 영변 핵시설의 사찰 조건으로 남한 내 미군기지 사찰을 요구하는 등 여러 이유를 댔으나 결국 3차에 걸친 남북 핵협상과 남북핵통제공동위원회 합의 등을 통해 이를 수용하였고, 결국 1992년 안전조치협정에도 서명하겠다고 발표한다. 그러나 그로부터 1년 뒤 북한은 한미 합동훈련의 재개에 반대하며 IAEA의 특별사찰을 거부하고 NPT를 탈퇴한다. 이에 UN 안보리는 대북 제재를 실행하면서 1994년 제네바 합의 전까지 남북 관계는 극도로 경직되게 된다.

본 총서는 외교부에서 작성하여 최근 공개한 1991~1992년 북한 핵 문제 관련 자료를 담고 있다. 북한의 핵안전조치협정의 체결 과정과 북한 핵시설 사찰 과정, 그와 관련된 미국의 동향과 일본, 러시아, 중국 등 우방국 협조와 관련한 자료까지 총 14권으로 구성되었다. 전체 분량은 약 7천여 쪽에 이른다.

2024년 3월

한국학술정보(주)

| 일러두기

· 본 총서에 실린 자료는 2022년 4월과 2023년 4월에 각각 공개한 외교문서 4,827권, 76만여 쪽 가운데 일부를 발췌한 것이다.

· 각 권의 제목과 순서는 공개된 원본을 최대한 반영하였으나, 주제에 따라 일부는 적절히 변경하였다.

· 원본 자료는 A4 판형에 맞게 축소하거나 원본 비율을 유지한 채 A4 페이지 안에 삽입하였다. 또한 현재 시점에선 공개되지 않아 '공란'이란 표기만 있는 페이지 역시 그대로 실었다.

· 외교부가 공개한 문서 각 권의 첫 페이지에는 '정리 보존 문서 목록'이란 이름으로 기록물 종류, 일자, 명칭, 간단한 내용 등의 정보가 수록되어 있으며, 이를 기준으로 0001번부터 번호가 매겨져 있다. 이는 삭제하지 않고 총서에 그대로 수록하였다.

· 보고서 내용에 관한 더 자세한 정보가 필요하다면, 외교부가 온라인상에 제공하는 『대한민국 외교사료요약집』 1991년과 1992년 자료를 참조할 수 있다.

| 차례

정 리 보 존 문 서 목 록					
기록물종류	일반공문서철	등록번호	2020040099	등록일자	2020-04-10
분류번호	726.62	국가코드		보존기간	영구
명 칭	북한.IAEA(국제원자력기구) 간의 핵안전조치협정 체결, 1991-92. 전15권				
생 산 과	국제기구과/국제연합1과	생산년도	1991~1992	담당그룹	
권 차 명	V.14 IAEA 2월 이사회 관련 협조 요청				
내용목차	* 대북한 비준 촉구 발언 교섭				

0001

공 란

공 란

공 란

공 란

공 란

공 란

공 란

공 란

공 란

공 란

공 란

공 란

공 란

공 란

공 란

공 란

공 란

공 란

공 란

공 란

공 란

공 란

공　란

공 란

공　　란

공 란

공 

공 란

공 란

공 란

공 란

공 란

공 란

공 란

공 란

공 란

공 란

공　　　란

공　　란

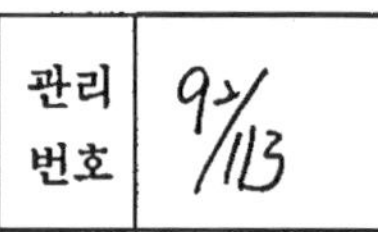

외 무 부

종 별 :

번 호 : COW-0057 일 시 : 92 0217 1705

수 신 : 장관(국기,미중) 사본:주오스트리아대사-중계필

발 신 : 주 코스타리카 대사

제 목 : IAEA 2월 이사회 대책

대:WCO-0018

1. 금 17 일 정참사관은 외무성 MONGE 국기과장을 방문, 대호 관련 구상서를 수교, 협조 요청한바 동 과장은 상부에 적극 건의, 조치하겠다고 하였음.

2. 소직은 MELVIN SAENZ 대외정책국장(2.18), 외상대리(외무차관)등 면담코, 동건 재 다짐 확인후 결과 추보하겠음. 끝.

(대사 김창근-장관)

예고:92.6.30 일반

일반문서로 재분류(1992.6.30.) 이

국기국 미주국 중계

PAGE 1

92.02.18 08:39

외신 2과 통제관 BN

0040

공 란

공 란

공 란

2/19 신

관리 번호	92-113

원 본

외 무 부

3

종 별 :

번 호 : IRW-0091 일 시 : 92 0218 1630

수 신 : 장관(국기,사본:주오지리대사-중계필)

발 신 : 주 이란 대사

제 목 : IAEA 이사회 대책

대:WIR-0089

1. 당관 엄공사는 금 2.18 1400-1500 SCHAVESTERI 주재국 외무부 한국과장을 접촉(김서기관동석) 대호 지시에의거 표제회의와 관련한 아측입장을 상세설명하고, 주재국이 이사국으로서 금번회의시 아측입장을 강력지지하는 발언을 하여줄것을 요청함.

2. 동인은 주관부서에 동요청사항을 상세전달, 회의참석 자국대표단이 아국대표단과 긴밀히 협조 아국의 입장이 반영될수있도록 하겠다고 하였음. 끝

(대사정경일-국장)

예고:92.12.31 일반

국기국 중계

PAGE 1

92.02.19 04:56

외신 2과 통제관 FM

0044

공　　　란

공 란

관리 번호 121

원 본

외 무 부

종 별 :

번 호 : MXW-0170 일 시 : 92 0218 1700

수 신 : 장관(국기,미중,기정,사본:주오지리대사-중계필)

발 신 : 주 멕시코 대사

제 목 : IAEA 2월이사회 대책

대:WMX-0080,0074, EM-5

1. 본직은 금 2.18. 12:30 부터 약 30 분간 외무성 유엔국장 O.PELLICER 대사를 면담하고 북한이 핵안정협정 서명후에도 비준, 발효 일정에대한 입장이 모호하고 시일을 끌고있어 국제적으로 북한 진의에대한 의구심과 우려가 대두되고 있음을 지적, 주재국이 세계적으로 최초의 지역 비핵화노력(TREATY OF TLALTELOLCO)의 이니시아티브를 창출한 국가로서 또한 남. 북간의 한반도 비핵화 공동선언에대한 중요성을 부여. 주재국으로서는 이례적인 외무성 환영 성명(92.1.7. 자)을 발표한 사례등에도 언급, 2 월 이사회에서 대호 2. 가, 나항 요지에따라 강력 발언하여 줄것을 요청하고 아울러 최근의 한-멕 실질관계 발전사항등에 관해 설명해줌.

2. 국장은 최근 비엔나 주재 자국대사가 업무협의차 일시귀국, 작 2.17 귀임하였음을 알리고 아측 입장의 타당성을 충분히 이해한다 하면서 금명 비엔나에타전, 대호 요지를 알리고 아국대사와 긴밀히 협조토록 하겠다고 약속함.

(대사이복형-국장)

예고:1992.12.31. 일반

검토필 (1992.6.20)

국기국	장관	차관	1차보	2차보	미주국	외정실	분석관	청와대
안기부	중계							

PAGE 1 92.02.19 08:32

외신 2과 통제관 BX

0047

2/19 신

관리번호	92-117

원 본

외 무 부

3

종 별 :

번 호 : COW-0059 일 시 : 92 0218 1715

수 신 : 장관(국기,미중)사본:주오스트리아대사-중계필

발 신 : 주 코스타리카 대사

제 목 : IAEA 2월이사회 대책

연:COW-0057

대:WCO-0018

1. 연호 외무성 VICTOR MONGE 국제기구과장은 금 18 일 주 IAEA "코"대표부FELIX PRZEBORSKI 대사에게 IAEA 2 월 이사회에 참석, 대호 "2"항의 아국입장 지지발언과 동건 관련 비엔나주재 아국대표부와의 긴밀한 협조를 하고, 동 조치결과를 보고토록 지시하는 요지의 공문(연호 DGPE/SGPM/0111/92, 92.2.18)을 발송(FAX 편) 하였음.

2. 입수된 동 공한사본 파편 송부 위계임.끝.

(대사 김창근-장관)

예고:92.6.30 일반

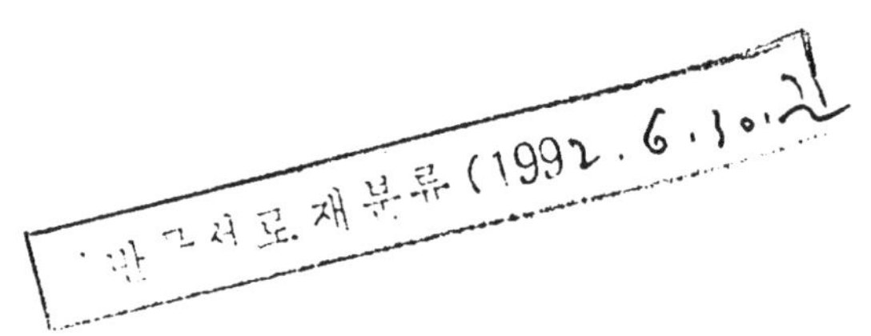

국기국	1차보	미주국	외정실	분석관	청와대	안기부	중계

PAGE 1

92.02.19 08:48

외신 2과 통제관 BX

0048

2/19.신

관리 번호	92-119

원 본

외 무 부

종 별 :

번 호 : MOW-0078 일 시 : 92 0218 1530

수 신 : 장관(국기,중동이)사본:주오지리대사(본부중계필)

발 신 : 주 모로코대사

제 목 : IAEA 2월 이사회

대:WM 주재국(047)0035,0040

대호 IAEA 2 월 이사회의 핵안전조치 강화 방안및 북한의 핵안전협정 비준문제에 대하여 2.18. 당관 박대원 참사관의 주재국 외무성 베라다 국제기구 과장접촉 결과를 다음과 같이 보고함.

1. 핵안전조치 강화문제

-주재국의 기본 입장은 지구상에서 핵무기가 존재하지 않도록 하는 것임.

-따라서 금번 이사회에서의 핵안전 조치 강화 협의를 대 환영함.

-그러나 핵안전 조치와 사찰등이 강화될수록 많은 예산이 소요될 것이며 모로코와 같은 개발도상국가는 동 예산이 기술협력비용에 더 사용되기를 바라고 있음.

-모로코는 금번 회의에서 핵안전 조치가 더욱 강화되기를 바라는 입장이나 아울러 자금 사용이 개도국에 적절하게 부여되는 방안도 아울러 제기할 것이라함.

2. 북한의 핵안전협정 비준 문제

-국제협약의 비준은 전적으로 국내문제에 해당하는 사항임으로 모로코는 북한에 대하여 압력을 행사할수가 없으나 금번 회의에서 북한대표에게 남북한의 불신을 해소하는 지름길이 북한의 핵협정 조속 비준임을 설득시킬 예정이라고함.

3. 당지 미국대사관은 핵안전조치 강화문제에 대하여, 일본및 호주대사관은북한의 협정 비준문제에 대하여 각각일신로 외무성을 접촉한바 위와 같은 모로코의 입장을 설명하였다하며 금번 회의시 아국 대표단이 모로코대표단(대표: 주오지리 모로코대사)을 접촉해 줄것을 요망함. 끝

(대사허리훈-국장)

예고:92.6.30 일반

국기국	장관	차관	1차보	2차보	중아국	외정실	분석관	청와대
안기부	중계							

PAGE 1 92.02.19 10:36

외신 2과 통제관 BX

0049

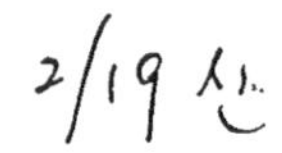

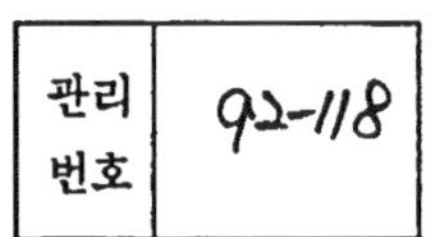

원 본

외 무 부

종 별 :

번 호 : DEW-0079　　　　일 시 : 92 0218 1600

수 신 : 장관(국기)

발 신 : 주 덴마크 대사

제 목 : IAEA 2월 이사회 대책

대:WDE-0058

1. 본직은 금 2.18. 주재국 외무부 HENRIK WOHLK 차관을 면담(김성엽 참사관 배석), 대호 관련 아측 입장을 설명하는 메모렌덤을 수교하고 주재국의 협조를 요청한바, 동 차관은 아측 요청이 덴마크 외교정책과도 부합한다고 말하고 현지(비엔나) 대표로 하여금 최대한을 아측 입장지지토록 지시하겠다고 말함.

2. 동 차관은 동 건이 EC 차원에서도 면밀히 주시 대처해야 할 사항이라말함. 끝.

(대사 김세택-국장)

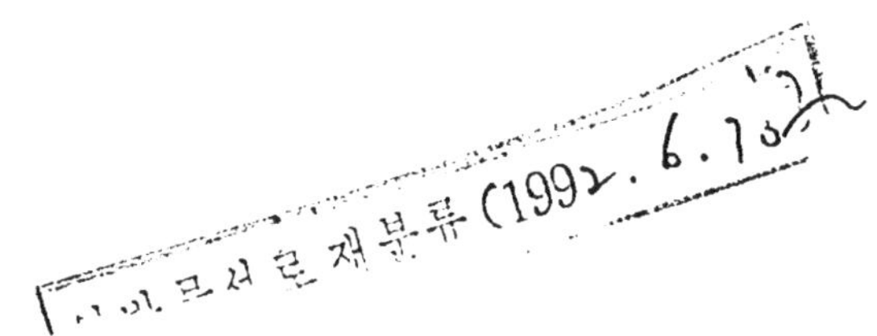

국기국　장관　차관　구주국　외정실　분석관

PAGE 1　　　　92.02.19　10:51

외신 2과　통제관 BN

0050

공 란

공 란

2/19 신

관리번호	92-132

3 원 본

외 무 부

종 별 :

번 호 : RMW-0080 일 시 : 92 0218 1810

수 신 : 장관(국기, 사본:주오지리 대사)

발 신 : 주 루마니아 대사

제 목 : IAEA 2월이사회 대책

대:WRM-0068

1. 본직(채참사관 수행))은 금 2.18 ENE 외무차관 (국제기구 관할)을 면담하고 대호 훈령관련 주재국의 지지를 요청함.

2. 동차관은 아국입장을 지지하며 자국대표단에게도 아국대표단과 접촉, 아국입장 지지토록 훈령하겠다고 약속함.

3. 동차관에 의하면 수일전 주재국 주재 북한대사가 자기를 방문, 북한이 조속 핵안전협정을 비준토록 압력을 받고 있다고 말하면서 자국내 절차에 의하여2-3 개월이 소요될 것이라며 북한측 입장을 이행해 주도록 요청이 있었다함. 동대사는 이어 일본의 북로토늄 소유현실을 언급하면서 이를 북한의 비준입장과 연계시키는 듯한 의견제시가 있었는바, 동차관은 비준문제와 직접 관련이없는 문제가 아니냐고 그 비논리성을 지적하였다함.

4. 동차관은 명 2.19 주재국 주재 미국, 일본, 카나다 대사의 요청에 의해 본건관련 이들과 면담예정이라 함. 끝.

(대사 이현홍-장관)

예고:92.12.31 일반

검토필 (1992.6.20.)

국기국	장관	차관	1차보	2차보	구주국	청와대	안기부	중계

PAGE 1 92.02.19 14:14

외신 2과 통제관 BN

0053

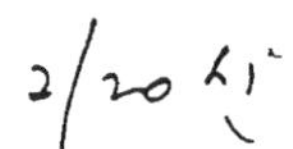

관리 번호	92-132

원 본

외 무 부

종 별 :

번 호 : CAW-0157 일 시 : 92 0219 1345

수 신 : 장 관(국기) 사본:주오지리대사-중계필

발 신 : 주 카이로 총영사

제 목 : IAEA 2월 이사회 대책

대:WCA-0074

.1. 대호관련 2.19 당관 공선섭부총영사가 주재국 외무부 본건담당 AWADALLAH 참사관에 그 협조를 요청하였던바, 이를 현지 공관에 훈령 협조토록 하겠다고 하였음.

2. 동회의에 본부인사는 파견되지 않는다함.

3. 본직은 92.2.22 국제기구국장을 면담 본건 재확인 예정임.끝.

(총영사 박동순-국장)

예고:92.6.30. 일반

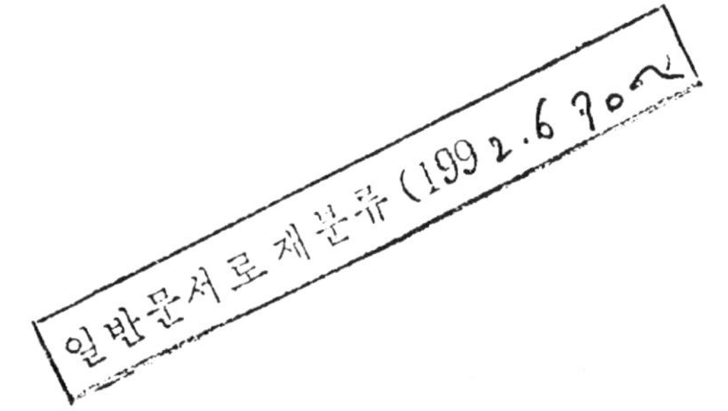

국기국 중계

PAGE 1

92.02.19 20:50

외신 2과 통제관 BS

0054

2/20 신

관리번호	92-134

원 본

외 무 부

종 별 :

번 호 : GEW-0330 일 시 : 92 0219 1130

수 신 : 장관(국기) 사본:주오지리대사(직송필)

발 신 : 주 독 대사

제 목 : IAEA 2월 이사회대책

대:WGE-0204

1. 대호관련 2.18. 안공사는 연구기술부 LOOSCH 국장(IAEA 독일측 이사)을 면담 협의한바 아래보고함

가. 안공사는 대호내용을 상세히 설명하고, 독일측의 적극적인 협조를 당부한바, 동국장은 가능한 협조를 다하겠다고 함

0 90.6 월 및 9 월 IAEA 이사회에서 동국장은 북한의 조속한 핵안전협정 서명, 발효조치(비준)및 이행을 촉구하여 온바 있으며, 북한이 이제 서명은 하였음으로 나머지 두가지(발효조치 및 이행)를 강력히 촉구코자 함

0 IAEA 이사회에서 분명한 대북한 입장을 이룩함이 중요한바, 이를 위해 적극 노력코자함

0 북한이 핵안전협정 비준 이전이라도 비준후의 이행을 위한 사전준비 조치로서 북한내 핵시설에 관한 자료(정보)를 제출토록 하는 방안 추진을 구상하고 있음

나. LOOSCH 국장(이사)는 2.21(금) 오전 10 시에 개최예정인 IAEA 이사회 비공식 회합에 참석예정이라고 하는바, 현지에서 동인과 접촉, 구체적인 협조방안 협의를 건의함

2. 2.19. 전부관 참사관은 상기 이사회에 LOOSCH 국장을 수행, 참석예정인 외무부 DR.PREISINGER 핵문제담당 부과장을 면담한바, 동인은 주재국 대표가 북한이 핵안전협정 비준및 이행을 강력 촉구하는 발언을 하도록 적극 협조하겠다고말함. 동인에 의하면 본건 관련 비엔나 현지에서 EC 회원국간 상호 긴밀한 협의가 있을 것이라고 함을 참고로 보고함. 끝 (대사-장관)

예고:92.12.31. 일반

국기국 장관 차관 분석관 안기부

PAGE 1

92.02.20 00:37

외신 2과 통제관 FK

0055

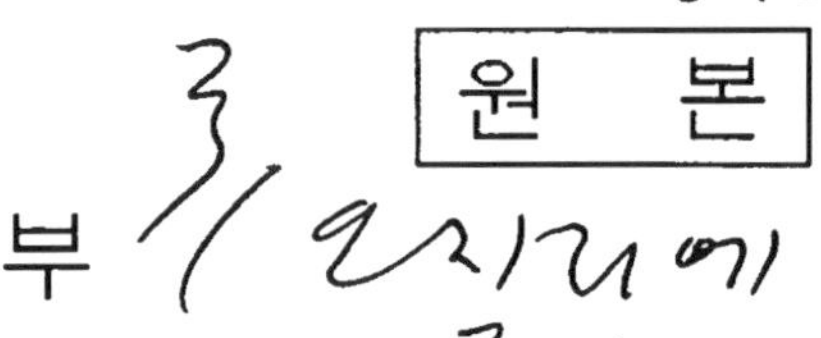

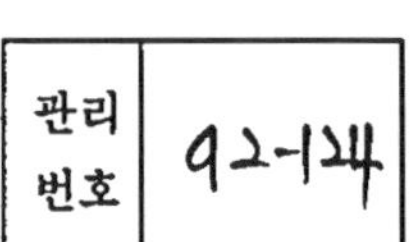

외 무 부

종 별 :

번 호 : EQW-0053 일 시 : 92 0219 1200

수 신 : 장관(국기,미남)

발 신 : 주 에쿠아돌 대사

제 목 : IAEA 이사회

대: WEQ-0020, 0022, 0026

1. 본직은 금 2. 19 외무부 RAMIRO SILVA 국제기구국장을 면담, 표제회의에대호 내용의 아국입장 지지를 요청한 바, 동국장은 관계관과 협의, 현지 대표단에게 아국입장을 지지토록 금명간 훈령하겠다고 함.

2. 주재국은 금번 표제회의에 주 오지리 대사 및 참사관이 대표단으로 참석예정이라 하는 바, 현지에서도 주재국 대표단에 재확인 바람. 끝.

(대사 정해융 - 국장)

예고 : 92. 6. 30 일반

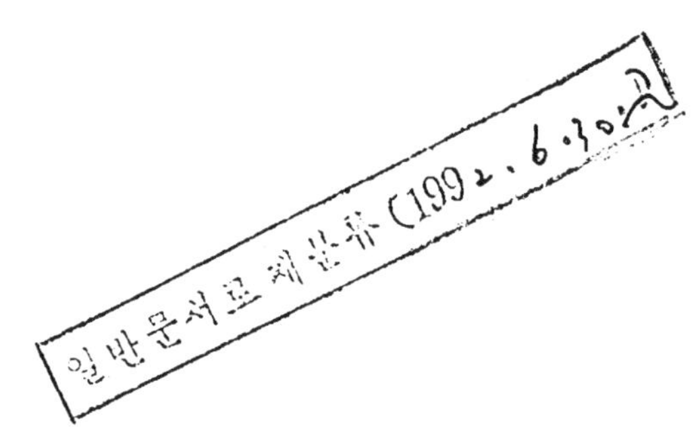

국기국 미주국

PAGE 1

92.02.20 04:25

외신 2과 통제관 FK

0056

2/20 신

관리번호	92-131

원 본

외 무 부

종 별 :

번 호 : BLW-0131 일 시 : 92 0219 1730

수 신 : 장관(국기,동구이)사본:주오지리대사(중계필)

발 신 : 주 불가리아 대사

제 목 : IAEA 이사회 대책

대:WBL-0074

1. 당관 방참사관은 2.19(목) 주재국 외무부 제 6 국(국제기구 및 유엔 담당) RADOSLAV DEYANOV 국장대리를 방문, 대호 이사회 회의시 불가리아 정부의 대북한 핵안전협정 조기비준 및 완전이행 강력 촉구 등을 요청한 바, 동 국장대리는 자국정부가 아국정부와 같은 LINE 의 핵안전 정책을 추구하고 있다고 하면서,비엔나에 있는 자국 대표단에게 아측 요청 내용을 통보, 아국대표와 적극 협력하도록 지시하겠다고 함.

2. 동 국장대리는 최근 EC 국가가 북한에 대하여 핵안전협정 조기비준 및 완전이행을 촉구하는 내용의 성명을 이미 발표한 바 있다고 설명하면서, 동 촉구가 이미 국제여론화되고 있음을 시사함. 끝.

(대사 김좌수-국장)

예고:92.6.30 일반

일반문서로 재분류 (1992. 6. 30.)

국기국 구주국 중계

PAGE 1

92.02.20 04:39

외신 2과 통제관 FK

0057

2/20 신이

관리번호	92-127

원 본

외 무 부

종 별 :

번 호 : HGW-0121 일 시 : 92 0219 1800

수 신 : 장관(국기,동구이,사본:주오지리대사-중계필)

발 신 : 주 헝가리 대사

제 목 : IAEA 2월 이사회 대책

대:WHG-0083

본직은 금 2.19. 외무부 국제기구국 ENDREFFY 국장을 방문(이원형 참사관 배석), 금번 IAEA 2 월 이사회에서 주재국이 IAEA 의 옵서버국으로서 대호(2 항)요지로 발언하여 줄것을 강력히 요청한바, 동국장의 발언요지 다음 보고함.

1. 헝정부로서는 북한당국이 IAEA 와의 핵안전협정에 서명한것을 환영하며,동협정의 조속한 이행을 촉구하는 입장임.

2. 북한당국이 핵안전협정에 서명한 예를 보더라도 동 협정의 조속한 비준과 이행을 위하여서는 국제적 압력이 필요하다고 봄.

3. 헝가리는 옵서버국으로서 IAEA 2 월 이사회에서 발언할수 있는 기회가 주어질런지는 확실하지 않으로, 발언기회가 주어지는 경우에는 핵무기 비확산문제에 관한 헝정부의 입장과 함께 북한의 핵사찰문제도 언급하는데 최선을 다하겠음.

4. 본직의 요청을 비엔나소재 IAEA 상주대표인 VILMOS CSERVENY (IAEA 2 월이사회 헝정부 수석대표)에게도 통보하고, 현지(비엔나)에서 한국대표와 긴밀해 협조하도록 훈령하겠음. 끝.

(대사 박영우-장관)

예고:92.12.31. 일반

국기국 구주국 중계

PAGE 1 92.02.20 04:47

외신 2과 통제관 FK

0058

2/20 신
서열 수요

관리 번호	92-126

원 본

외 무 부

종 별 :

번 호 : ITW-0196 일 시 : 92 0219 1820

수 신 : 장관(국기)

발 신 : 주 이태리 대사

제 목 : IAEA 2월 이사회대책

대:WIT-0114

1. 당관 문참사관은 금 2.19. 주재국 외무성 IAEA 담당관 DELLA CROCE 참사관과 면담, 북한이 아직도 핵안전 협정 비준및 발효에 관한 명확한 일정을 밝히지 않고 있음에 우려를 표명하면서 대호 아측 입장을 설명하고 금번 이사회에서 북한에 대한 강력한 발언과 현지 아국대표와의 긴밀한 협조를 하여 줄것을 요청하였음.

2. 동참사관은 지난 1.31. EPC 회의에서 채택, 발표한 대북한 조기비준촉구선언문을 상기하면서 당시 EPC 회의에서 일부대표는 서명후 비준까지는 다소의시일이 소요될것임을 감안 조기 비준을 촉구하는 내용을 포함시키는데에 회의적인 태도를 보였으나 1 개국 대표가 북한의 정치체제로 보아 비준의사만 있으면곧 비준할 수 있다는 점을 강조하여 동 내용이 채택되었다고 밝히고 이태리도 동문제에 깊은 관심을 가지고 있으며 아국의 입장에 동의하나 자국이 옵서버국임에 비추어 아국의 요청사항을 협의한 후 방침이 결정되는 대로 알려 주겠다고 답하였음.

3. 한편 본직은 작 2.18. BUTINI 정무차관에 대한 이임인사시 상기 아국 입장을 설명하고 이태리측의 적극적인 지원을 요청한 바, 동차관은 아국의 입장에 동조하면서 이것이 이태리의 PERMANENT LINE 이라고 밝힘.끝

(대사 김석규-국장)

예고:92.6.30. 일반

국기국

PAGE 1

92.02.20 04:49

외신 2과 통제관 FK

0059

2/20 신

관리번호	92-130

원 본

외 무 부

종 별 :

번 호 : PDW-0159 일 시 : 92 0219 1500

수 신 : 장관(국기, 사본 : 주 오지리 대사(중계필))

발 신 : 주 폴란드 대사

제 목 : IAEA 이사회

대 : WPD-0096

대호관련, 최참사관은 2.19 외무성 핵문제담당 TADEUSZ STRULAK 대사(91 년초까지 비엔나주재 국제기구 대사역임)와 면담, 2 월말 IAEA 이사회시 발언 및 아국 대표단과의 긴밀 협조를 요청한바, 폴란드는 기존의 북한 핵개발 반대 정책에 따라 동 회의에 임할것이며 현지 대표부(폴측은 외무성 대표는 예산관계로 파견치 않는다고 함)에 아측과의 협조를 지시하겠다고 함. 끝 (참사관 최병효-국장)

예 고 : 92.6.30. 일반

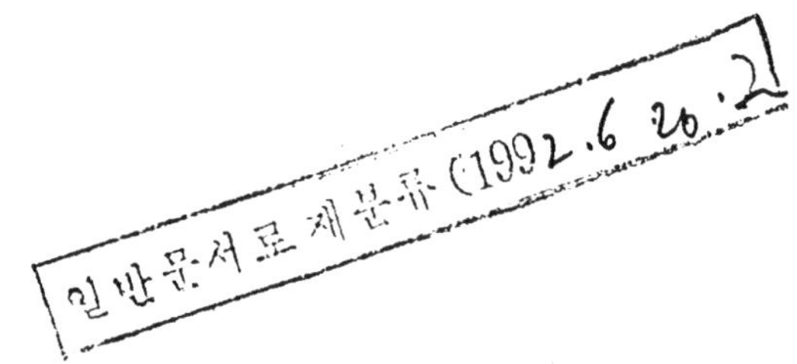

국기국 중계

PAGE 1

92.02.20 05:26

외신 2과 통제관 FK

0060

2/20 신.

관리번호	92-129

원 본

외 무 부

종 별 :

번 호 : IDW-0039 일 시 : 99 2 0219 1615

수 신 : 장관(국기)사본:주오지리대사관(직송필)

발 신 : 주 아일랜드대사

제 목 : IAEA 2월 이사회대책

대:WID-0030

1. 당관 유참사관은 2.19 P.MURNAGHAN 외무성 아태국장을 면담, 대호내용을설명하고 이에대한 주재국의협조를 요청하였음.

2. 동국장은 주재국은 한반도를 포함한 세계적인 군축및(054)비핵화등 세계평화를위한 노력에 특히관심이 높음을 설명하고 북한이 IAEA 이사회이전에 비준절차를 거치지않을경우 동이사회의 EC 회원국들과도 협의, 북한으로하여금 조속한비준및 국제핵사찰 허용을촉구토록 노력하겠다고 약속하였음. 연이나 동이사회이전에 비준절차가 완료되었을경우, 1.30 서명이후 단기간내에 동절차를 완료한점에 비추어 국제핵사찰도 조만간에 허용할것으로 간주될것이므로 일정기간 INTERVENTION 을 자제함이 좋을것 이라고언급 하였음. 끝

(대사민형기-국장)

예고:92.6.30 일반

일반문서로 재분류(1992.6.30.)

국기국

PAGE 1

92.02.20 06:16

외신 2과 통제관 FK

0061

2/20 신

관리 번호	92-128

원 본

외 무 부

종 별 :

번 호 : UKW-0279 일 시 : 92 0219 1830

수 신 : 장관(국기) 사본:주오지리대사-직송필

발 신 : 주 영 대사

제 목 : IAEA 2월 이사회대책

대: WUK-0281

2.19. 당관 최참사관은 BATEMAN 외무성 NPT 과장대리를 면담하고 대호 협조를 요청한 바, 동인은 주재국으로서도 북한의 핵개발 우려 해소를 위해 핵안전협정의 조기비준과 핵사찰 이행을 촉구하는 국제적인 노력이 필요하다고 보며, 이와같은 입장은 1.31. EC 선언문에서도 표명된바 있다하고, 대호 발언등에 관해 영국은 최대한 협조하겠으며 동 대책관련 한. 영간의 긴밀한 협의를 위해 비엔나주재 IAEA 자국대표부와도 협조하여 주기바란다고 하였음. 끝

(대사 이홍구-국장)

예고: 92.6.30 일반

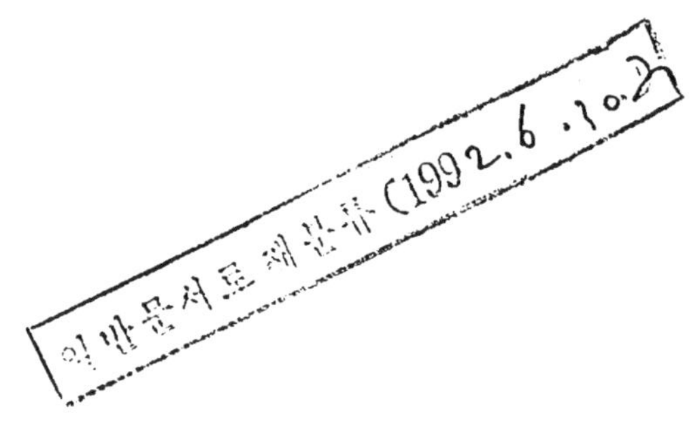

국기국

PAGE 1 92.02.20 06:20

외신 2과 통제관 FK

0062

2/20신

관리번호	92-137

3

외 무 부

종 별 :

번 호 : COW-0061 일 시 : 92 0219 1710

수 신 : 장관(미중,국기)

발 신 : 주 코스타리카 대사

제 목 : 외상대리 면담

대:WCO-0018

연:COW-0059

금 19 일 소직은 CASTRO 외상대리를 방문, 연호 IAEA 이사회에서의 자국대표에 대한 북한 핵안전협정 비준 및 핵사찰 수락촉구 연설지시 및 대전박람회 국제회의에 주재국 대표 파견결정에 사의를 표하고, 신임 주한대사 파견건 타진한바, CASTRO 차관은 (1)코스타리카가 북한 핵개발에 관심을 갖고 주시하고 있다면서 모든 협조를 하겠다하고, (2)신임대사건 현재 인선이 EXELENT 한 인물로 결정, 가급적 내주중 아그레망을 당관에 요청하겠다고 언급하였음(동 후임대사 성명등 외무성등 요로에 타진하였으나 상금 확인되지 않으며, 금일 사업가이며, DEPORTIVO SAPRISSA 프로 축구팀 PRESIDENT 인 FABIO GARNIER 씨가 당관을 방문, 대통령이 자기를 주한대사로 결정하였다면서 한국관계 자료등을 요청하였기 참고로보고함). 끝.

(대사 김창근-국장)

예고:92.12.31 일반

검토필 (1992. 6. 30.)

미주국 차관 국기국 의전장

PAGE 1 92.02.20 10:29

외신 2과 통제관 BN

0063

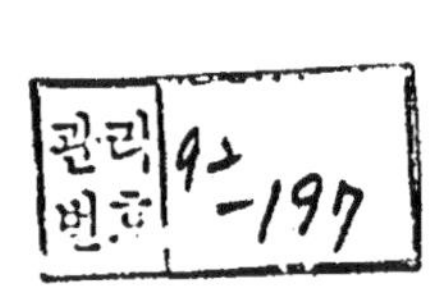

2/25신.

신뢰받는 정부되고 받쳐주는 국민되자

주 코 스 타 리 카 대 사 관

코스타(정)20332- 14 1992. 2. 20

수 신 장 관

참 조 국제기구국장, 미주국장

제 목 IAEA 2월 이사회 대책

연 : COW-0059

대 : WCO-0018

연호 표제 관련 주재국 외무성의 주 IAEA 대표부 앞 공문사본을 별첨 송부합니다.

첨 부 동 공문사본 1부.

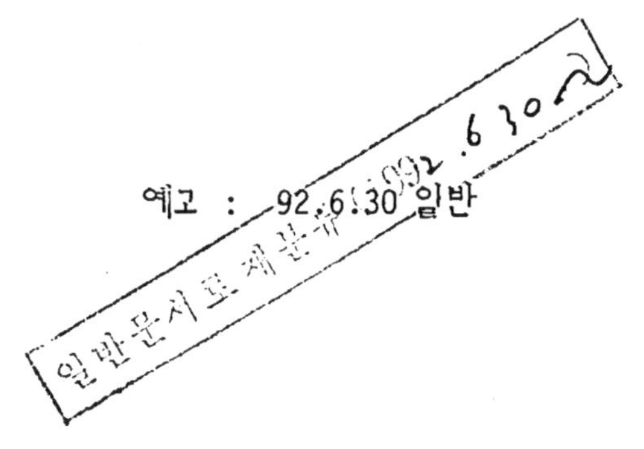

예고 : 92.6.30 일반

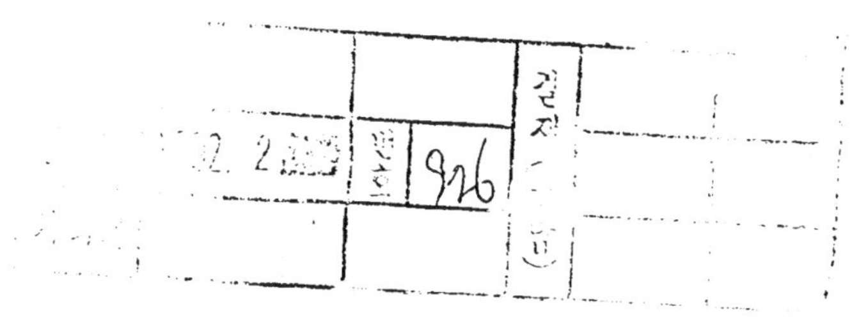

주 코 스 타 리 카 대

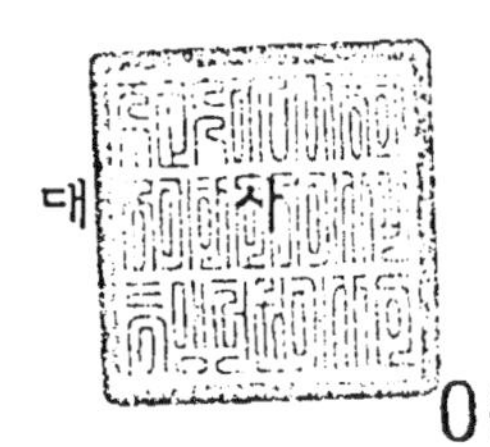

0064

DGPE/SGPM/0111/92

F.A.C.S.I.M.I.L.

PARA: SR. FELIX PRZEBORSKI,
EMBAJADOR, REPRESENTANTE PERMANENTE DE COSTA RICA
ANTE LA ORGANIZACION INTERNACIONAL DE ENERGIA
ATOMICA
FAX NO. 004317130541
VIENA, AUSTRIA

DE: SR. VICTOR ML. MONGE CHACON,
SUBDIRECTOR GENERAL DE POLITICA MULTILATERAL

FECHA: 18 DE FEBRERO DE 1992

NO. PAGINAS: 2

ASUNTO:

Hago de su conocimiento que el pasado 30 de enero del año en curso, Corea del Norte firmò el Acuerdo de Seguridad Nuclear y mencionò aceptar la ratificaciòn del Acuerdo y la inspecciòn internacional de sus facilidades nucleares por parte de la Agencia Internacional para la Energía Atómica.

A pesar de su compromiso, hasta la fecha, no ha mencionado una fecha concreta para que se lleve a cabo la ratificación y puesta en vigor del acuerdo.

En vista de lo anterior, ruego participar en la Junta de Gobernadores a efectuarse del 24 al 28 de febrero y cooperar estrechamente con la representación permanente de Corea del Sur y hacer uso de la palabra en los siguientes términos:

1.-) En caso de que Corea del Norte no ratifique el Acuerdo antes de la Junta de Gobernadores de febrero:

a) Expresar los sentimientos de bienvenida a Corea del Norte por la firma del Acuerdo de Seguridad Nuclear el pasado 30 de enero;

b) Urgir a Corea del Norte a ratificar y cumplir este Acuerdo, en un período de corto plazo, tal y como se mencionó en la Resolución de la Junta de Gobernadores de setiembre de 1991

02/18/92 15:07 ☎ 506 23 93 28 MINIST REL EXT.

0065

c) Solicitar al Secretario General informar a los países miembros de la Junta de Gobernadores, la situación de la ratificación y cumplimiento y dar el seguimiento oportuno por parte de Corea del Norte.

2.-) En caso que Corea del Norte ratifique el Acuerdo antes de la Junta de Gobernadores de febrero:

a) Expresar los sentimientos de bienvenida a Corea del Norte por la firma y la ratificación del Acuerdo de Seguridad Nuclear;

b) Urgir que la totalidad del material, instalaciones y facilidades nucleares en Corea del Norte sean sometidos a la inspección internacional en forma completa en un período de corto plazo.

Ruego comunicar los resultados de estas gestiones.

Saludos,

VM/gemr

cc: Embajada de la República de Corea en Costa Rica
Archivo

0066

92. 2. 20
카나다 Stephen 참사관 내방 전달. IAEA 2월 이사회 기세리 카측 발언문

PROPOSED CANADIAN STATEMENT AT IAEA BOG MEETING

We are pleased that the DPRK has finally signed (on January 30, 1992) a full-scope safeguards agreement with the IAEA.

We are concerned that the DPRK has not indicated specific dates for either ratifying or implementing the agreement.

We strongly urge the DPRK, according to the resolution which was adopted by an overwhelming majority at the last BOG meeting in September 1991, to take prompt action to ratify and implement the agreement, without any pre-conditions, and without further delay.

We expect the DPRK to take the necessary steps as soon as possible after ratification and implementation of the agreement to ensure that the IAEA's safeguards will be applied to all materials and facilities within its territory, under its jurisdiction, or carried out under its control anywhere, including that of Yongbyon.

We urge the DPRK to respond politively to the statement made by Dr. Hans Blix (Director-General of IAEA) at General Conference 35, in which he expressed his readiness to receive any relevant information, such as the initial inventory of facilities and materials, even before the agreement by the DPRK has entered into force.

0067

2/20 신

2. 카나다.北韓 外交官 接觸

o 2.19 카나다 外務部는 北韓側 要請에 따라 2.20(목) 北京에서 北韓 外交官과 接觸 예정임을 아래와 같이 우리측에 알려옴.

- 北韓側은 카.北韓 兩者問題 協議를 요청함.

- 카側은 北韓側에게 核安全協定의 批准과 履行 및 韓國과의 2개 合意書 履行을 위한 具體的 措置를 要求함과 동시에, 2.25 開催 예정인 IAEA 理事會에 對備한 4개국(카.美.日.濠洲)의 北韓 核問題 관련 共同對應策도 北韓側에 傳達 예정임.

(駐카나다大使 報告)

0068

2/21 신

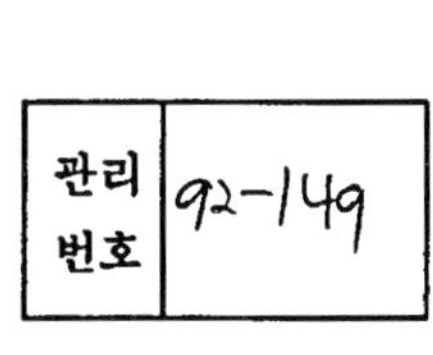

원 본

외 무 부

종 별 :

번 호 : DJW-0263 일 시 : 92 0220 1540

수 신 : 장관(국기) 사본:주오지리대사(본부중계필)

발 신 : 주 인니 대사

제 목 : IAEA 2월 이사회 대책

대:WDJ-0156

1. 당관 이참사관은 2.20. ARIF HARAHAP 외무성 국제기구과장을 방문, 대호내용을 설명하고 주재국이 IAEA 이사국으로써 북한의 핵안전협정 비준등을 촉구하는 발언을 하여줄 것을 거듭 요청하였음.

2. 동 과장은 우리측 요청 사항을 상부에 보고하고 주오지리 대사관에도 통보하겠으며, 이사회와 관련된 구체적 협조사항은 주오지리대사(JOHN LOUHANAPESSY)나 정무참사관(MINISTER COUNSELLOR MR. GHAFFAR FADYL)과 협의하기 바란다고말하였음.

3. 주재국 외상, 정무차관보 및 국제기구국장은 외유중이며, 국제기구국 부국장은 와병중임을 첨언 함. 끝.

(대사 김재춘-국장)

예고:92.6.30. 일반

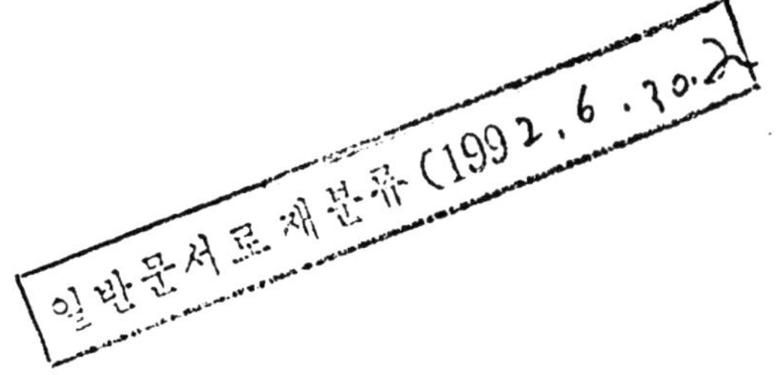

국기국 아주국 중계

PAGE 1

92.02.20 18:28

외신 2과 통제관 CH

0069

2/21신

관리번호	92-150

원 본

외 무 부

종 별 :

번 호 : THW-0362　　　　일 시 : 92 0220 1600

수 신 : 장 관(국기,사본:주오스트리아대사-중계필)

발 신 : 주 태국 대사

제 목 : IAEA 2월 이사회 대책

3

대 : WTH-0222,0251

1. 2.20 주공사는 외무성 국제기구국 SUPHOT 국제개발과장을 면담(이상팔서기관배석)하고 금번 이사회에서 논의될 특별 사찰제도 강화문제에 관한 아측입장을 설명, 지지를 요청하는 한편, 북한의 조속한 IAEA 협정이행을 촉구하는 발언을 해줄것을 요청함

2. 상기관련, 동과장은 아국입장을 충분히 이해하겠다고 말하고 이를 상부에 보고, 금번 이사회에 참석할 자국 실무대표단(원자력위원회)및 현지 주재 대표부에 아국대표단과 긴밀히 협조토록 훈령하겠다고 약속하였음.

(대사 정주년-국장)

예 고 : 92.6.30 일반

국기국　아주국　중계

PAGE 1　　　　92.02.20 18:25

외신 2과 통제관 BW

0070

공 란

공　　　란

공 란

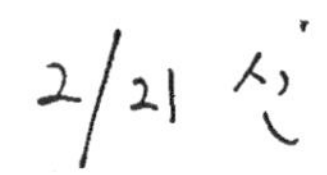

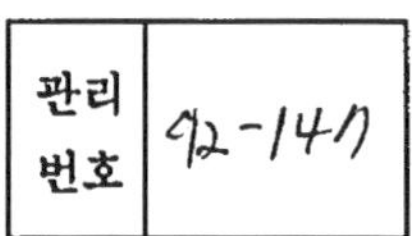

원 본

외 무 부

종 별 :

번 호 : NDW-0291 일 시 : 92 0220 1800

수 신 : 장 관(국기, 아서) 사본:주오스트리아대사:중계필

발 신 : 주 인도 대사

제 목 : IAEA 2월이사회 대책

대:WND-0134

대호관련, 당관 박경태공사는 2.20. 주재국 외무부 SREENIVASAN 유엔국장을면담, 인도측의 협조를 요청하였는 바, 동인의 반응 아래 보고함.

1. 한국측의 입장은 잘알고 있으나, 다음과 같은 사정으로 인도정부로서는 이문제에 대해 발언할 입장이 아님을 이해해 주기바람.

가. NPT 불가입정책등 핵문제에 대한 인도정부의 기본입장과 제반 관련사정상 인도정부로서는 핵문제와 관련한 국제적 압력에 소극적 입장일 수 밖에 없음.(동인은 관련사정에 대해 구체적 언급은하지 않았으나 최근 핵문제관련 미국등의 대인도 압력이 계속되는 상황을 시사하는 것으로 감촉됨)

나. 인도정부는 현재로서는 UN 헌장에 규정된 이외의 국제적 강제사찰은 반대하며, 당초 원자력의 평화적 이용을 증진하기 위한 IAEA 의 기능이 현재는 핵의 사찰기능으로 변질되어 가고 있다고 봄.

2. 다만, 인도정부로서는 북한핵문제의 민감성을 인식, 작년 북한의 군축담당 외무차관 방인접수를 거부한 바 있는바, 표제회의시 인도는 중립적인 관망자세를 견지할 것임.(특히 동인은 지난 IAEA 이사회시 인도측이 북한측의 입장을 편드는 듯한 인상을 주었다는 우리측의 지적을 인식, 이번에는 인도대표로 하여금 조용히 있도록(KEEP QUITE) 훈령 하겠다고 함)

(대사 이정빈-국장)

예고:92.12.31. 일반

국기국 아주국 중계

PAGE 1

92.02.20 22:30

외신 2과 통제관 CH

0074

2/21 신

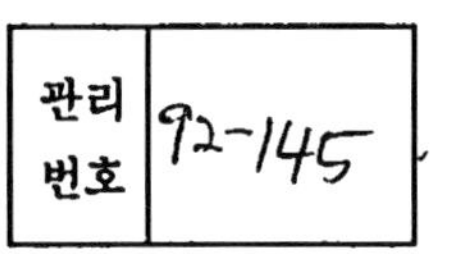
관리번호 92-145

원 본

외 무 부

종 별 :

번 호 : ARW-0141 일 시 : 92 0220 1230

수 신 : 장관(국기), 사본:주오지리대사(본부중계필)

발 신 : 주 아르헨티나대사

제 목 : IAEA 2월 이사회 대책

대:WAR-56,61,68

1. 본직은 2.19. 신공사를 대동, 외무부 FERNANDO PETRELLA 정무차관보를 면담한데이어, PFIRTER 핵에너지 및 전략국장을 오찬에 초청하고 대호건 교섭한 결과를 아래 보고함.

2.PFIRTER 국장은

가. 당지주재 일본 및 호주대사관 직원이 함께 동국장을 방문, 북한의 핵안전협정 조속비준 및 핵사찰을 수락하기위한 아르헨티나 정부의 협력을 요청하였다고 하면서

나. 아르헨티나는 91.12.13.IAEA 와 핵안전협정을 서명하였으나(국회 휴회중)아직 비준을 하지 못하고 있는 입장으로서 북한에 대해 조속한 비준을 촉구하는것이 어폐가 있으나 최선을 다하겠다고 하였음.

다. 특별사찰 제도 강화 관련, 동 국장은 아르헨티나와 브라질이 핵문제에 관한한 동일 입장(정책)을 취하게 되어있음을 상기시키고, 동국장이 지난주 브라질을 방문, 브라질 정부와 핵정책에 관해 의견을 협의하였다고 하면서, 브라질 정부는 아직 부정적이나 기본정책에서는 아르헨티나와 같기 때문에 현지 상황을 보아가면서 대호(WAR-56)의 3 의 가항 및 나항을 지지 하는데 큰 어려움은 없을것이라고 하였음.

라. 동 국장은 2 월회의에 아르헨티나 대표단으로 참석예정이며, PETRELLA 차관보로부터 본직과의 면담내용을 설명받았다고 추가 설명하면서 아국 입장 적극 지지하겠다고 약속하였음.

(대사 김해선-국장)

예고:92.6.30. 일반

국기국 아주국 중계

PAGE 1

92.02.21 01:02

외신 2과 통제관 FM

0075

관리 번호 92-1144

원 본

외 무 부

종 별 :

번 호 : NRW-0101 일 시 : 92 0220 1310

수 신 : 장관(국기,사본:주오스트리아대사-본부중계필)

발 신 : 주 노르웨이대사

제 목 : IAEA 2월 이사회대책

대:WNR-48

1.2.19. 본직및 유창현참사관은 주재국 외무부 군축담당 SAETHER 대사 및 IAEA 담당 NORENDAL 과장을 각각 면담, 대호 북한의 핵안전협정 조기 비준 국제핵사찰 조기 수락에 대한 우리의 입장을 설명하고 금번 IAEA 이사회에서 대호 요지를 강력 발언하여줄것과 우리대표들과의 긴밀 협조를 요청하였음.

2. 이에대해 동인들은 주재국은 북한의 핵문제에 대하여 지대한 관심을 갖고있다고 말하면서, 아측 입장에 찬동을 표명하고, 이번 IAEA 이사회 회의시 주재국대표가 아국대표를 비롯 미국, 카나다, 일본, 호주등과 긴밀히 협조, 아측입장을 지지 발언토록 하겠다고 말함. 또한 동 NORENDAL 과장은 북경주재 노르웨이대사가 최근 평양방문시 북한의 핵안전협정 조기 비준등 핵문제를 제기한바 있다고 첨언함.

3. 상기에 비추어 금번 IAEA 이사회 회의 아측 대표단이 주재국 대표단과 현지에서 사전 긴밀협조할것을 건의함. 끝

(대사 김병연-국장)

예고:92.6.30 일반

국기국 구주국 중계

PAGE 1

92.02.21 01:12

외신 2과 통제관 FM

0076

2/21 신

관리 번호	92-142

원 본

외 무 부

종 별 :

번 호 : CZW-0128 일 시 : 92 0220 1450

수 신 : 장 관(국기,동구이)사본:주오지리,항가리대사-필

발 신 : 주 체코대사

제 목 : IAEA 이사회

대:WCZ-0063

1. 최승호참사관이 2.20 주재국 외무부 NEJEDLY 국제기구국장 방문, 대호 요청한 바, 동 국장은, 북한핵문제 관련, 항가리측이 체코.폴란드등 3 국을 대표하여 발언하기로 되어 있다하고, 항가리측이 발언치 않을 경우, 체코가 발언토록 대표단에 바로 지시하겠으며, 이를위해 당관이 전달한 TALKING POINTS 내용을그대로 주오지대표부에 전해 두겠다하였음(체코가 옵서버국이지만 발언하는데 지장없다하고, 그렇더라도 이사회 회의시 발언토록 INVITE 하는 것도 방법이라고부언하였음).

2. 동 국장은 2.12. 당지 북한대사대리가 자신을 방문, 본국정부가 1.30 IAEA 와 안전조치 협정을 체결하였으며, 비준을 위한 국내절차가 이루어지는대로 조속 비준하고 실제 사찰이 이루어질수 있도록 추진한다는 입장이라고 알려왔다하였음. 동 대사대리의 언동중 주한미군 문제등 여타 정치적 발언이 없었으며, 한국 또는 미국등 제 3 국 비난도 없었던 것이 과거와는 다른 새로운 자세였다고 말하였음. 끝.

(대사 선준영-국장)

예고:92.6.30

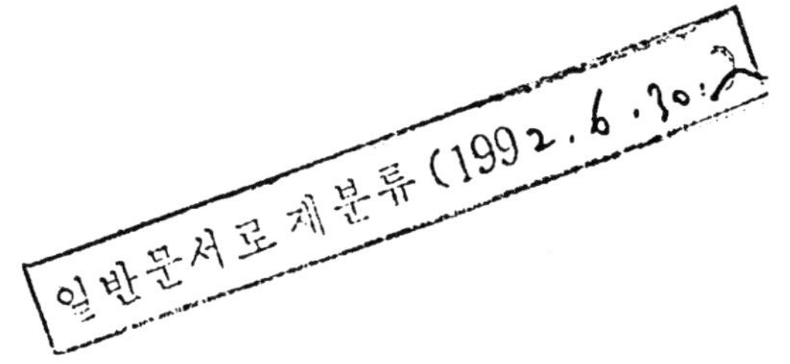

국기국 구주국 중계

PAGE 1

92.02.21 06:33

외신 2과 통제관 FM

0077

공 란

공 란

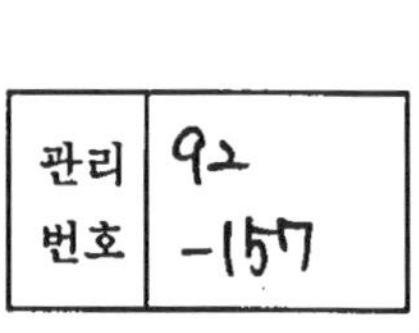

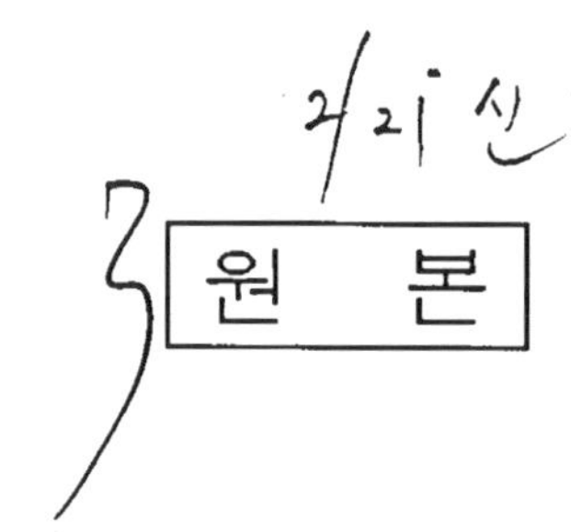

외 무 부

종 별 :

번 호 : MAW-0189 일 시 : 92 0221 1100

수 신 : 장관(국기,사본:주 오지리 대사-본부 중계요)

발 신 : 주 말련 대사

제 목 : IAEA 2월 이사회

대:WMA-147

1. 2.21(금) 장참사관은 외무부 국제기구 과장에게 금번 IAEA 이사회 (764)전까지 북한의 핵 안전협정 비준치 않은경우 말련 대표가 동 이사회에서 조속한 비준을 촉구하는 발언을 해주도록 요청함.

2. 동 과장은 한국측이 결의안을 제출할 계획이 있는지를 문의함. 장참사관은 확인해 보겠으며 북한의 협정 비준 문제가 내용상의 문제가 아니라 서명후 비준하는 국내 절차상의 문제이므로 말련이 IAEA 의 보편적 원칙에 따라 발언해 주기를 희망한다고 언급함. 또한 현재까지 북한의 핵 개발 계속 여부가 의구심을 받고 있는 상황에서 동 비준의 지연은 더욱 그러한 의심을 불러 일으키게 될것임을 설명함.

3. 동 과장은 핵 문제에 대한 말련의 입장은 분명하나 금번 이사회에서의 발언 지침여부는 2.24(월) 당관에 알려주겠다고 하였음. 끝

(대사 홍순영-국장)

92.6.30 까지

국기국 아주국 중계

PAGE 1

92.02.21 14:40

외신 2과 통제관 BN

0080

2/21. 신.

관리 번호	92-156

원 본

외 무 부

종 별 : 지 급

번 호 : PAW-0148 일 시 : 92 0221 1400

수 신 : 장관(국기,아서)사본;주 오스트리아 대사-중계필

발 신 : 주 파키스탄 대사

제 목 : IAEA이사회 대책

대;WPA-76

1. 당관 이상완 공사는 2.20. 오후 SHAUKAT UMAR 주재국외무성 유엔국장을 면담한바, 아래보고함.

가. 양국간의 경제관계, 국제기구에서의 협조를 통한 양국간의 우호관계 긴밀화등을 언급하고, 북한의 핵안전협정비준및 시행에관한 불부명성이 아국및 동북아안보에 위협요소임을 지적하면서, 금번 IAEA 이사회에서 주재국이 대호사항을 지원하여 줄것을 요청하였음.

나. 이에대해 동국장은 현지에서 우리대표와 긴밀히 협조토록하고, 금번 비엔나 이사회에서 주재국 대표연설시 이를 포함하도록 적극고려하겠다고 약속함. 주재국은 PAKISTAN ATOMIC ENERGY COMMISSION 의장을 단장으로한 대표단(현지 공관원포함)을 금번 이사회에 파견할 예정이라고 함.

2. 한편, 주재국 외무성실무자(유엔과장)는 북한의 핵안전협정서명이 일천함에 비추어 금번 IAEA 이사회에서 동문제를 재거론하는것보다는 좀더 시간을 주고 북한측을 설득하는것이 더욱효과적일것이라는 견해를 당관 박서기관 면담시 피력한바 있음을 참고로 보고함. 동과장에 의하면 동건관련 당지 미국및 일본대사관에서도 주재국 외무성에 협조요청한바있다고함. 끝.

(대사 전순규-국장)

예고;92.12.31 까지

검토필(92.6.30.)

국기국 아주국 중계

PAGE 1

92.02.21 16:55

외신 2과 통제관 BW

0081

신 . (2/24 신

관리 번호	92-166

원 본

외 무 부

종 별 :

번 호 : CMW-0051 일 시 : 92 021 1020

수 신 : 장관(국기,사본:주오스트리아대사-중계필)

발 신 : 주 카메룬 대사

제 목 : IAEA 2월 이사회대책

대: WCM-0052

1. 본직은 2.20 SAO 주재국 외무부 국제 기구 국장을 면담, 대호 발언 및 아국대표와의 긴밀한 협조를 요청하였음.

2. 동국장은 북한으로 하여금 핵안정협정을 조속 비준.이행토록 격려 및 촉구하는 의미에서 아측의요청을 검토, 자국대표에게 훈령하겠다고 말하였는 바, 회의 기간중 주재국 대표와 접촉, 협의바람.

(대사 황남자-국장)

예고:92.6.30 일반

일반문서로 재분류 (1992.6.30.)

검토필 (1992.6.30.)

국기국 중아국 중계

PAGE 1

92.02.21 18:43

외신 2과 통제관 BW

0082

공 란

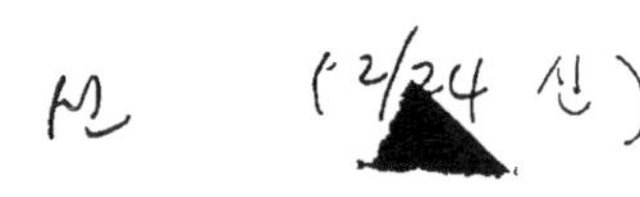

관리 번호	92-168

원 본

외 무 부

종 별 :

번 호 : POW-0101 일 시 : 92 0221 1500

수 신 : 장관(국기,구이,기정)

발 신 : 주 폴부갈 대사

제 목 : IAEA이사회

당지 일본대사관 SHIMIZU 참사관이 금일 당관에 전화로 알려온바에 의하면,당지주재 일.미.호주 및 카나다대사관측에서 주재국 외무성 SANTANA CARLOS 다자관계 국장을 방문, 92.2 IAEA 이사회 회의시, 주재국이 종전과 같이 북한이 기서명한 핵사찰 수용협정을 조속히 비준하도록 촉구하는 발언을 하여줄것을 요청하였는바, 동 CARLOS 국장은 현지 주재국 정부대표에게 상기 내용대로 훈령을 내리겠음을 약속하였다함. 끝

(대사조광제-국장)

예고:92.12.31 일반

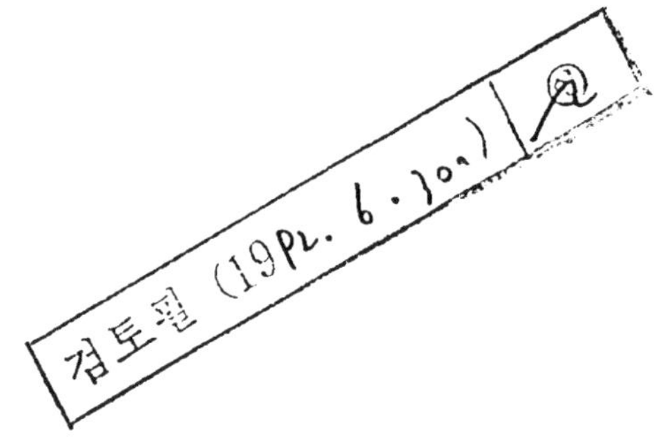

국기국 구주국 안기부

PAGE 1

92.02.22 07:03

외신 2과 통제관 CB

0084

관리번호	92-256

외 무 부

종 별 :

번 호 : NDW-0319　　　　일 시 : 92 0224 1830

수 신 : 장 관(국기,정안,미이,통일,아서)사본:주오스트리아대사-중계필

발 신 : 주 인도 대사

제 목 : IAEA 2월이사회 대책

대:WND-0134

연:NDW-0291

1. 본직은 2.23. 주재국 외무부 MEHROTRA 차관과 SREENIVASAN 유엔국장을 접촉한 기회에 북한의 핵문제와 관련하여 우리정부가 남북한 관계의 차원과 병행하여 다자차원에서 취하고 있는 조치를 설명하고, 다음과 같이 IAEA 이사회시 인도측의 신중한 대응을 재차 당부함.

가. 인도가 핵문제에 대해 특수한 입장을 갖고 있음은 이해하나, 국제사회에서 큰 물의를 이르키고 있는 북한의 핵개발을 옹호하는 듯한 인상을 주는 것은우리와 국제사회의 민감한 여론에 비추어 볼때 바람직하지 못함을 지적하고

나. 특히 최근 인도와 우리간에 활발한 경제협력이 이루어지고 있으며, 현재 한국기업의 10 억불이상 대인도 수주와 관련, 한국수출입은행의 연불수출금융지원문제등에 대해 양국간 협의가 진행중인 상황에서 북한의 핵문제와 관련, 자칫 오해를 불러 이르킬수 있는 인도입장이 우리의 민감한 여론을 자극하여 한, 인간 실리관계에 불필요한 손상을 끼치는 일이 없도록 인도측의 신중한 대응이 필요함을 강조해 두었음.

검토필(1992.6.30)

2. 이에대해 인도측(유엔국장)은 지난번 IAEA 이사회시 자국대표가 본부의 승인없이 불필요한 발언을 하게 된 것을 미안하게 생각한다고 하고 금번회의시에는 침묵을 지키도록 조처하겠다고함.

3. 본직은 현재 한, 인간 경제현안에 대해 인도정부가 매우 큰 관심을 가지고 있고 우리의 적극적인 협조를 요망하고 있음을 감안, 이러한 측면을 북한의 핵문제에대해 인도의 신중한 대응과 관련지어 외교적으로 활용하는 것이 바람직하다는 고려에서 상기와 같이 언급하였음을 참고로 보고함.

국기국　아주국　미주국　통상국　외정실　중계

0085

PAGE 1　　　　92.02.24　23:12

외신 2과　통제관 FK

(대사 이정빈-장관)

예고:92.12.31. 일반

관리 번호	92-170

	분류번호	보존기간

발 신 전 보

번 호 : WFR-0385 920222 1102 WH 종별 : 지급

수 신 : 주 수신처참조 대사. 총영사

WGR -0052 WUR -0031
WRF -0519 WAG -0062
WZR -0206

발 신 : 장 관 (국기)

제 목 : IAEA 2월이사회 대책

연 : 수신처 참조

연호, 귀주재국에 대한 교섭결과를 지급 보고바람. (사본: 주오스트리아 대사)

예고 : 92.6.30 일반

(국제기구국장 김 재 섭)

일반문서로 재분류(1992.6.30.)

수신처 : 주불란서(WFR-0345), 그리스(WGR-0046), ~~우크라이나(WAV-0173)~~
우루과이(WUR-0030), 러시아(WRF-0448), 알제리(WAG-0056),
자이레(WZR-0176)대사

보안 통제	

앙 고 재	92년 2월 22일	국제기구과	기안자 성명		과 장	심의관	국 장		차 관	장 관
			신동익				전결			

외신과통제

0087

공 란

공 란

공 란

2/24신

3 원 본

관리 번호	92-178

외 무 부

종 별 :

번 호 : CAW-0164 일 시 : 92 0222 1545

수 신 : 장관(국기)사본:주 오스트리아대사:중계필

발 신 : 주 카이로 총영사

제 목 : IAEA 2월 이사회대책

대:WCA-0080,0074,0064, 연:CAW-0157

1. 본직은 금 92.2.22(토)주재국 외무부 국제기구국장 REDA SHEHTA 대사를 방문, 대호 특별사찰제도 강화및 북한의 핵안전조치협정 비준문제에 관한 아측입장을 설명하고 2 월이사회에서 아측 입장지지를 요청한바, 동국장은 모든 핵시설을 IAEA 에 사찰하에 두는것이 주재국의 입장이므로 동이사회에서 아국입장을 지지하도록 최대한 협조토록 현지 대표에게 지시하겠다고 하였음.

2. 한편 당지 미국, 일본, 카나다및 호주대사는 92.2.18 상기 SHEHTA 국장을 방문 상기 특별사찰 및 북한의 핵안전조치 협정의 조기 비준 및 이행촉구를 위해 2 월이사회에서 주재국이 최대한 협조해줄것을 요청했다고 함. 끝.

(총영사 박동순-국장)

예고:92.6.30. 일반

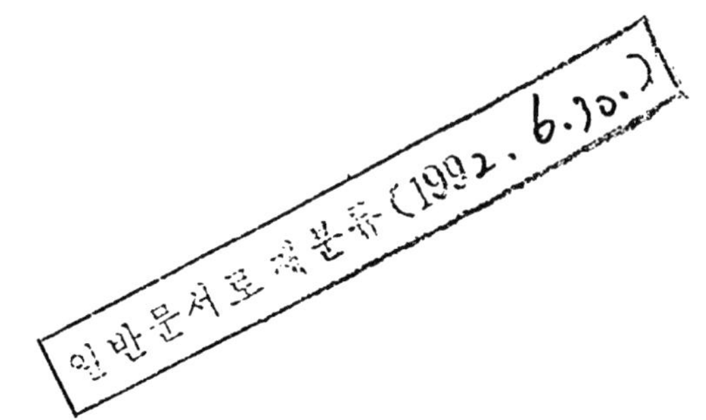

국기국 중아국 중계

PAGE 1

92.02.22 23:26

외신 2과 통제관 CH

0091

2/24 신

관리 번호	92-176

원 본

외 무 부

종 별 : 지 급

번 호 : AGW-0097　　　　일 시 : 92 0222 1600

수 신 : 장관(국기, 사본;주오스트리아대사:중계필)

발 신 : 주 알제리 대사

제 목 : IAEA 2월 이사회 대책

대:WAG-0062

연:AGW-0006(92.1.7)

1. 본직은 2.18. 외무부 MESLOUB 국제기구 총국장을 대통령 리셉션에서 만난 자리에서 대호건 타진하였던바, 동인은 최대한 노력하겠다고 하면서도 확답은회피하였음.

2. 동 총국장은 선진국들이 알제리를 핵무기 개발국으로 몰아 붙이는데 대해 강한 불만을 표시하면서 알제리는 주권 수호와 외세의 간섭을 배격한다는 원칙하에 상금 NPT 에 서명하지 않았다고 자랑스럽게 말하고, 이스라엘이 엄연히 핵무기를 보유하고 있는데대해서는 아무런 말이 없으면서 다른 나라에 대해서는 과민한 반응을 보이고 있다고 비난하였음.

3. 상기 및 연호에 비추어 주재국측의 대 북한 발언은 기대하기 어려운 형편이니 양찰바람. 끝.

(대사 한석진-국장)

예고;1992.6.30. 일반.

일반문서로 재분류 (1992. 6. 30)

국기국　구주국　중계

PAGE 1　　　　92.02.23 07:58

외신 2과 통제관 CH

0092

관리번호	92-175

외 무 부

종 별 : 지 급

번 호 : CPW-0674 일 시 : 92 0223 1430

수 신 : 장관(정특,아이,국기,기정)

발 신 : 주 북경 대표

제 목 : 북한 대내외 관계

연: CPW-0672(2.22)

연호(주중핀랜드, 노르웨이대사 면담 내용) "2 항 가"의 두번째 줄을 "2 원적 핵사찰 구조를 교묘히 악이용하여 완전한 사찰을 피할 가능성이 있다고 언급함"으로 수정 바람. 끝.

예고: 92.12.31. 일반

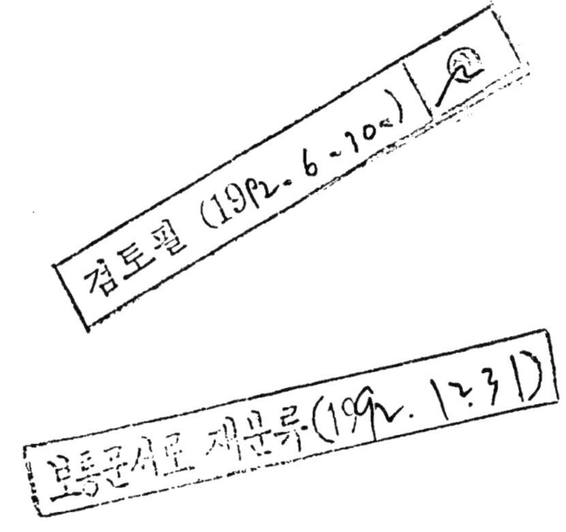

외정실	장관	차관	1차보	2차보	아주국	국기국	분석관	청와대
안기부								

PAGE 1

92.02.23 22:53

외신 2과 통제관 FM

0093

공 란

공 란

2/24 신,

관리 번호	92 -182

원 본

외 무 부

3 (오지시)

종 별 : 지 급

번 호 : THW-0385 일 시 : 92 0224 1130

수 신 : 장 관(국기, 사본:주 오지리 대사-중계필)

발 신 : 주 태국 대사대리

제 목 : 북한의 핵문제

대 : WTH-(1)0292,(2) 0222,(3)0251,(4)0287

연 : THW-0362

1. 표제 대 주재국 교섭은 대호(2),(3) 본부훈령에 의거 2.20 연호 보고와 같이 기시행한바 있음

2. 대호(1) 주 오스트리아 대사 보고와 관련, 대호(4) 훈령에 따라 계속교섭 여부 지급 하시바람.끝.

(대사대리 주진엽-국장)

예 고 : 92.6.30 일반

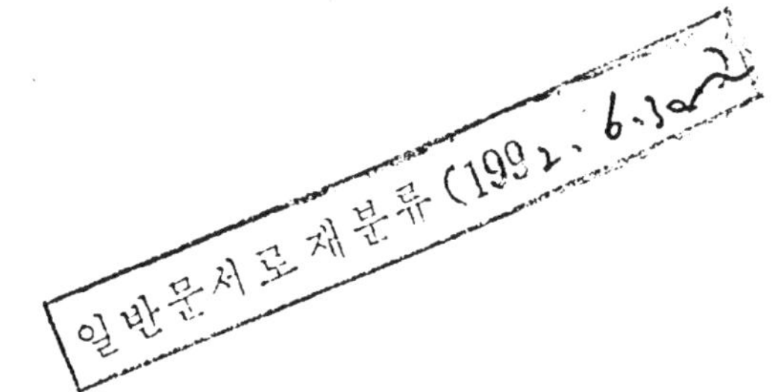

국기국 중계

PAGE 1

92.02.24 14:06

외신 2과 통제관 BS

0096

관리 번호	92-55

분류번호	보존기간

발 신 전 보

번 호 : WTH-0295 920224 1706 CJ 종별 : 지급

WAV -0248

수 신 : 주 태국대사 대리 대사. ~~총영사~~ (사본: 주오스트리아 대사)

발 신 : 장 관 (국기)

제 목 : 북한의 핵문제

대 : THW-0385

대호 ~~2항~~ 주오스트리아 대사의 건의를 감안, ~~하여 주재국을 상대로 한~~ 추가 교섭을 시행하지 말기 바람. 끝.

(국제기구국장 김 재 섭)

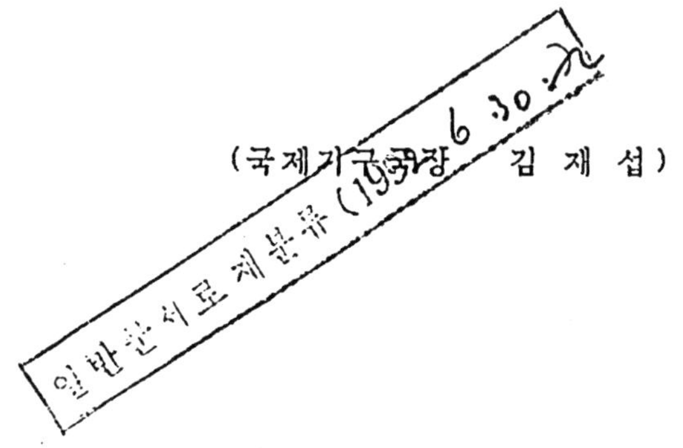

보 안 통 제	

앙 고 재	92년 2월 24일	국제기구과	기안자 성 명		과 장	심의관	국 장		차 관	장 관
			김종영							

외신과통제

0097

2/24 신

관리번호	92-183

원 본

외 무 부

종 별 : 지 급

번 호 : KUW-0133　　　　일 시 : 92 0224 0900

수 신 : 장 관(국기,중동일 사본:주오지리대사(중계필))

발 신 : 주 쿠웨이트대사

제 목 : IAEA 2월 이사회대책

대:WKU-51

연:KUW-116

2.24 쿠웨이트 외무부 MARAD 국기국장에게 확인하였는바, 쿠웨이트 대표에게 IAEA 이사회에 참석, 가능한대로 연호 SPECIAL INSPECTION 을 지지하도록 지시 하였다고 말하였음을 보고함.끝.

(대사소병용-차관)

예고:92.6.30. 일반

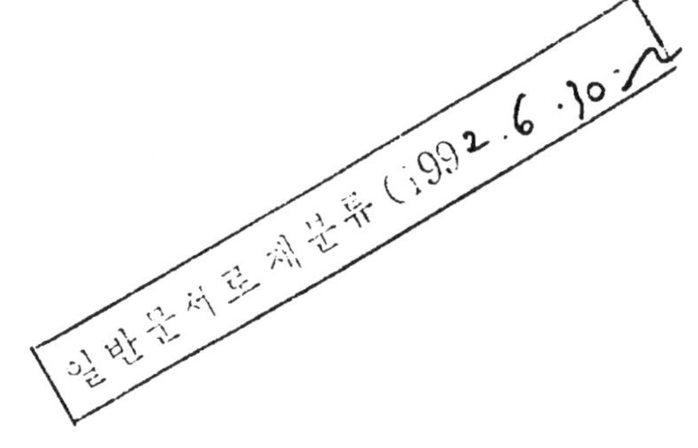

국기국　중아국　중계　차관

92.02.24 15:27

외신 2과 통제관 BS

0098

2/25 신.

3

관리 번호	92 -186

원 본

외 무 부

종 별 :

번 호 : THW-0389 일 시 : 92 0224 1630

수 신 : 장 관(국기,사본:주오지리대사-중계필)

발 신 : 주 태국 대사대리

제 목 : IAEA 2월 이사회대책

연 : THW-0362,0385

1. 2.24 주공사가 외무성 국제기구국 SUPHOT 국제개발 과장에게 확인한바, 주재국 정부는 주오지리 자국 대표부에 연호 관련, 현지 아국대표단과 긴밀히 협조, 대응토록 훈령하였다고함

2. 동건관련 2.20 당지 미국 및 일본대사관 측도 동 과장에게 특별사찰 강화문제에 관한 태국측 협조를 요청한바, 협조하겠다고 언급하였다함

(대사대리 주진엽-국장)

예 고 : 92.6.30 일반

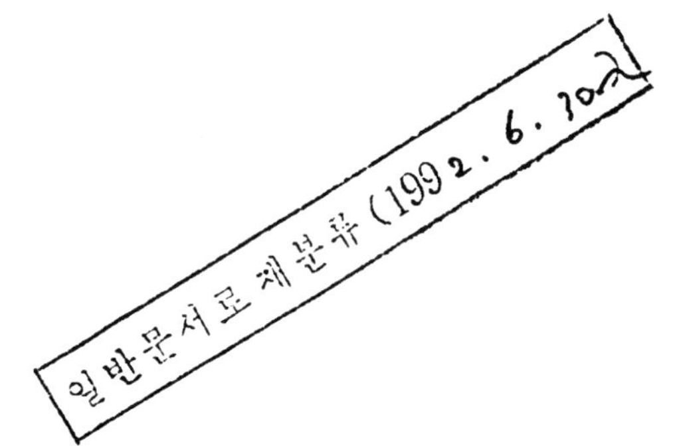

국기국 아주국 중계

PAGE 1

92.02.24 19:30

외신 2과 통제관 BW

0099

2/25 신

관리번호	92-185

원 본

외 무 부

종 별 : 지 급

번 호 : DJW-0283 일 시 : 92 0224 1600

수 신 : 장관(국기)(사본:주오지리대사-중계필)

발 신 : 주 인니 대사

제 목 : IAEA 2월 이사회 대책

대:WDJ-0156,0188

연:DJW-0263

1. 본직은 2.24. HADI WAYARABI 외무성 국제기구국장을 오찬에 초청(이참사관 배석), IAEA 이사회 대책과 관련 북한의 핵안전협정 비준문제 및 핵안전조치 제도강화를 위한 특별사찰문제에 대한 우리측 입장을 설명하고, 특히 북한이 핵안전협정을 조속히 비준할 것을 주재국이 강력히 촉구하여 줄 것을 요청하였음(우리측 요청사항을 TALKING POINTS 형식으로 전달).

2. 동 국장은 북한이 현단계에서 IAEA 의 핵사찰을 받을 시간표(TIME SCHEDULE)를 제시하는 것이 바람직하다고 하면서 우리측 입장을 지지하는데 별 문제가 없으며, 우리측 요청사항을 주오지리대사에게 통보 지지토록 하겠다고 말하였음. 끝.

(대사 김재춘-국장)

예고:92.6.30. 일반.

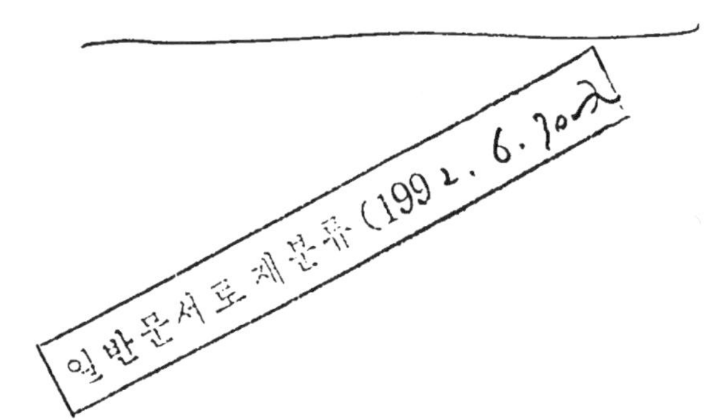

국기국 아주국 중계

PAGE 1

92.02.24 21:31

외신 2과 통제관 CE

0100

2/25 신

관리 번호	92 -189

원 본

외 무 부

종 별 :

번 호 : NDW-0319 일 시 : 92 0224 1830

수 신 : 장 관(국기,정안,미이,통일,아서)사본:주오스트리아대사-중계필

발 신 : 주 인도 대사

제 목 : IAEA 2월이사회 대책

대:WND-0134

연:NDW-0291

1. 본직은 2.23. 주재국 외무부 MEHROTRA 차관과 SREENIVASAN 유엔국장을 접촉한 기회에 북한의 핵문제와 관련하여 우리정부가 남북한 관계의 차원과 병행하여 다자차원에서 취하고 있는 조치를 설명하고, 다음과 같이 IAEA 이사회시 인도측의 신중한 대응을 재차 당부함.

가. 인도가 핵문제에 대해 특수한 입장을 갖고 있음은 이해하나, 국제사회에서 큰 물의를 이르키고 있는 북한의 핵개발을 옹호하는 듯한 인상을 주는 것은우리와 국제사회의 민감한 여론에 비추어 볼때 바람직하지 못함을 지적하고

나. 특히 최근 인도와 우리간에 활발한 경제협력이 이루어지고 있으며, 현재 한국기업의 10 억불이상 대인도 수주와 관련, 한국수출입은행의 연불수출금융지원문제등에 대해 양국간 협의가 진행중인 상황에서 북한의 핵문제와 관련, 자칫 오해를 불러 이르킬수 있는 인도입장이 우리의 민감한 여론을 자극하여 한, 인간 실리관계에 불필요한 손상을 끼치는 일이 없도록 인도측의 신중한 대응이 필요함을 강조해 두었음.

2. 이에대해 인도측(유엔국장)은 지난번 IAEA 이사회시 자국대표가 본부의 승인없이 불필요한 발언을 하게 된 것을 미안하게 생각한다고 하고 금번회의시에는 침묵을 지키도록 조처하겠다고함.

3. 본직은 현재 한, 인간 경제현안에 대해 인도정부가 매우 큰 관심을 가지고 있고 우리의 적극적인 협조를 요망하고 있음을 감안, 이러한 측면을 북한의 핵문제에대해 인도의 신중한 대응과 관련지어 외교적으로 활용하는 것이 바람직하다는 고려에서 상기와 같이 언급하였음을 참고로 보고함.

국기국 아주국 미주국 통상국 외정실 중계

PAGE 1 92.02.24 23:12

외신 2과 통제관 FK

0101

(대사 이정빈-장관)
예고:92.12.31. 일반

외 무 부

종 별 :
번 호 : URW-0042 일 시 : 92 0224 1200
수 신 : 장관(국기)
발 신 : 주 우루과이 대사
제 목 : IAEA 이사회

대:WUR-0031

1. 본직은 2.24 GROA 외상을 면담, 대호건 재확인한 바, 동 외상은 북한의 조속한 IAEA 협정 이행을 촉구하는 내용의 발언 훈령을 지난 주 주재국 대표단에하달했다 하며, 필요시 RIET 현지 우루과이 대표와 협조할 수 있음을 조언함.

(대사-국장)

예고:92.6.30일반

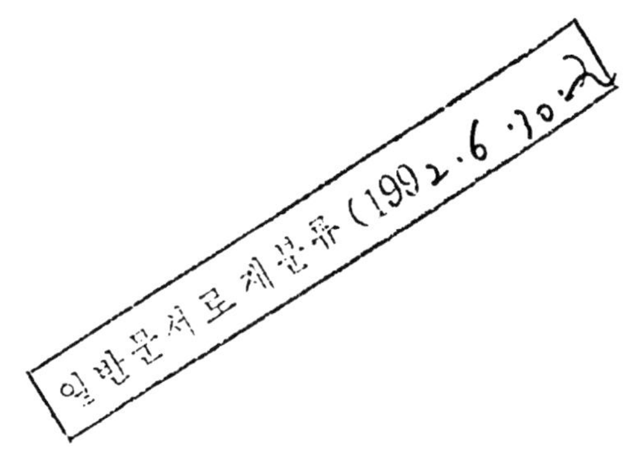

국기국

PAGE 1

92.02.24 23:15
외신 2과 통제관 FK

0103

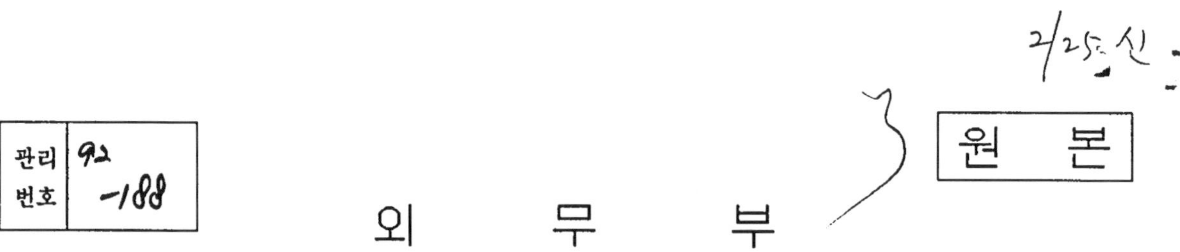

외 무 부

종 별 : 지 급

번 호 : FRW-0391　　　　　　　　일 시 : 92 0224 1430

수 신 : 장관(국기,구일),사본:주오스트리아대사-직송필

발 신 : 주 불 대사

제 목 : IAEA 2월 이사회

대:WFR-0386

1. 당관 정해웅 서기관이 금 2.24 주재국 외무부 BOISSY 한국담당관을 면담,남북고위급 회담에서도 핵문제에 관하여는 북측이 성의를 보이지 않았으며, 핵안전협정 비준도 지연시키고 있음을 설명하고, 이번 2 월 IAEA 이사회에서 동 협정의 조속한 비준을 촉구하는데 주재국이 적극 협조해 줄것을 요청하였음.

2. BOISSY 담당관은 북한의 핵개발 저지 문제에 관해서는 주재국이 단호한 입장을 보여 왔으며, 이번 이사회에서도 북한의 핵안전협정 비준 촉구에 동참할 것이라 함. 국기국과 협의, EC 대표를 지원하는 별도의 발언을 하도록 훈령하겠다 함. 끝.

(대사 노영찬-국장)

예고:92.12.31. 일반

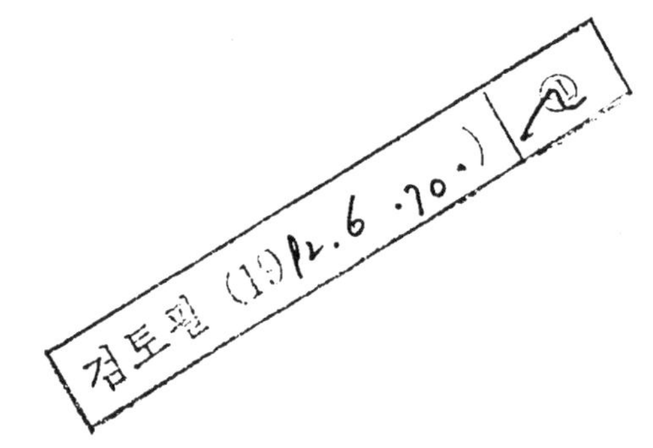

국기국　　구주국

PAGE 1　　　　92.02.25　00:09

외신 2과　통제관 FK

0104

2/25 신.

3

관리 번호	92-189

원 본

외 무 부

종 별 : 지 급

번 호 : RFW-0784 일 시 : 92 0224 1910

수 신 : 장 관(국기,사본:주오스트리아대사-중계필)

발 신 : 주 러 대사

제 목 : IAEA 2월 이사회 대책

대:WRF-448

1. 표제관련 당관 김성환서기관은 92.2.24(월) 주재국 외무성 국제과학기술협력국 MESHKOV 담당관을 접촉 대호 지침에따라 금번 IAEA 이사회에서 북한이 핵안전 협정을 조속히 이행할것을 주재국이 촉구해 줄것과 아측대표단과 긴밀히 협조해 줄 것을 요청함.

2. MESHKOV 담당관은 러시아 정부도 북한의 비준치 이의 완전한 이행이 조속히 이루어져야 한다는 입장하에 지난 1 월 로가쵸프 특사의북한방문시 북한측에 이러한 러시아측의 입장을 이미 전달한바 있음을 언급하고 금번 회의시에도 북한 대표단에게 이를 재차 전달할 예정이라고 하는바, 러시아측은 늦어도금년 봄까지는 반드시 비준이 이뤄져야 함을 촉구할것이라 함.

3. 러측대표단의 회의시 발언 요청관련, MESHKOV 담당관은 아국대표단이 VIENNA 현지에서 러측대표단고바 접촉할것을 권유함. 끝

(주러대사홍순영-국장)

예고:92.6.30 일반

일반문서로 재분류(1992.12.31.)

국기국 중계

PAGE 1

92.02.25 02:17

외신 2과 통제관 FK

0105

2/25 신

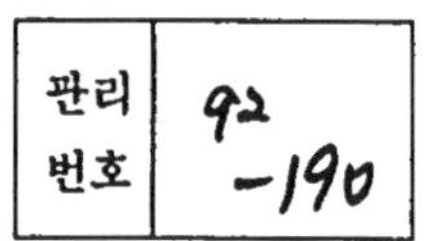

외 무 부

종 별 : 지 급

번 호 : GEW-0369 일 시 : 92 0224 1500

수 신 : 장관(국기) 사본:주오지리대사(직송필)

발 신 : 주 독 대사

제 목 : IAEA 2월 이사회

연:GEW-0330

대:WGE-0234

1. 대호 관련 2.24. 전부관 참사관은 외무부 핵문제 담당 NOCKER 과장을 접촉한바, 주재국 IAEA 대표단은 EC 의장국으로서 폴뮤갈의 EC 를 대표한 대북한 촉구 발언과는 별도로, 북한의 핵사찰 조기비준및 이행을 촉구하는 발언을 하도록 준비하여 비엔나 현지로 떠난바 있다함

2. 동과장에 의하면 비엔나 현지에서의 주재국 대표의 발언여부는 LOOSCH 수석대표의 현지상황 판단에 따라 결정된다고 하는바, 현지에서 주재국 대표단과긴밀히 접촉할 것을 건의함. 끝

(대사-국장)

예고:92.12.31. 일반

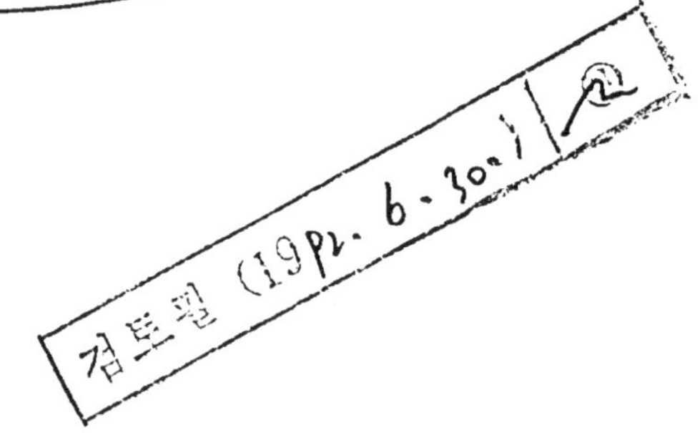

국기국

PAGE 1

92.02.25 06:05

외신 2과 통제관 FK

0106

2/25 신

관리번호	92-192

원 본

외 무 부

3

종 별 :

번 호 : BBW-0127 일 시 : 92 0224 1700

수 신 : 장관(국기,구일,사본:주오지리대사-직송필)

발 신 : 주 벨기에 대사

제 목 : IAEA 2월이사회 대책

대호건, 2.24(월) SAVERYS 주재국 핵문제 담당관에게 요청하였는바(최근 담당국장이 정년퇴직, 신임국장은 3.2. 부터 근무 예정임), 동인은 EC 회원국이 91.12. MAASTRICHT EC 정상회담 이후, 국제무대에서 공동 발언을 하기로 합의, 이번 이사회에서도 대북한 촉구 발언을 폴부갈 대표가 하도록 되어있으나, 한국측의 거듭된 요청을 고려하여, 비엔나주재 동국 대표의 의견을 들은후 단독 발언 여부를 결정, 아측에 통보하여 주겠다고 답변함. 끝.

(대사 정우영-국장)

예고:92.12.31. 일반

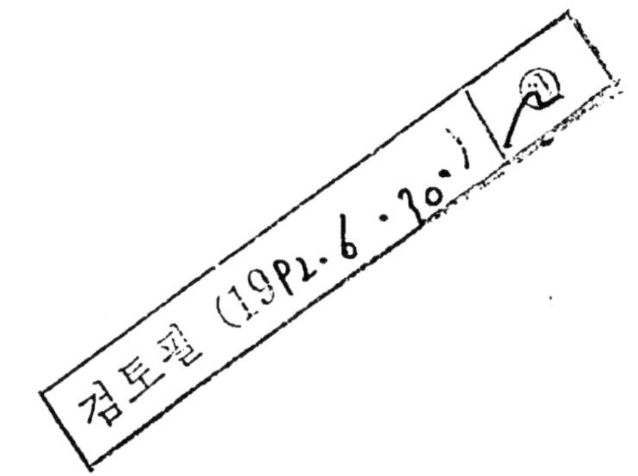

국기국 구주국

PAGE 1

92.02.25 06:16

외신 2과 통제관 FK

0107

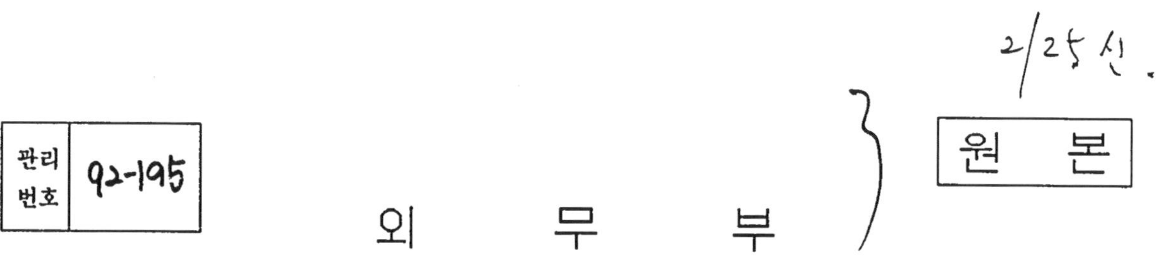

외 무 부

종 별 :

번 호 : MOW-0086 일 시 : 92 0224 1800

수 신 : 장관(국기,중동이, 사본:주오지리대사(중계필))

발 신 : 주 모로코대사

제 목 : IAEA 이사회 대책

대:WMO-0045

1. 본직은 금 2.24(월) 주재국 외무부 WARZAZI 국제기구 국장을 방문(박참사관 동행) 특별사찰 제도 강화문제에 대하여 모로코측이 적극 참여하여 줄것과 북한의 핵안전협정 조기 비준 실현을 위하여 금차 IAEA 이사회에서 적극 발언해줄것을 당부하였음.

2. 동 국장은 북한의 비준지연 술책에 관한 본직의 설명을 경청한후 북한만을 지적하여 핵안전협정 조기 비준을 촉구하기는 어려우나 모든 협정비준 미이행국(이스라엘 포함)에 대하여 조속한 비준을 촉구하는 발언을 하겠다고 하였음.

3. 북한을 특별히 지적하여 촉구하는 것이 어렵다면 제일 최근에 협정에 가입한 북한을 예시하는 방법으로 언급하는 방안을 제시한데 대하여 동 국장은 적극 검토하겠다고 약속하였는바 비엔나 현지에서 모로코 대표단과 접촉이 바람직함을 첨언함. 끝

(대사허리훈-국장)

예고:92.12.31 일반

검토필 (1992. 6. 30.)

국기국 중아국 중계

PAGE 1

92.02.25 07:15

외신 2과 통제관 BN

0108

공　　　　란

공 란

2/2.7 신.

관리 번호	92 -204

원 본

외 무 부

종 별 : 지 급

번 호 : GRW-0141 일 시 : 92 0224 1500

수 신 : 장 관(국기)

발 신 : 주 희랍 대사

제 목 : IAEA 2월 이사회대책

대:WGR-46

2.24 당관 박참사관은 외무성 국제기구국 CARAFOTIAS 참사관을 접촉 대호 교섭결과를 문의한바 동인은 아래와 같이 답변했음.

-아 래-

1. 주재국은 현지 대표단에 아국대표와 긴밀히 협조해 주도록 지시했음.

2. 주재국은 대호 아국의 요청사항을 EC 제국과 협의한바 EC 는 공동명의로 북한이 동협정을 조속히 비준하고 이행할것을 촉구하는 성명서를 발표할예정임.끝.

(대사 박남균-국장)

예고:92.6.30 일반

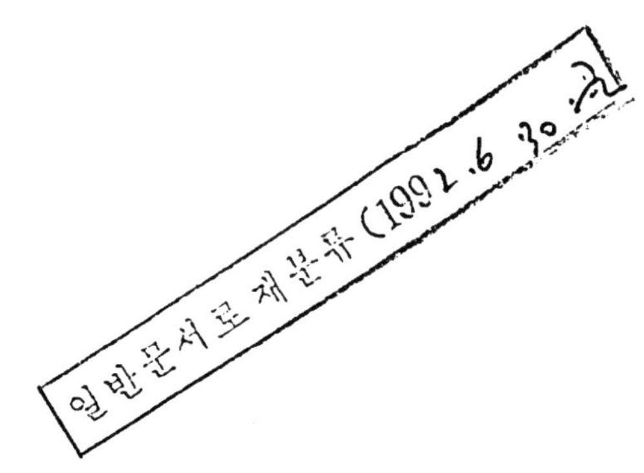

국기국 장관 차관 구주국 분석관 청와대

PAGE 1

92.02.26 19:42

외신 2과 통제관 BS

0111

2/26 신

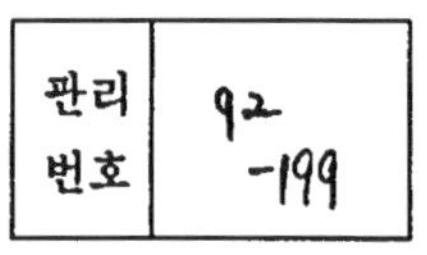

원 본

외 무 부

종 별 :

번 호 : MAW-0209 일 시 : 92 0225 1500

수 신 : 장관(국기,아동,사본:주 오지리대사-중계필)

발 신 : 주 말련 대사대리

제 목 : IAEA 2월 이사회

연:MAW-189

대:MAW-147

1. 금 2.25(화) 장참사관은 외무부 CHOO ENG GUAN 국제기구국장을 재차 면담하고 연호와 같이 말련 대표가 반언해 주도록 요청하였으며, 동 국장은 오지리에 훈령을 보내겠다고 하였음.

2. 동 국장은 말련이 지난번 뉴욕에서 이락의 핵 개발 관련 IAEA 보고서 채택시 기권한바 있음을 상기 시키면서 핵 확산 반대입장은 분명하나 이락과 함께 이스라엘도 동등하게 규탄되어야 한다는 것이 말련의 입장임에 따라 IAEA 보고서에 기원하게 된 것임을 언급하고, 핵 문제에 대한 정책이 여타 정책과 연관되어 있어 말련이 이 문제에 높은 TONE 으로 지지하지 못함을 설명하였음. 끝

(대사대리 장철균-국장)

92.6.30 일반

일반문서로 재분류 (1992. 6.30 .)

국기국 아주국 중계

PAGE 1 92.02.25 16:35

외신 2과 통제관 BW

0112

2/25 신

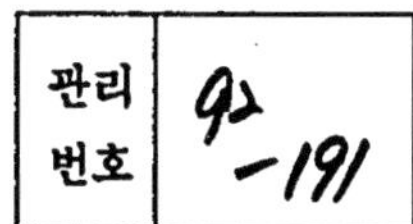

원 본

외 무 부

종 별 : 지 급

번 호 : HGW-0128 일 시 : 92 0225 1630

수 신 : 장관(국기,동구이)사본:주오지리,체코대사-중계필

발 신 : 주 헝가리대사

제 목 : IAEA 2월 이사회 대책

대: WHG-0083

연:HGW-0121

관련: CZW-0128

본직은 금 2.24(월) 오후 외무부 국제기구국 ENDREFFY 국장과 접촉, 대호 북한의 핵사찰문제관련 발언여부를 탐문한바, 동 국장은 헝가리대표의 INITIATIVE 로 중구 3 개국(헝가리, 체코, 폴란드) 대표들이 오늘 오전 비엔나에서 만나 협의한 결과, 중구 3 개국을 대표하여 헝가리대표는 핵무기 비확산문제(ITEM 2-A)에 관하여 발언하고, 체코대표는 북한의 핵안전협정 이행문제(ITEM 2-C)에 관하여 발언하기로 하였다고 함. 끝

(대사 박영우-국장)

92.12.31. 일반

검토필(1992. 6.30.)

국기국 구주국 중계

PAGE 1

92.02.26 02:13

외신 2과 통제관 FK

0113

2/26 신

3

관리번호	92-201

원 본

외 무 부

종 별 :

번 호 : UKW-0311 일 시 : 92 0225 1600

수 신 : 장관(국기),사본: 주오지리대사-직송필

발 신 : 주 영 대사

제 목 : IAEA 2월이사회

대: WUK-0332

2.25. 당관 최참사관은 BATEMAN 외무성 NPD 과장대리를 면담하고 주재국대표가 적절한 기회에 개별적으로 대호 추가발언을 하여줄 것을 요청한 바, 동인은아측 요청에 적극 협조토록하겠으며, 금번회의에 참가중인 BRIAN DONELY NPD 과장에게도 추가발언을 하도록 연락하겠다고 하였음. 끝

(대사 이홍구-국장)

예고: 92.6.30 일반

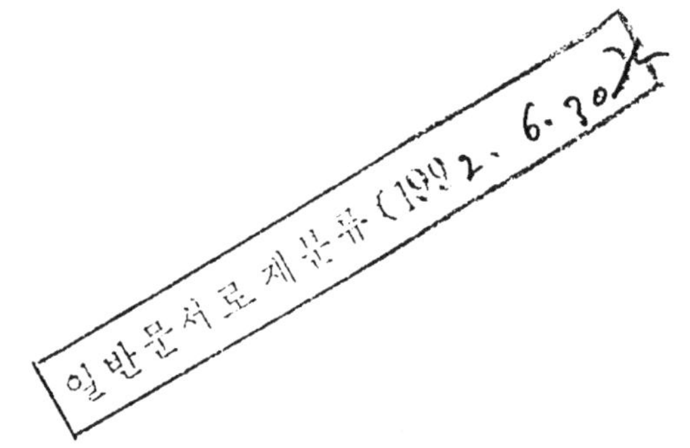

국기국

PAGE 1

92.02.26 06:56

외신 2과 통제관 FM

0114

공　　　　　란

공　　　　란

공　　　란

공 란

WPO-0074 920226 1820 CJ

WTH -0311 WRM -0080 WNR -0060 WFR -0413 WUK -0362

WGE -0249 WRF -0563 WAR -0090 WMO -0052 WBL -0089

WEQ -0037 WDJ -0209 WUR -0033 WCZ -0081 WCO -0026

WAV -0267

0119

WZR-0224 920226 1822 CJ

0120

공　　　란

공　　　란

공 란

공 란

WUS-0899   920226 1807 CJ

WCN -0185 WJA -0822 WBB -0099 WAU -0164 WCP -0438

WCA -0086 WND -0157 WMX -0105 WBR -0129 WGR -0055

WAG -0065 WCM -0059 WPA -0090 WIR -0105 WUN -0451

WGV -0320 WDE -0069 WHG -0108 WID -0035 WPD -0114

WMA -0188

0125

2/28 신

관리번호	92-208

원 본

외 무 부

종 별 : 지 급

번 호 : CPW-0743 일 시 : 92 0227 1400

수 신 : 장 관(국기,아이)

발 신 : 주 북경 대표

제 목 : IAEA 기술협력 담당 사무차장

대:WCP-0419

1. 대호 2.26. 이시영대사 주최 주재국 외교부 WAN YONGXIANG 차관보를 위한 만찬석상에서 당관 김하중 참사관이 동 만찬에 참석한 국제기구국 CHEN JIAN 부국장에게 표제입후보에 대한 아측의 협조 의사를 통보하였음.

2. CHEN 부국장은 아측의 협조의사에 감사를 표하면서 상부에 즉각 보고 하겠다고 하였음. 끝.

(대사 노재원-국장)

예고:92.12.31 일반

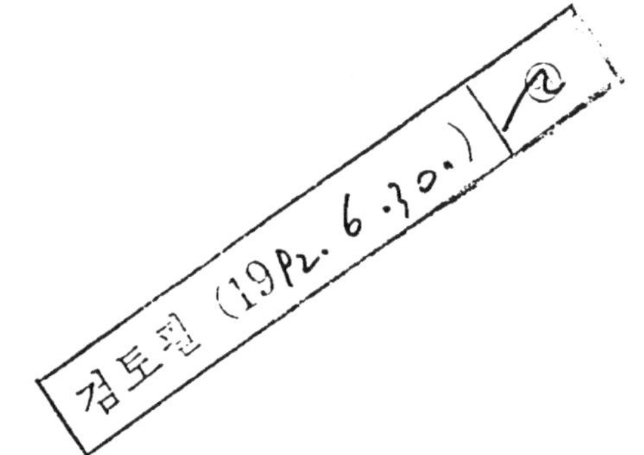

국기국 아주국

PAGE 1

92.02.27 15:55

외신 2과 통제관 BS

0126

관리 번호 92-209

3 2/28 신

원 본

외 무 부

종 별 :

번 호 : FRW-0430 일 시 : 92 0227 1800

수 신 : 장관(국기,구일,기정),사본:주오지리대사-직송필

발 신 : 주 불 대사

제 목 : IAEA 2월이사회

대:WFR-0413

연:FRW-0391

1. 당관 정해웅서기관이 2.27 대호 4 항에 따라, 금번 IAEA 이사회에서의 북한 핵안전협정 비준 및 핵사찰 관련 주재국의 효과적인 협조에 대한 아국정부의 사의를 BOISSY 외무성 한국담당관에게 전하였음.

2. DE LA FORRELLE, IAEA 대표 귀임하는대로 별도로 동인에게 사의를 표할 계획임.끝.

(대사 노영찬-국장)

예고:92.12.31. 일반

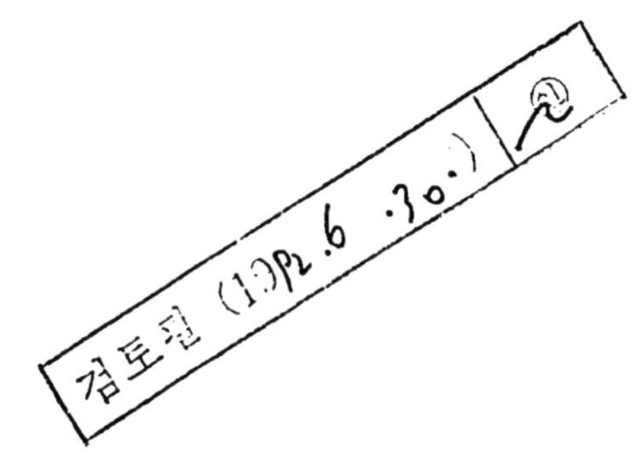

국기국 구주국 안기부

PAGE 1

92.02.28 05:46

외신 2과 통제관 FM

0127

관리번호	92-222

원 본

3/2 신.

외 무 부

종 별 : 지 급

번 호 : KUW-0138 일 시 : 92 0229 1200

수 신 : 장관(국기,중동일)

발 신 : 주 쿠웨이트 대사

제 목 : IAEA 2월 이사회

대:WKU-51

연:KUW-133

쿠웨이트외무부 MURAD 국기국장은 쿠웨이트대표가 표제에 출석하여 SPECIALINSPECTION 을 지지하는 발언을 하였다고 2.29 본직에게 말했음. 끝

(대사소병용-국장)

예고:92.6.30. 일반

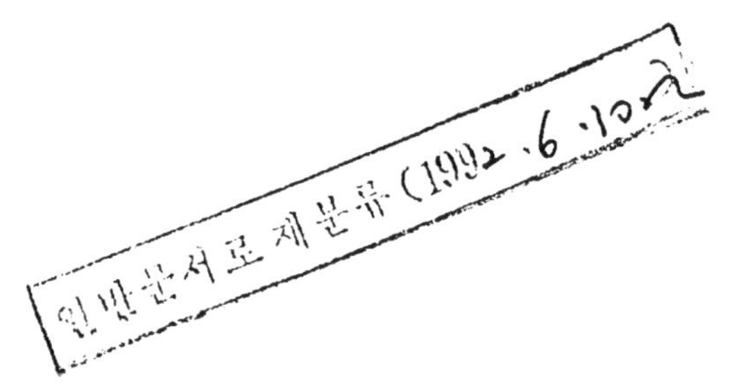

국기국 차관 중아국

PAGE 1

92.02.29 18:59

외신 2과 통제관 CE

0128

관리번호 92-233

주 쿠 웨 이 트 대 사 관

문서번호 : 주쿠웨이트(정) 10200-83

시행일자 : 1992 . 3 . 2

수 신 : 장 관

참 조 : 국제기구국장,중동아프리카국장

제 목 : IAEA 2월 이사회 대책

선결			지시	
접수	일자 시간			
	번호	10663	결재·공람	
처리과				
담당자		3/6		

대 : WKU - 51

연 : KUW - 116

표제 고섭시 본직이 쿠웨이트 AL - MINAYES 수전력부차관 및 외무부 AL-MURAD 국제기구국장에게 전달한 문서를 별첨으로 송부합니다.

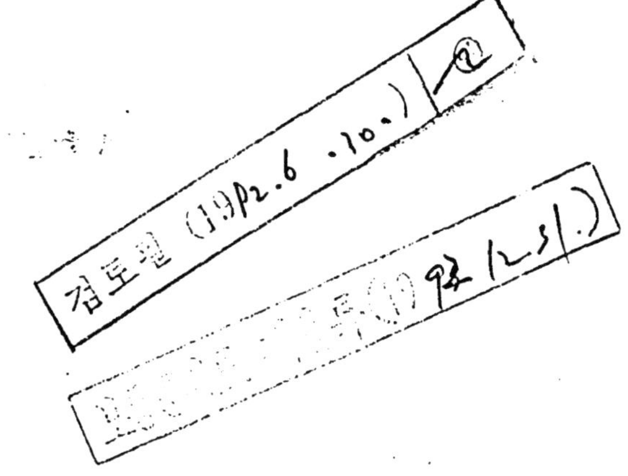

첨 부 : 상기문서 2매. 끝.

주 쿠 웨 이 트 대 사

0129

EMBASSY OF THE REPUBLIC OF KOREA
KUWAIT

17 February 1992

Dear Mr. Under-Secretary,

The Board of Governors of IAEA will deliberate on the agenda item of Strengthening of Safeguards System at its meeting on 24 - 29 February in Vienna. That the IAEA shall be able to make special inspections of the undeclared nuclear facilities and materials as well under article 73 of current Safeguards Agreement is the question to be considered at the meeting.

Given the ongoing United Nations' exercise to control nuclear weapons development in Iraq and the increased risk of nuclear weapons proliferation in the wake of the breakup of the former USSR, the special inspection only of the nuclear facilities and materials which are declared by host states should not suffice for preventing proliferation of nuclear weapons. In order for the IAEA to fulfil its responsibility under the Safeguards Agreement, and article 2 thereof in particular, undeclared facilities and materials should also be made subject to special inspections by it, when necessary. The IAEA should have the right to access to additional information and locations of such facilities and materials in the territory of a contracting party to the Safeguards Agreement, and to all credible information of them, when it believes they are for development or manufacturing nuclear weapons or other nuclear explosive devices. We are of the opinion that article 73 of the Safeguards Agreement could be so interpreted as to allow IAEA to make such special inspection.

Having said the above, I would like to request, under my Government's instruction, you to consider favourably the possibility of having the representative

0130

of Kuwait at IAEA present at the forthcoming Board of Governors' meeting as an observer and intervene in support of IAEA's right to make special inspections of undeclared facilities and materials.

I thank you for your attention to this matter and renew my high regard.

Sincerely yours,

Byung Yong Soh
Ambassador

His Excellency
Abdulla M. Al-Minayes
Under-Secretary
Ministry of Electricity & Water
Kuwait

0131

EMBASSY OF THE REPUBLIC OF KOREA
KUWAIT

17 February 1992

Dear Mr. Director,

The Board of Governors of IAEA will deliberate on the agenda item of Strengthening of Safeguards System at its meeting on 24 - 29 February in Vienna. That the IAEA shall be able to make special inspections of the undeclared nuclear facilities and materials as well under article 73 of current Safeguards Agreement is the question to be considered at the meeting.

Given the ongoing United Nations' exercise to control nuclear weapons development in Iraq and the increased risk of nuclear weapons proliferation in the wake of the breakup of the former USSR, the special inspection only of the nuclear facilities and materials which are declared by host states should not suffice for preventing proliferation of nuclear weapons. In order for the IAEA to fulfil its responsibility under the Safeguards Agreement, and article 2 thereof in particular, undeclared facilities and materials should also be made subject to special inspections by it, when necessary. The IAEA should have the right to access to additional information and locations of such facilities and materials in the territory of a contracting party to the Safeguards Agreement, and to all credible information of them, when it believes they are for development or manufacturing nuclear weapons or other nuclear explosive devices. We are of the opinion that article 73 of the Safeguards Agreement could be so interpreted as to allow IAEA to make such special inspection.

Having said the above, I would like to request, under my Government's instruction, you to consider favourably the possibility of having the representative

0132

of Kuwait at IAEA present at the forthcoming Board of Governors' meeting as an observer and intervene in support of IAEA's right to make special inspections of undeclared facilities and materials.

I thank you for your attention to this matter and renew my high regard.

Sincerely yours,

Byung Yong Soh
Ambassador

His Excellency
Abdulla A. Al-Murad
Director of International
Organizations Department
Ministry of Foreign Affairs
Kuwait

0133

정 리 보 존 문 서 목 록					
기록물종류	일반공문서철	등록번호	2020010106	등록일자	2020-01-16
분류번호	726.62	국가코드		보존기간	영구
명 칭	북한.IAEA(국제원자력기구) 간의 핵안전조치협정 체결, 1991-92. 전15권				
생 산 과	국제기구과/국제연합1과	생산년도	1991~1992	담당그룹	
권 차 명	V.15 1992.3-4월				
내용목차	* 4.10 북한, IAEA에 협정 비준 사실 통보(발효)				

0001

3/3 신

원 본

외 무 부

종 별 :

번 호 : UNW-0585 일 시 : 92 0302 1800

수 신 : 장 관(국기,연일,미이,기정)사본:유종하 대사

발 신 : 주 유엔 대사대리

제 목 : 북한핵관련기사

북한 핵관련 금 3.2.(월)자 NYT 지 사설을별첨 FAX 송부함

(대사대리 신기복-국장)

첨부: UNW(F)-0212

국기국 미주국 국기국 안기부 차관실

PAGE 1

92.03.03 08:52 FE

외신 1과 통제관

0002

UNW(ㄱ)-0212 20302 1800
(국기, 연인, 미이, 기획)

92. 3. 2. (月) NYT 사설

Fearing North Korea Too Fast

Is North Korea rushing to develop nuclear arms while deceitfully fending off international inspection with promises? That suspicion gained a little altitude last week after testimony by Robert Gates, the Director of Central Intelligence. It was possible to infer that the North Koreans are within a couple of months of nuclear pay dirt.

But that's not what Mr. Gates said and that's not what the intelligence community judges to be the fact. Even if North Korea bargains hard in the talks with South Korea to resume tomorrow, it is nowhere near building The Bomb.

Scaremongers failed to convince the intelligence community that North Korea was about to get a nuclear device. In his carefully cleared statement, Mr. Gates said, "*Even after North Korea accumulates enough plutonium,* making a device would require several additional steps that could require months or even years." It won't begin amassing that plutonium unless a reprocessing plant at Yongbyon starts operating.

That means there's plenty of time to gauge whether Pyongyang intends to live up to its obligations. It knows what it has to do: ratify the nuclear safeguards accord it signed with the International Atomic Energy Agency and open all suspect sites to intrusive inspection. And it could allay suspicion by advancing the date for ratification to late March and expediting the start of inspection.

Some intelligence analysts, having underestimated Iraq's nuclear program, may be particularly edgy about North Korea. But Pyongyang has been keeping its promises to Washington. If it is proceeding on course, premature pressure could backfire. If it is not, there will be plenty of time for Washington to prepare the way for stern international sanctions.

UNW-0585 접수

2/2-1-1

0003

의 추가분

The Washington Post

AN INDEPENDENT NEWSPAPER

North Korea's Run for a Bomb ...

THE AMERICAN government has now gone public with its concern over secret nuclear-bomb development in Communist North Korea. The chief of intelligence discloses indications of a nuclear "deception plan" and suggests a bomb could be as close as a "few months" away. North Korea is a completely closed society with a notoriously treacherous government—and a legendary tunnel-digging capacity. Its recent diplomacy of smile and maneuver has encouraged the hope, especially in South Korea, that it was exchanging its go-it-alone nuclear ambitions for broader security guarantees that would integrate it in its region. But its diplomacy is also consistent with a policy of nuclear concealment. Particularly disturbing is its evasion of the prompt and full international inspection that would ease, though it would not end, anxieties about its nuclear intentions.

What this means is that a major crisis is building in east Asia precisely at a moment when most people elsewhere are still relaxing in the glow of the end of the Cold War. For even the strong suspicion of North Korean accession to nuclear status would be taken as menacing not simply by South Korea but also by nearby Japan, China and Russia and by remote America as well. That North Korea might be able to sneak-build a nuclear force over the active objections of all of them would be a stunning blow to regional stability. It would give Kim Il Sung or a successor dangerous new options of nuclear diplomacy and nuclear threat, not to speak of commercial sale. For the first time, American troops protecting South Korea would be under a direct nuclear gun.

North Korea has no security justification for a bomb. The United States squeezed South Korea out of its nuclear program years ago. More recently, in a so-far unreciprocated gesture of strategic respect for North Korea, Washington withdrew its own nuclear weapons from the peninsula. The North's reach for a bomb, while pretending to reach for regional accommodation, could only be regarded as intimidating and hostile.

Perhaps the North's nuclear works can still be brought under effective inspection—although whether intelligence is good enough to make inspection foolproof is a question. Otherwise, it becomes necessary for the countries that deal with North Korea to isolate it with tough Security Council sanctions. A new collective guarantee of South Korea would be in order. So would a collaborative military option, although again much depends on the intelligence. Every nation everywhere has a powerful interest in halting a rogue regime's run to nuclear daylight.

212-1-1

0004

북한 외교부 대변인, IAEA 관리이사회 회의 관련 중앙통신과의 회견에서 아래와 같이 절차에 따른 지체없는 핵사찰 재천명

(3.3 중방)

o "우리는 최고인민회의 제9기 제3차회의에서 우리의 핵담보협정이 심의되고, 그에 따라 그것이 비준되면, 핵담보협정 조항에 따라 국제원자력기구에 효력발생과 관련한 서면통지를 하게 될 것이며, 기구와 합의되는 실무적 절차에 따라, 지체없이 핵사찰을 받을 것이라는 점을 다시금 명백히 한다."

0005

제 140 호

외교부대변인,IAEA관리이사회 회의 관련 중앙통신과 회견 (3.2)

'92. 3. 3,06:15,중 방

조선민주주의인민공화국 외교부대변인은 국제원자력기구 2월관리이사회 회의와 관련하여 어제 조선중앙통신사 기자가 제기한 질문에 다음과 같이 대답했습니다.

지난 2월 24일부터 26일까지 오지리의 윈에서 국제원자력기구 2월 관리이사회 회의가 진행되었다.

회의에서 우리나라대표단은 핵무기전파방지조약에 따르는 의무를 성실히 이행하기 위한 우리 공화국정부의 주동적인 조치와 성의있는 노력에 대하여 언급하고 핵담보협정의 비준문제와 관련한 우리의 원칙적 입장을 밝히었다.

우리 대표단은 핵사찰 문제와 관련한 우리의 원칙적인 요구가 실현된데 따라 우리가 담보협정에 서명하였으며,이어 지난 2월18일 최고인민회의 상설회의 제9기 제16차회의에서 우리와 국제원자력기구 사이에 체결된 담보협정에 대하여 토의하고 이를 최고인민회의 제9기 제3차 회의 심의에 제출하기로 결정하였다는 것을 언급하고 이것이 심의되고 그에 따라 비준되면 국제원자력기구의 핵사찰을 받기 위한 실무적 조치

-1-

0006

들을 지체없이 취할 것이라는 데 대하여 천명하였다.

「회의에 참가한 절대다수의 나라들은 핵담보협정의 비준절차와 관련한 우리의 자주적이며 전진적인 계획에 대하여 열렬히 환영하였다. 지난시기 관리이사회 회의들에서 핵문제와 관련한 우리의 조치들에 대하여 의심하면서 우리에게 내정간섭적인 부당한 발언을 하던 나라들까지도 우리의 핵담보협정의 비준절차에 대하여 이해와 동감을 표시하였다.

이것은 핵담보협정 이행문제와 관련하여 우리가 일관하게 견지하여 온 입장이 매우 정당한 것이었으며, 담보협정 비준절차와 관련하여 우리가 내놓은 주동적인 계획들이 국제적인 기정사실로 인정을 받고 있다는 것을 명백히 보여 주고 있다.」

그런데 핵사찰 문제와 관련하여 우리와 국제원자력기구 사이에 협상과 합의가 순조롭게 진척되어 가고 있고 우리의 담보협정 문제가 최고인민회의에 제기되어 곧 심의를 거치게 된 지금에 와서까지도 미국을 비롯한 극히 몇몇 나라들은 우리의 핵담보협정비준이 절차상 공정으로 보아도 오래 걸리지 않는다는 것을 뻔히 알면서도 우리의 핵무기 개발 의심에 대하여 떠들어대면서 심히 도발적이고 내정간섭적인 태도를 취하고 있다.

우리는 남조선으로부터 미국의 핵무기를 철수해 갈 데 대한 전체 조선민족의 정당한 요구를 외면한 채 30년이상이나 버티오던 미국이 핵무기전파방지조약을 위반한 종래의 위법행위에 대해서 사죄할 대신 우리의 담보협정 비준문제가 최고인민회의의 심의에 제출

-2-

0007

된 오늘날에 와서까지도 우리에 대하여 이러쿵 저러쿵 시비 중상하면서 도발적인 압력을 가하는 것은 우리의 핵담보협정의 이행에 해가 되면 되었지 이롭지 못하다는 것을 알아야 할 것이라고 생각한다.

미 국회 하원의원 솔라즈는 지난해 12월에 우리나라에 와서 우리와 마주앉았을때에는 우리의 핵사찰 문제가 공정하게 해결되어야 한다는 우리의 원칙적 주장에 동의하였으나, 지금에 와서는 우리 나라에 대한 이른바 무력행사의 필요성에 대하여서까지 떠벌여댔다.

지금 미국의 일부 사람들이 우리의 핵담보협정 이행문제를 가지고 터무니없이 우리를 걸고드는 것을 보면 그들이 어떻게해서든지 세계여론을 오도하여 우리를 모해함으로써, 우리로 하여금 핵사찰을 받지 못하게 하고 조.미관계 개선에 제동기적 작용을 하자는 것이 아닌지 의심하지 않을 수 없다. 우리는 그들이 정치인들이라면 법률이행과 관련한 초보적인 상식이라도 가지고 좀 더 자중해야 할 것이라고 생각한다.

매개나라마다 체결된 협정을 비준 승인하는 절차가 있는 법이다.

이것은 자주권에 관한 문제이다. 우리에게도 체결된 조약의 비준 승인과 관련한 구체적인 절차 규정이 있다.

우리는 최고인민회의 제9기 제3차회의에서 우리의 핵담보협정이 심의되고 그에 따라 그것이 비준되면 핵담보협정 조항에 따라 국제원자력기구에 효력 발생과 관련한 서면통지를 하게 될 것이며, 기구와 합의되는 실무적 절차에 따라 지체없이 핵사찰을 받을 것이라는 것을 다시금 명백히 한다.

최근 남조선 당국자들은 온 민족앞에 서명한 북남사이의 역사적 합의사항을 난폭하게 위반하면서 우리를 비방중상하고 자극하는 발언들을

-3-

0008

서슴치 않고 하고 있다.

남조선 당국자들이 전체 조선민족에게 있어서 현실적인 위협으로 되는 일본의 핵무장화 시도에 대해서는 애써 외면하면서도 남의 장단에 맞춰 춤을 추면서 동족인 우리의 핵사찰 문제를 가지고 우리를 걸고드는 것을 보면 그들에게 과연 자주성과 민족성이 있고 조선반도의 비핵화에 관한 공동선언을 이행하려는 의사가 있는가 하는 데 대하여 생각해 보지 않을 수 없다.

남조선 당국자들은 저들의 이러한 태도가 북남 사이에 합의한 조선반도의 비핵화에 관한 공동선언 이행에 엄중한 장애만을 조성할 뿐이라는 것을 똑똑히 알아야 한다.

우리는 국제 사회의 공정성과 평등성의 원칙에 어긋나게 우리에게 일방적인 압력을 가하거나 우리의 내정에 간섭하며 우리 나라의 자주권과 민족의 존엄을 모독하는 행위에 대하여서는 절대로 용허하지 않을 것이다.

우리 공화국정부는 앞으로도 핵무기전파방지조약에 의하여 지닌 자기의 의무를 성실히 이행하여 나갈것이다.

공　　란

공 란

공　　　란

공 란

IAEA 92.2월 이사회 토의 동향 분석

92. 3.

국 제 기 구 과

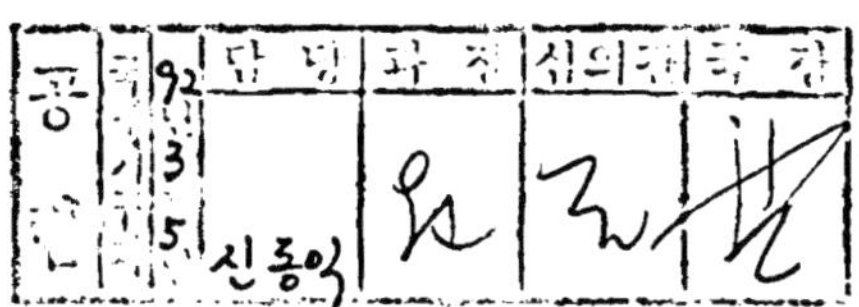

0014

1. 주요 의제별 이사회 토의결과(summing-up)

가. 북한의 핵 안전 협정 발효 및 이행문제

o 이사회는 북한이 4월 최고인민회의에서의 협정 심의후 다른 추가 조치 없이 협정 발효 및 이행할것을 희망

o 이사회는 북한이 협정 발효 이전에 IAEA에 핵 재고정보(Inventory)를 제출할것을 촉구

o 북한의 협정 비준 및 이행상황에 대해 사무총장이 6월이사회에서 보고할것을 요청

나. 안전조치제도(Safeguards System) 강화 방안

1) 특별사찰(special inspection)제도 확립

o IAEA헌장과 안전조치 협정에 따라 평화적 핵 활동에 사용되는 모든 핵물질(all nuclear materials)에 대한 안전조치 적용과 특별사찰을 위한 IAEA의 권한을 재확인

- 핵관련 추가정보를 입수하고 관련 장소를 사찰할수 있는 권한도 재확인

o 이사회는 사무총장에게 특별사찰을 실시할 경우 소요예산 내역을 보고하고, 기존 예산정책 테두리내에서 여타 IAEA사업용 예산을 손상하지 않는 범위내에서 실시할것을 요청

2) 설계정보(design information)

o 신설 또는 기존시설 개축에 관한 설계정보를 조기 입수하기 위해 IAEA가 안전조치협정 당사국과 보조약정(subsidiary arrangement)을 개정하는데 필요한 조치를 취할것을 요청

ㅇ 협정 당사국은 보조약정 개정시까지 아래와 같이 설계정보를 제출할 것을 요청

- 핵시설 건설 계획, 승인 및 개축의 결정이 나는대로 IAEA에 예비적인 시설정보(preliminary design information)를 제공
- 핵시설 건설의 각 단계별(계획, 예비설계, 건축, 가동) 추가정보를 IAEA에 조기제출
- 신설 핵시설에 대하여는 예비 건설계획을 늦어도 건축시작 180일전에 완전한 설계정보 설문서(completed Design Information Questionnaires)로 IAEA에 제출하여, 완성된(as-built)시설에 관한 설계정보 설문서(DIQ)는 동 시설용 핵물질 접수 180일전에 제출해야 함.

ㅇ 일부 이사국들은 상기 시한 설정의 실현성과 동 방안의 경비효과면에서 문제점 제기

3) 핵, 비핵 물질 및 민감장비의 수출입과 생산의 신고 및 검증

ㅇ 동제도의 충분한 검토를 위해 IAEA 6월 이사회시 재심의키로함.

3. 92. 2월 이사회 토의 동향

가. 전반적인 회의 진행 상황

ㅇ 금번 이사회의 가장 중요한 토의 의제는 안전조치제도 강화 문제였고, 작년 12월이사회시 동 강화 방안관련 사무국 작성 paper(GOV/2554)에 대해 77그룹 중심으로 반발이 있었던 점에 비추어, 이에 대한 논란이 심할것으로 예상하여 사무국은 당초 회의기간(2.25-27)을 2.24-28로 연장하였음.

o 금번 이사회에서는 이라크와 같은 미신고 핵개발 국가들의 출현을 방지 하기 위한 IAEA의 규제적 활동(regulatory activities)을 강화하자는 여론에 따라 안전조치제도 강화에 초점을 두고, 이를 구체화 하기 위한 방안 채택을 위해 여타의제(기구 재정상태, 핵안전 협약 제정등)를 먼저 처리하고 안전조치제도에 대해서는 2-3일간 충분한 시간을 갖고 본격 토의 예정이었음.

o 그러나 예상외로 특별사찰 강화와 설계정보 제출에 관한 서방 - 77그룹 간 의견 조정이 쉽게 이루어졌고, 핵물질 보고 검증제에 대해서는 심의 시기를 6월이사회로 연기시킴에 따라, 당초 계획했던 회의기간을 2일 단축하여 폐회하였음.

* 회의기간 단축에는 심각한 재정난에 직면해 있는 IAEA가 소모적인 회의로 인한 불필요한 예산지출을 방지해야 한다는 여론을 의식한 이유도 있음.

나. 회의 의제별 토의 동향 분석

1) IAEA의 재정 상태

o IAEA 재정위기에 관한 토의시 분담금 미납국(러시아, 우크라이나등)의 증가로 인한 금년도 예산의 13% 감액 집행문제와 관련 미국, 카나다, 영국등은 핵안전조치협정 체결국의 증가로 안전조치 예산증가의 불가피성을 주장한 반면, 중국, 인도, 멕시코등은 핵의 평화적 목적사용을 위한 기술협력 분야(TACF)예산의 감축은 불가하다고 주장.

o 따라서 이사회는 사무총장에게 6월이사회시 13% 예산 삭감을 위한 예산지출 항목별조정(readjustment) 결과를 보고토록 하였으나, 앞으로 감액 예산균형 집행문제를 둘러싸고 그룹간 의견대립이 예상됨.

o 이러한 상황에서 77그룹은 안전조치 예산증액으로 인해 대개도국 지원 예산이 삭감되는 것을 우려, 미국을 중심으로한 선진국들이 정책결정을 주도하는 IAEA 이사회에서 여타의제들 토의시 서방국들과 불필요한 마찰을 피하려는 경향을 띠었음.

2) 북한의 협정 비준 및 이행문제

o 본래 토의계획과는 달리 안전조치강화 방안 심의 이전에 토의된 북한의 협정 체결 문제는 사무총장의 보고(1.30. 서명 환영, 4월 최고인민회의에서 비준 기대)에도 불구, 북한대표(오창림 본부 대사)의 미온적 발언(명확한 비준시기 미제시)에 따라 우리를 비롯한 다수이사국들의 강경한 비준 촉구 발언들을 유발하였음.

o 북한의 협정서명에도 불구 35개 이사국중 31개 이사국 및 2개 옵서버국이 조속한 비준촉구 발언을 행한것은 아래와 같이 분석될 수 있음.

- 이라크의 비밀 핵개발 사실 발견후 북한의 핵개발 위험성에 대한 국제적 우려 고조
- 91.9월 이사회 결의(27개국 찬성)는 북한의 조속한 협정서명, 비준 및 이행을 촉구했음에도 불구하고 92.2월 이사회전까지 북한은 서명 절차만 완료함으로써 앞으로 협정 비준, 이행시까지 계속적인 대북한 압력이 필요하다는 이사국간 공동 인식 형성
- 우리를 비롯한 미국, 호주, 카나다, 일본등이 전 이사국 수도를 통해 대북한 비준 촉구발언 교섭을 적극적으로 시행한 결과로 다수 이사국 지지 확보
  (이사회 현장에서 현지 대표단의 촉구발언 교섭 활동도 주효)

4

0018

- 인도, 파키스탄, 중국, 큐바, 베트남등 그동안 북한 입장에 동조하던 국가들까지 조속한 협정 비준을 촉구한것은 이사회의 전반적인 분위기가 북한에 대한 강력한 압력이 필요하다는 쪽으로 기울자 북한의 협정의무 이행을 일반적으로 강조함으로써 대부분이 NPT 비가입국인 자신들에 대한 비난을 피해 보려는 의도로 분석.
- 회의의제 토의순서가 안전조치강화 방안 심의에 앞서 북한 문제를 토의하게 됨으로써, 서방국가들과 비동맹 이사국들간 대립 분위기가 나타나지 않은 객관적인 상황에서 이사국들은 북한의 협정비준 압력에 집중할수 있었음.

3) 특별사찰 제도 확립

o 77그룹이 특별사찰강화 문제에 대해 타협하여 특별사찰과 추가정보 입수 및 관련장소 사찰에 대한 IAEA의 권한확인에 동의한 것은 서방 국가들과 불필요한 마찰을 피하기 위해 기존 핵안전 협정문안을 수정하지 않은 상태에서 해석자체에만 조금 양보한 것으로 볼수 있음.
  - 미신고 핵시설 및 물질에 대한 정보입수를 통해 특별사찰이 실시하게 되더라도 핵안전협정 9조에 따라 사찰관 임명시에는 당사국의 사전 동의가 필요하므로 최악의 경우 특별사찰을 거부할수 있다고 판단.

o 또한 향후 예산 지출 조정문제관련 특별사찰에 필요한 안전조치 예산이 기존 예산정책 테두리내에서 여타 기존 IAEA사업(개도국 기술협력 사업 등)용 예산을 손상시키지 않아야함을 못박음으로써 77그룹이 우려하는 개도국용 예산 삭감문제는 해결한 셈임.

o 77그룹 소속국가들이 많으나 인도, 파키스탄, 멕시코등 일부국가들을 제외하고는 사실상 핵개발 능력이 없기 때문에 특별사찰제도를 포함한 안전조치제도 강화가 기타 77그룹국가들에게 미치는 영향은 미미하다고 볼수 있음.

4) 설계정보 조기 제공

o 설계정보 조기제공 문제에 대해서는 사무국 작성 paper(GOV/2554/Attach 2/ Rev.1)에 대해 이사국들간 완전한 합의가 이루어지지 않은 상태에서 일부 국가들의 유보하에 결론을 내렸고, 앞으로 이를 시행하기 위해서는 보조약정 개정절차를 각 협정당사국 별로 밟아야하는 기술적인 어려움이 있기 때문에 완전한 시행까지는 많은 시간이 소요될 것으로 예상

o 특히 시설 건설시작 180일전의 설계정보 제출 시한설정에 대해서는 일부 국가들은 각기 다른 자국사정을 고려해야함을 강조하였고, 일본, 불란서, 멕시코등은 그 실현가능성과 경비 효과적 측면에서의 의문을 제기하고 있어 앞으로도 계속 논란이 많을 것으로 예상됨.

5) 핵. 비핵물질 및 민감장비 수출입과 생산의 신고 및 검증

o 안전조치제도 강화를 위한 세번째 방안인 상기 제도의 도입에 대해서 77그룹은 특별사찰, 설계정보 제공 문제에 대해 2월이사회가 이미 결론을 내린 상황에서, 핵.비핵물질 신고제도의 내용은 광범위하고 복잡하기 때문에 검토에 충분한 시간이 필요하고, 또한 최근 들어 IAEA의 활동이 개도국에 유리한 원자력개발과 같은 촉진적 활동(promotional activities)보다는 안전조치와 같은 규제적 활동(regulatory activities)에 지나치게 많은 시간과 예산을 소모하고 있음을 지적, 상기 방안에 대한 토의자체를 6월이사회부터 시작하자는 공동입장을 제시

o 또한 일본, 독일과 같이 비공개적으로 핵개발을 추진하고 있는 선진국들은 핵물질 신고 및 검증제도가 기존의 핵안전협정을 개정하거나 새로운 형태의 의정서(protocol) 형식으로 채택되는 것에 반대하며,

6

0020

특히 비핵물질 및 민간장비 수출입 신고 및 검증제도는 기존의 '런던 가이드라인'이 존재하기 때문에 불필요하다고 강력히 반발하고 있어 앞으로 동 강화 방안의 채택에는 많은 난관이 있을 것이며, 채택시에도 그 내용이 대폭 완화되고 단순화 될것으로 예상됨.

4. 92.6월이사회 대책 : 상기 분석과 IAEA 작성 회의 결과보고서(report)를 참고 5월 초 종합 마련 예정.

첨부 : 상기 의제별 이사회의장 토의요약(summing up) 4매. 끝.

BOARD OF GOVERNORS
Notes for the Chairman
4304289/47

Meetings starting on
Monday, 24 February 1992

Item 2(c)

Report on the status of implementation of the safeguards agreement with the Democratic People's Republic of Korea
(4)

CONCLUSION

THE CHAIRMAN

There are no more speakers and we have concluded discussion on this sub-item. As always all observations and comments will, of course, be reproduced in our summary records.

Many speakers expressed satisfaction that the safeguards agreement required under NPT has been signed by the Democratic People's Republic of Korea. However, the fact was stressed that the DPRK Government still has the important - and urgent - task of bringing the agreement into force and ensuring its full implementation without further delay and in this connection many speakers noted the statement made by the distinguished representative of the DPRK that the Standing Committee of the Supreme National Assembly had reviewed the safeguards agreement and had decided to submit it to the Assembly for consideration at its forthcoming session, in April. The Board hopes that this is the only outstanding formality to be completed before the entry into force and full implementation of the agreement by the DPRK and urges the Government of the DPRK to have the agreement brought into force without delay and, in the meantime, to co-operate with the Agency by providing the requisite initial information.

May I therefore further take it that the Board wishes to request the Director General to keep in close contact with the authorities of the DPRK, and report to the Board in June on developments in the ratification and implementation of the safeguards agreement with the DPRK?

- brief pause and, if no comments -

It is so agreed.
1992-02-25, 11.40hrs

0022

BOARD OF GOVERNORS

Meetings starting on
Monday, 24 February 1992

"SPECIAL INSPECTIONS

The Board recalled the various views expressed by members during its discussions on special inspections at its December 1991 meetings.

The Board urged the full exercise of all Agency rights and obligations as provided under the Statute and in all comprehensive safeguards agreements*. The Board reaffirmed the Agency's right to undertake special inspections, when necessary and appropriate as described in the above-mentioned agreements and to ensure that all nuclear materials in peaceful nuclear activities are under safeguards. The Board anticipates that these special inspections should only occur on rare occasions. The Board further reaffirmed the Agency's rights to obtain and to have access to additional information and locations in accordance with the Agency's Statute and all comprehensive safeguards agreements.

The Board requested the Director General to keep it informed of any budgetary implications of the steps envisaged for this purpose and further requested that they be limited to the framework of existing budgetary policies, carried out without affecting the funds available for other Agency activities and in accordance with resolution GC(XXXV)/RES/569.

Footnote

(*Comprehensive safeguards agreement - those which are based on the guidelines set forth in INFCIRC/153. (Corrected), as well as others which provide for the application of Agency safeguards to all nuclear materials in all peaceful nuclear activities within a State.)

****

0023

MD

BOARD OF GOVERNORS
Notes for the Chairman
4304289/64

Meetings starting on
Monday, 24 February 1992

Design information

CONCLUSION

There was support for the action proposed by the Secretariat.

However, a few reservations were expressed. Also, comments were made relating, for example, to the practicability of complying with prescribed time limits and to the cost effectiveness of the proposals. Some members wondered whether the 180-day time limit should apply to all facility types, but were willing to leave the matter as it stood at present and revert to it in the light of experience if necessary.

A few members suggested that a working group be set up, and some stated that they would like the Director General to report to the Board routinely on the implementation of the proposals.

* * *

The Board accepts the Secretariat's revised proposals. However, some textual amendments to the recommended action in document GOV/2554/Attachment 2/Rev.1 were proposed by Germany. They involve the switching of sub-paragraphs (a) and (b) and some other changes. The resulting text is as follows:

It is recommended that the Board:

(a) call upon all parties to comprehensive safeguards agreements to provide the information described in paragraph 6 above; and

(b) request the Secretariat and all parties to comprehensive safeguards agreements to adapt, where appropriate, the related Subsidiary Arrangements.

0024

BOARD OF GOVERNORS
Notes for the Chairman
4304289/32

Meetings starting on
Monday, 24 February 1992

Item 2(a)
Strengthening of Agency safeguards
Papers relating to nuclear material and sensitive equipment and non-nuclear material
Summing-up

THE CHAIRMAN

I have no more speakers. So, let me sum up our discussion on the papers relating to reporting of the export, import and production of nuclear material and of sensitive equipment and non-nuclear material.

The discussion was a multifaceted one, with a political component, a technical component and, finally, a philosophical component - a fact that complicates the task of summing up.

The discussion evoked many interesting and useful comments which the Secretariat will, no doubt, take into account when revising the two papers for our June meetings.

The modifications which the Director General proposed to his original proposals were welcomed by some members. However, there were other members who recognized that the details of the proposed scheme needed more careful examination. Also, some members were not ready to engage in more than a preliminary discussion at our present meetings.

Having said this, let us decide to revert to these two matters in June on the basis of revised documentation. I hope that sufficient consultations in the intervening period between the Secretariat and the different groups of Member States and within those groups will facilitate a positive outcome to our discussion of these matters in June.

1992-02-27, 10.15hrs
92-00772

0025

26 February 1992
PR 92/12
FOR IMMEDIATE RELEASE

INTERNATIONAL ATOMIC ENERGY AGENCY
WAGRAMERSTRASSE 5, P.O. BOX 100, A-1400 VIENNA, AUSTRIA,
TELEPHONE: 1 2360, TELEX: 1-12645, CABLE: INATOM VIENNA,
TELEFAX: 431 234564

PRESS RELEASE FOR USE OF INFORMATION MEDIA • NOT AN OFFICIAL RECORD

IAEA BOARD OF GOVERNORS STRENGTHENS NUCLEAR SAFEGUARDS INSPECTION REGIME

The International Atomic Energy (IAEA) Board of Governors has agreed to a number of measures intended to strengthen the Agency's safeguards system, including the ability of the Agency to conduct special inspections and expanded requirements on the provision and use of nuclear facility design information.

The Board, recalling its earlier discussion of this issue in December last year, reaffirmed the Agency's right to undertake special inspections in Member States with comprehensive safeguards agreements, when necessary and appropriate, and to ensure that all nuclear materials in peaceful nuclear activities are under safeguards.

The Board further reaffirmed the Agency's rights to obtain and to have access to additional information and locations in accordance with the Agency's Statute and all comprehensive safeguards agreements.

The Board, which met in Vienna from 24-26 February, called on parties to comprehensive safeguards agreements to provide preliminary information as early as possible on programmes for new nuclear facilities and activities, as well as modifications to existing facilities as soon as the decision to construct, to authorize construction or to modify a facility has been taken. This information would be updated during project definition, preliminary design, construction and commissioning phases.

The Board also addressed Secretariat proposals on reporting and verification of the export, import and production of nuclear material, of sensitive equipment and certain non-nuclear materials. The proposals included measures under which States would provide the IAEA with information to enable it to verify that reported inventories in a given State are consistent with the State's declared nuclear activities. The Board agreed to continue to review these proposals at its next meeting in June.

The Board further discussed a report by the Director General on the conclusion of an international convention in the field of nuclear safety. The Board authorized the Director General to set up an open-ended working group to begin necessary preparations for such a convention and report to the Board on its progress.

During the week of the Board's meeting, a safeguards agreement was signed by the Syrian Arab Republic pursuant to the latter's obligation under the Non-proliferation Treaty.

The transfer by the Government of the People's Republic of China to the Government of the Syrian Arab Republic, through the Agency, of a 30kW miniature neutron source reactor was also approved by the Board.

0026

2

관리 번호 92-414

외 무 부

종 별 :

번 호 : JAW-1254 일 시 : 92 0305 1147

수 신 : 장관(아일,정특) 사본:주일대사

발 신 : 주 일 대사(일정)

제 목 : 북한핵문제(일외상 국회답변)

연 : JAW(F)-0781

연호, '외상, 북한의 핵의혹관련 북한을 일응 신용'제하 와타나베외상의 작3.4 중원예산위 발언관련 금 3.5(목)자 산께이 조간 보도에 대해 외무성측에 확인한 발언요지를 아래 보고함.

0 질문(민사당 이또에세 의원) : 북한의 핵문제에 어떻게 대처할 할것인지,IAEA 특별사찰 실시는 ?

0 외상답변 : (북한의 핵사찰 수락의 중요성을 언급한후) 북한측은 핵을 갖고 있지않으며 핵개발 능력도 없다고 말하고 있음. 북한측의 말을 믿고싶으나, 현재로서 중요한 것은 북한이 핵사찰을 수락하여 북한측 주장을 제기될 문제로서현재는 북한이 아직 IAEA 핵안전협정에 비준도 하지 않은 단계이므로 우선은 북한이 협정에 비준하고 핵사찰을 받도록 해야할 것임.끝

(대사대리 남홍우-국장)

예고:92.12.31. 일반

검토필(1992.6.30.)

아주국	장관	차관	1차보	2차보	아주국	외정실	분석관	청와대
안기부								

PAGE 1 92.03.05 13:22

외신 2과 통제관 BX

0027

공　　　란

공　　란

공 란

공 란

관리번호	92-431

분류번호	보존기간

발 신 전 보

번 호 : AM-0042 920309 1726 FO 종별 :

수 신 : 주 전재외공관장 대사. 총영사

발 신 : 장 관 (정특)

제 목 : 북한, 핵안전협정 4.8. 비준 심의

3.8 북한 중앙방송은 북한 최고인민회의 상설회의가 최고인민회의 제9기 제3차 전체회의의 4.8 평양 소집을 결정하였으며, 의안은 예년과 같은 결산 및 예산안 이외에 "핵안전협정의 비준 심의"가 포함된 것으로 보도하였으니 업무에 참고바람. 끝.

(91년도 최고인민회의 전체회의는 4.11-13간 개최)

(외정실장 이 승 곤)

WMI-0054 920309 1726 FO

WZR -0263

보안통제	

국기주장 ...

앙고재	92년 3월 9일	특수정책과	기안자 성명		과 장	심의관	국 장	실장	차 관	장 관
			박동상					전결		

시보: 강한설

외신과통제

0032

	분류번호	보존기간

발 신 전 보

번 호 : WAV-0325 920309 1943 FO 종별 :

수 신 : 주 오스트리아 대사. 총영사

발 신 : 장 관 (국기)

제 목 : 북한 핵안전 협정 비준

1. 3.8. 북한 중앙방송은 4.8. 최고 인민회의 제9기 제3차 회의를 소집, 표제 협정비준 문제를 심의할 예정이라고 보도하였음.

2. 상기 북한 방송문과 관련 국내기사를 별첨 fax 송부하니 참고 바람.

별첨 : 상기 fax 5 매. 끝. AV(F)-35

(국제기구국장 김 재 섭)

보안통제	

앙고재	92년 3월 9일	국제기구과	기안자 성명		과 장	심의관	국 장		차 관	장 관
			신동익				전결			

외신과통제

0033

제 151 호

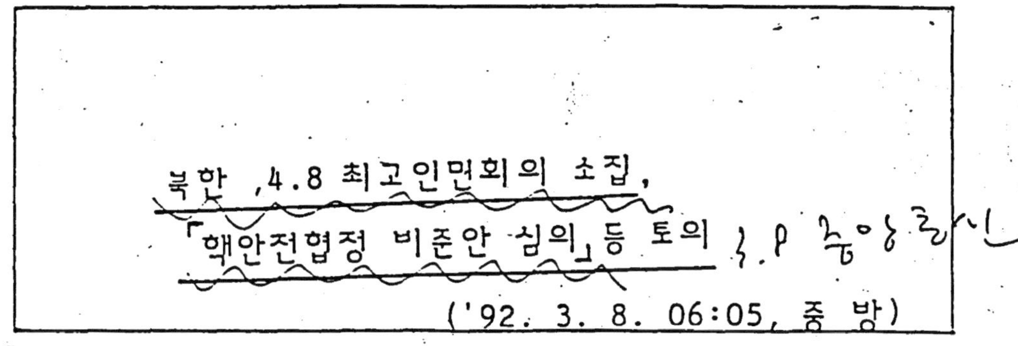
북한, 4.8 최고인민회의 소집,
「핵안전협정 비준안 심의」등 토의 3.8 중앙방송
('92. 3. 8. 06:05, 중 방)

「조선민주주의인민공화국 최고인민회의상설회의 결정」

-조선민주주의인민공화국 최고인민회의를 소집함에 대하여

조선민주주의인민공화국 최고인민회의 상설회의는 다음과 같이 결정한다

조선민주주의인민공화국 최고인민회의 제9기 제3차회의를 1992. 4. 8 평양에서 소집한다.

조선민주주의인민공화국 최고인민회의 상설회의

1992. 3. 7. 평양

조선민주주의인민공화국 최고인민회의 소집에 대한 공시

조선민주주의인민공화국 최고인민회의 상설회의는 최고인민회의 제9기 제3차회의를 1992. 4. 8 평양에서 소집함을 최고인민회의 대의원들에게 알린다.

회의에서 토의하게 될 의안은 다음과 같다.

1)조선민주주의인민공화국 1991년 국가예산 집행의 결산과 1992년

-1-

0034

국가예산에 대하여

2)최고인민회의 휴회기간 조선민주주의인민공화국 최고인민회의 상설회의가 심의 결정한 법들을 승인함에 대하여

3)조선민주주의인민공화국 정부와 국제원자력기구 사이에 맺은 핵무기전파방지조약에 따르는 담보협정을 비준할 데 대한 제안 심의에 대하여

대의원등록은 1992년 4월 6일과 7일에 만수대의사당에서 한다.

조선민주주의인민공화국 최고인민회의 상설회의

1992. 3. 7. 평양

南北韓 정치분과委 첫회의

「연락사무소」 중점논의

南측「설치·운영합의서」초안 제시

「화해」실천방안 교환·절충

오늘 板門店서 양측 6명씩 참석

【板門店=安熙昌기자】南北韓은 9일 오전 板門店 南측 지역인 평화의 집에서 고위급회담 정치분과위원회 제1차 회의를 열고 南北화해를 위한 구체적인 이행방안에 대해 논의했다.

9일 오전 板門店 南측지역「평화의 집」에서 열린 南北정치분과위 첫 정기회의에서 우리측 李東馥위원장(右)과 北측 白南俊위원장이 회의에 앞서 인사를 나누고 있다. 【板門店=[illegible]】

지난 2월19일 발효된 南北기본합의서에 따라 구성돼있는 정치·군사·교류-협력분과위중 처음으로 열린 이날회의에서 南北韓은▲상대방에 대한 체제존중▲내정불간섭▲상대방에 대한 비방·중상중지▲파괴전복행위금지등 南北화해에 관한 실천과제와 집행기구인 南北연락사무소의 구성문제를 놓고절충을 벌였다. 우리측 李東馥총리특별보좌관과 北측 白南俊조국평화통일위원회서기국장을 위원장으로, 양측에서 6명씩의 위원이 참석한 가운데 열린 이날 회의에서 南北양측은 위원장의 기조발언을 통해 南北화해분야를 이행하기 위한 서로의 입장과 실천방안을 제시했다.

우리측의 李위원장은 南北합의서이행을 위한 3대원칙을 제시하고 합의내용을 구체적으로 이행하는 집행기구인「南北연락사무소의 설치·운영에 관한 합의서」초안을 제시했다.

李위원장은『南北화해는 기본합의서를 이행·준수하는데 있어 핵심적인 과제』라고 전제, 『이를 위해 南北은▲상대방 체제와 법질서존중▲당사자해결▲南北호혜등 3개원칙을 준수해야 할것』이라고 말했다.

우리측이 이날 제시한 남북연락사무소 설치·운영에 관한 합의서」의 초안에 따르면▲명칭은「남북연락사무소 서울측 사무소」「남북연락사무소 平壤측 사무소」로 하며▲우리측 사무소는 板門店 북측 지역에, 북측사무소는 板門店 우리측 지역에 각각 교환 설치토록돼있다.

또 사무소 구성과 관련, 차관 또는 차관보급의 소장 1명밑에 부소장 1명과 연락관 5명및 기타 필요한 인원을 두면서▲남북간의 제반연락과 협의▲남북직통전화설치·운영▲남북간 왕래및 접촉에 따른 안내·편의제공·절차협의▲각분과위및 공동위 위임사항등의 기능을 수행토록 했다.

이와함께 각자의 연락사무소에▲연락관실▲왕래·접촉안내실▲이산가족 면회실, 우편물교환실·전화교환실등의기구를 두고 연락사무소장간에 매주1회 정기회의를 갖도록 했다.

李위원장은 南北합의서의 南北화해분야에 규정된 상호체제인정등 7개항에 대한 이행과제로▲南北상호관계설정▲상호불간섭 대상선정▲비방·중상의 개념정의등을 제시하고『이같은 과제들이 쌍방의 법률적·지도적 문제와 연결돼 있으므로 이를위해「남북법률공동위원회」를 발족시키자』고 제의했다.

92. 3. 9 <월>

중앙 2면

0036

92.3.9 <월> 세계 1면

"北核안정협정 내달8일 비준"

최고인민회의 소집

【도쿄=朴英哲특파원】北韓은 4월8일 최고인민회의(의회)를 소집, 지난1월말 국제원자력기구(IAEA)와 체결한 核안전협정을 비준할 것이라고 北韓 관영 중앙통신이 8일 보도했다.

도쿄에서 수신된 중앙통신은 北韓 최고인민회의 상설회의의 발표를 인용, 4월8일 열리는 제9기 최고인민회의 3차회의 의제에는 核안전협정 비준과 92년도 예산안 및 법률안 심의가 포함될 것이라고 전했다.

0037

"北核시설 처리문제 내달 15일까지 斷案"

金容淳, 日 가네마루에 書信

【東京=夫址榮기자】북한이 金日成 북한 주석의 생일인 오는 4월15일 이전에 일본에게 核문제에 관한 최종해답을 주겠다는 서신을 일본의 가네마루(金丸信)自民党부총재에게 보낸 사실이 8일 오전 밝혀졌다.

東京의 믿을만한 외교소식통은 지난 2월말 金容淳 조선노동당국제부장이 직접 가네마루 自民党부총재에게 인편및 FAX서신을 통해 이같은 의사를 전했다고 밝혔다.

이같은 북한의 회답은 최근 핵문제로 난항을 겪고있는 日-北韓교섭과 관련, 북한이 핵문제만큼은 일본에게 일종의 보장을, 시한을 정해했다는 점에서 주목된다.

한편 북한은 이에앞서 金日成주석생일에 가네마루 부총재를 초청했다.

조선 (92. 3. 8).

0038

공 란

공　　　　란

공 란

공 란

공 란

공 란

공 란

공 란

공 란

관리 번호	92-617

외 무 부

종 별 :

번 호 : AUW-0245 일 시 : 92 0326 1700

수 신 : 장 관(아동)

발 신 : 주 호주 대사

제 목 : 호주 국립대 한반도 워크숍

대: WAU-0239

연: AUW-0229

1. 대호 워크숍은 작 3.25 WILENSKI 호주 외무차관의 개회사를 시작으로 개막되었으며, 작일 회의에서는 한반도에 대한 미.일.중.러 4 강의 입장에 관해서,금일 회의에서는 북한과 남한의 핵개발정책 및 군축정책에 관해서 각각 토의를가졌음.

2. 우리측 학자 4 인(안병준, 문정인, 노경수, 길정우)과 당관 김의택 서기관은 작 3.25 회의종료후, 북한측 참석자인 박현재와 배상학을 만찬에 초대하고,금번회의기간중 양측간에 명확하고 활발한 의견 개진이 이루어 질수있도록 상호 협조키로 함.

3. 금 3.26 회의에서 북한의 박현재(군축및 평화연구소 대외관계 책임자)는북한이 핵무기를 현재 보유하거나 제조하고 있지 않을뿐아니라 핵개발의 필요조차도 느끼지 않고 있다고 강조하고, 4.8 개최될 최고인민회의에서 금년 1.30 IAEA 와 체결한 핵안전협정이 비준되고나면 곧 이어 핵사찰을 받게될것이라고 언급함. 이어서 북한의 배상학은 주로 북한의 군축정책에 관해 언급하면서, 종래의북한입장을 요약 설명함. 이들의 발표내용중 새롭거나 특별히 주목을 끄는 사항은 없었으며, 남한을 자극하거나 비방하는 내용도 전혀 없었음(북한측 발표문 TEXT 별첨 FAX 송부함)

4. 북한측의 상기 입장 발표가 있은후, 토론 참석자들로부터 북한의 헌법상조약의 비준권한은 주석(김일성)에 있는데 유독 핵안전협정만은 왜 최고인민회의에서 비준하는가라는 질문이 있었으며, 이에대해 박현재는 통상적으로 주석이 비준하나, 북한핵문제에 관해서는 국제사회에서 큰 논란이 있기 때문에 최고인민회의에서 특별히 심의하여 비준키로 했다고 답변함. 또한 영변에 과연 핵재처리시설이 존재하는가라는

아주국 장관 차관 1차보 2차보 외정실 분석관 청와대 안기부

PAGE 1 92.03.26 17:43

외신 2과 통제관 EC

0048

질문에 대해서도 여사한 재처리시설은 절대로 존재하지않는다고 단호히 대답함. 그러나 박현재는 한질문자로부터 북한이 1985 년 NPT가입직후 IAEA 핵안전협정에 즉시 서명코저 하였으나 당시 IAEA 측이 북한측에그릇된 양식을 보냈기때문에 동안전협정 서명의 지연을 초래하였는데, 만약 그때 IAEA 측이 정확한 양식을 보냈더라면 즉각 서명하였을 것인가라는 질문에 대해서는 여사한 사실자체를 알지못한다고 답함으로서, 토론 참석자들에게 전문가로서의 신뢰도를 손상시킨 듯한 인상을 줌.

5. 한편 토론참석자들은 북한이 최근 들어 일본의 핵개발 저의(과도한 플루토니움 축적)를 비난하고 있으나, 이느 북한에 대한 국제사회의 비난과 압력을 분산시키려는 의도이며, 또한 북한이 IAEA 의 사찰을 받게된다해도, IAEA 로서는재처리 시설금지를 강요할수 없으므로, 핵재처리 시설금지를 위해 남북한간에 효과적인 양자적 핵사찰 협정을 체결하는것이 중요함을 지적함.

8. 한반도에 관한 미.일.러.중의 입장에 관한 토론 요지 및 명일 토의 예정인 남북관계 진전에 관한 토의 내용은 추보위계임.끝.

(대사 이창범-국장)

예고: 92.6.30. 까지.

19 92.6.30.에 예고문에
의거 일반문서로 재분류됨

검토필(19 . .)

5. 北韓의 核安全協定 批准 時期

o 3.31 '시아존' 유엔工業開發機構(UNIDO) 事務總長은 이시영 신임 駐오스트리아大使의 信任狀 提呈時 表題관련 아래 요지로 언급함.

- 北韓은 金日成 生日 雰圍氣를 손상시키지 않기 위해 4.8 最高人民會議에서 核安全協定을 批准하고, 늦어도 4.15 金日成 生日 以前에 이를 IAEA에 通報할 것으로 보임.

  * 同 事務總長은 4.14-17 訪北 예정임. (駐오스트리아大使 報告)

0050

북한의 핵안전조치 협정 발효에 대한 외무부 대변인 논평(안)

I . 발표문안

1. 북한이 국제원자력기구(IAEA)와 지난 1월 30일 서명한 핵 안전조치 협정을 92년4월10일자로 발효시킨것을 환영한다.

2. 우리는 북한이 핵 안전조치 협정에 규정된 절차에 따라 보유하고 있는 모든 핵물질과 시설 내용을 국제원자력기구(IAEA)에 성실히 신고하고 조속히 핵 사찰을 수락함으로써 핵 비확산 조약(NPT) 당사국으로서의 의무를 완전 이행 할것을 기대한다

II . 발표시기 : 북한의 협정 발효 당일 (92.4.10)

III . 발 표 자 : 공보관

IV . 발표대상 : 외무부 출입기자단

V . 사전협의 : 청와대

0051

최고인민회의, 『핵안전협정』 승인

(4. 9, 19:00 중방)

<보도 전문>

『핵무기전파방지조약에 따르는 담보적용에 관한 조선민주주의인민공화국 정부와 국제원자력기구 사이의 협정을 승인함에 대하여』

o " 조선민주주의인민공화국 최고인민회의는 핵무기전파방지조약에 따르는 담보적용에 관한 조선민주주의인민공화국 정부와 국제원자력기구 사이의 협정을 심의하고 다음과 같이 결정한다.

조선민주주의인민공화국 최고인민회의는 이 협정이 공화국 정부의 반핵평화정책에 부합되며, 조선반도의 비핵화를 실현하는데 크게 기여할 수 있으며, 핵에네르기의 평화적 이용 분야에서 국제적 협조를 강화하는데 이바지 하리라고 인정하면서, 핵무기전파방지조약 기탁국중 어느 한나라도 조선반도에 핵무기를 전개하지 않으며, 우리를 반대하여 핵위협을 하지 않으리라는 것을 전제로 하면서 핵무기전파방지조약에 따르는 담보적용에 관한 조선민주주의인민공화국정부와 국제원자력기구 사이의 협정을 비준할데 대한 공화국 정부의 제안을 심의하고 이를 승인한다"

※ 정무원 원자력공업부장 (최학근) 의 제안문 전문은 녹음·정리 중임.

[정보분석실]

0052

공 란

공　　　　란

공 란

9
1

9이

5. 北韓, 核安全協定 4.9 批准說

o 訪日中인 황장엽 北韓 勞動黨 書記는 4.4 요미우리新聞과의 會見에서 北韓이 IAEA와 署名한 核安全協定에 대한 批准이 4.9 最高人民會議에서 討議後 決定될 것이라고 말하였음.

- 한편, 황장엽 書記는 4.4 교도通信과의 會見에서 김정일에 대한 權力移讓 문제와 관련, 아래 要旨로 언급함.

. 두사람은 一心同體며, 김정일은 黨 事業을 總括, 실질적으로는 總書記와 같아서 지금 黨 總書記의 명칭만을 부여하는 것은 의미가 없음.

. 김정일의 軍 最高司令官 就任이 主席이나 黨 總書記職의 移讓과 결부된다고는 생각지 않음.

. (김정일에 대한 國家.軍의 首位라는 표현이 처음 사용된 것과 관련) 이는 사실상의 最高指導者라는 의미임.

(外信綜合)

끝.

0056

공 란

공 란

공 란

북한최고인민회의의 핵안전조치 협정 비준동의에 대한

외무부 당국자 반응

92. 4. 9

1. 북한의 최고인민회의가 4.9(~~화~~목) 제9기 제3차회의 이틀째 회의에서 북한과 국제원자력기구(IAEA)간 핵안전조치 협정에 대해 비준동의를 하였음.
   협정 발효를 위한 다음 절차는 김일성이 협정을 비준한후 동 비준사실을 IAEA에 서면통보해야하며, IAEA가 이를 접수한 일자에 협정이 정식 발효하게 됨.

2. 우리는 북한이 협정 비준후 발효 절차를 지체없이 취하고, 이어서 핵안전협정 규정에 따라 조속하고 완전한 사찰을 위한 절차를 밟기를 기대함. 끝.

0060

관리번호	92-301

분류번호	보존기간

발 신 전 보

번 호 : WAV-0484 920409 1144 WG 종별 :

수 신 : 주 오스트리아 대사. ~~총영사~~

발 신 : 장 관 (국기)

제 목 : 북한 핵안전 협정 발효

1. 북한최고인민회의는 금일(4.9) 제9기 제3차회의 이틀째회의에서 북한-IAEA 간 핵 안전조치협정 비준에 대한 동의를 할것으로 예상되며, 북한은 김일성의 비준후 가까운 시일내에 동 협정 비준사실을 IAEA에 서면 통보함으로써 협정 발효를 위한 조치를 취할것으로 봄.(최고인민회의 비준 동의에 대한 북한측 공식발표 내용은 금명간 별도 통보예정)

2. 이와관련 본부는 북한의 협정 발효 당일 외무부 대변인 성명을 발표할 계획으로 있으니, 귀관은 IAEA사무국이 북한의 상기 협정비준 통보서한을 받는대로 동내용을 즉시 파악하여 보고 바람. 끝.

예고 : 92.6.30 일반

일반문서로 재분류(1992.6.30.)

(국제기구국장 김 재 섭)

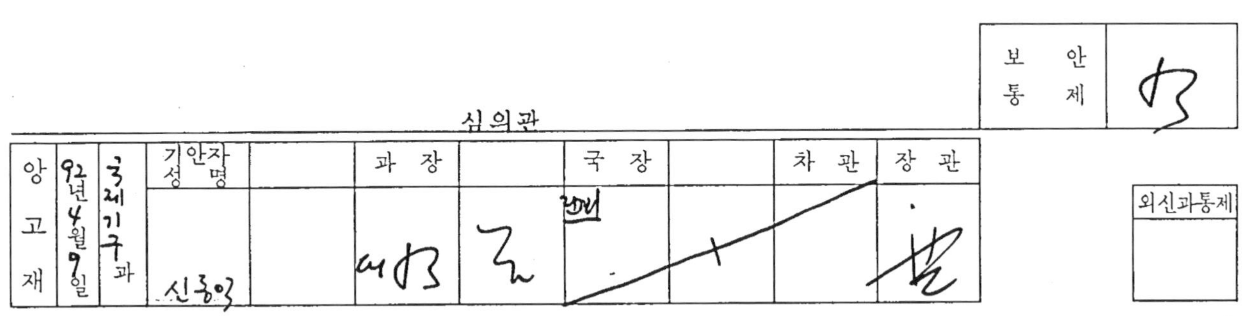

보안통제	

심의관

앙고재	92년 4월 9일	국제기구과	기안자 성명		과 장		국 장		차 관	장 관
			신동익							

외신과통제

0061

관리번호	92-305

원 본

외 무 부

종 별 : 긴 급

번 호 : AVW-0554 일 시 : 92 0409 2000

수 신 : 장 관(국기,미이,정특,기정,과기처)

발 신 : 주 오스트리아 대사

제 목 : 북한의 핵안전 협정 비준

4.9(목) 15:40 북한 대표부 윤호진 참사관은 허남 과학관에게 전화로 4.9(목) 북한 최고인민회의가 핵안전 협정을 비준했다는 사실을 알려 주면서 IAEA 사무국에 대한 통보 문제는 곧 지시를 보낼테니 기다리라는 평양의 지시가 있었다고 말하였음(북한 윤참사관은 금일 오전 IAEA 회의장에서 허 과학관과 조우시에 비준 관련 평양으로부터 통보가 있는데로 알려 주기로 약속한바 있었음). 끝.

(대사 이시영-국장)

예 고:92.12.31 일반.

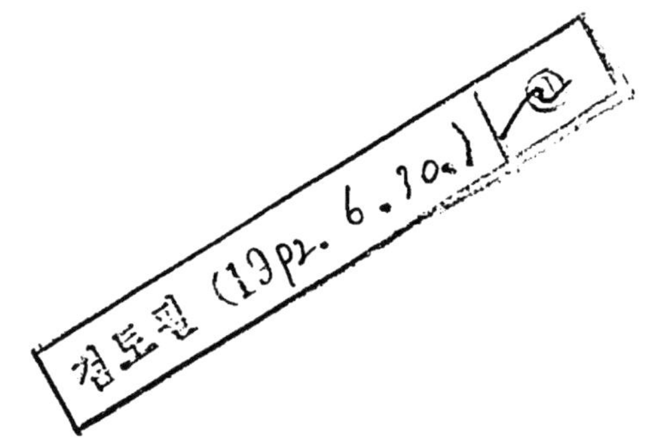

국기국	장관	차관	1차보	미주국	상황실	외정실	분석관	청와대
안기부	과기처							

PAGE 1

92.04.10 04:46

외신 2과 통제관 FM

0062

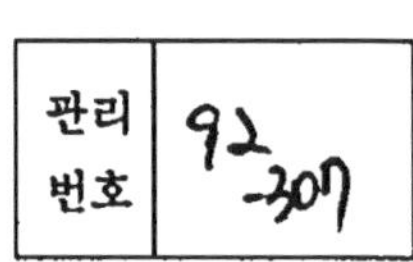

3 원 본

외 무 부

종 별 : 긴 급

번 호 : AVW-0555 일 시 : 92 0409 2000

수 신 : 장 관(국기,미이,정특,과기처)

발 신 : 주 오스트리아 대사

제 목 : 북한의 핵안전 협정 비준

대:WAV-0484

연:AVW-0554

1.4.9(목) 17:30 IAEA 사무국 ELBARADEI 섭외국장에게 확인한바, 동 시점 현재 북한 측으로 부터 비준에 관한 통보는 없다고 함을 중간 보고함.

2.IAEA 사무국측과 북한측의 통보가 있는데로 즉각 알려 주기로 하였는바 추보하겠음. 끝.

(대사 이시영-국장)

예 고:92.6.30 일반.

일반문서로 재분류 (1992.6.30)

국기국	장관	차관	1차보	미주국	외정실	분석관	청와대	안기부
과기처	상황실							

PAGE 1 92.04.10 04:47

외신 2과 통제관 FM

0063

공　　란

공 란

공

관리 번호	92 -304

원 본

외 무 부

종 별 : 지 급

번 호 : JAW-2085 일 시 : 92 0410 0003

수 신 : 장관(국기,아일,정특)

발 신 : 주 일 대사(일정)

제 목 : 북한의 IAEA 핵안전 협정 비준문제

1. 금 4.9(목) 저녁 당관 김영소 정무과장이 외무성 사다오까 원자력 과장에게 금일 북한의 IAEA 핵안전협정 비준관련 보도에 대한 일측반응을 타진한바, 동인의 언급 내용을 아래 보고함.

0 일정부는 금일 23:00 현재까지 북한이 IAEA 핵안전 협정에 비준했다는 사실을 확인하지 못하였으며, 따라서 정확한 내용을 확인중임.

0 금일 라디오 프레스는 '4.9 조선통신에 의하면, 평양에서 개최중인 북한최고인민회의는 동일 북한정부와 IAEA 간에 핵안전 협정비준에 관한 결정을 채택하였음.

비준에 관한 결정에서 최고인민회의는 NPT 에 가입한 모든 나라는 한반도에 핵무기를 배치하거나 북한에 핵위협을 초래하지 않는다는 것을 전제로 핵사찰 비준에 관한 정부 제안을 승인한다고 밝혔다'고 보도한바, 일측은 금일 북한측 조치가 비준을 의미하는지 확인하기 위해 평양방송을 청취하는등 노력하였으나 결국 확인하지 못했음.

0 금일 최고인민회의 결정내용이 상기 라디오 프레스 보도대로라면 '한반도에 핵무기를 배치하거나 북한에 핵위협을 초래하지 않는다는 것을 전제로 핵사찰 비준에 관한..' 부분에서 보듯이 북한이 또다시 전제를 제시함으로써 지연작전(DELAYING TACTICS)으로 나오는것으로 볼수도 있고, 동전제가 충족되지 않았다는 것을 이유로 김일성이 협정에 비준을 할수없다(동과장은 실제로 비준권이 누구에게 있는지도 확실하지 않다고 언급함)고 주장할수도 있으므로 일본으로서는 안전을 기하기 위해 금번 조치에 대해 평가한다는등의 담화를 발표하지 않기로 하였음.

0 일본으로서는 금후 북한이 핵안전조치 협정이 법적으로 발효되기 위한 조치인 IAEA 에 비준통지를 하게되면, 이는 북한이 협정에 비준했음을 의미하는 것이기

국기국	장관	차관	1차보	2차보	아주국	외정실	분석관	청와대
안기부								

PAGE 1 92.04.10 04:43

외신 2과 통제관 FM

0067

때문에, 평가한다는 요지의 담화를 북한의 동조치시 발표할 예정임

2. 한편, 동과장은 금일 북한이 핵안전조치협정에 비준할것에 대비 외무성으로서는 다음 요지의 외무보도관 담화를 준비해 놓고 있으나 상기와 같은 이유로 결국 발표하지 않기로 하였다고 첨언하였음.

0 '북한이 핵안전협정에 비준했다는 사실에 대한 보도가 있다는 것은 알고 있음. 동 보도가 사실이라면 일보 전진한것으로서 평가함. 그러나, 금후 IAEA 의 핵사찰 조기.무조건 수락, 작년말 채택된 한반도 비핵화 공동선언을 북한이 조속히 이행할것을 강력히 희망함. 끝

(대사 오재희-국장)

예고:92.12.31. 일반

PAGE 2

0068

a7743ALL r
u i BC-NUCLEAR-KOREA 10-04 0225
BC-NUCLEAR-KOREA
N.KOREAN NUCLEAR DELAY WOULD MEAN U.N. ROW - IAEA

TOKYO, April 10, Reuter - The International Atomic Energy Agency (IAEA) could take North Korea to the United Nations Security Council if it fails to open all nuclear facilities to inspection, a senior agency official said on Friday.

"It could go to the Security Council but so far indications are that North Korea wishes to cooperate," William Dircks, deputy director-general of the Vienna-based nuclear watchdog, told Reuters.

Dircks was in Japan attending a nuclear energy conference.

After months of suspense, North Korea on Thursday formally ratified an accord paving the way for international inspection of its secret nuclear plants. It must now send a list to the IAEA.

North Korea says it has built a research centre in the Yongbyon area, 90 km (60 miles) north of Pyongyang, for nuclear power generation. Washington, Seoul, and Tokyo suspect it is building a crude nuclear bomb there.

Dircks said the important question was whether North Korea would include the Yongbyon reactor on the list.

If there was a feeling that the list was incomplete, the IAEA would ask North Korea to show it everything, Dircks said.

If North Korea failed to comply the issue would be taken to the IAEA board of directors and if Pyongyang still refused to comply, the issue would go to the Security Council, he said.

REUTER VL SM JM
Reut07:03 10-04

0069

분류번호	보존기간

발 신 전 보

번 호 : WAV-0489 920410 0907 ED 종별 : 지급

수 신 : 주 수신처 참조 대사. 총영사

WUS -1653 WAU -0299
WJA -1569 WCN -0349
WUN -0822

발 신 : 장 관 (국기)

제 목 : 북한, 핵안전 협정 비준

1. 북한은 4.9(목) 개최된 최고인민회의 이틀째 회의에서 북한과 IAEA간 핵안전 조치 협정을 비준동의하였는바, 이와 관련한 북한 방송보도 내용을 별첨 fax 송부하니 참고바람.

2. 본부는 북한의 비준동의에 대한 당국자 반응을 별첨과 같이 발표하였으며, 공식논평은 북한의 협정 발효 당일 발표예정임을 참고바람.

첨부 : 상기 fax 매. 끝.

(국제기구국장 김 재 섭)

수신처 : 주오스트리아, 미국, 호주, 일본, 카나다, 유엔대사

보 안 통 제	(서명)

앙 고 재	92년 4월 9일	국제기구과	기안자 성명		과 장	심의관	국 장		차 관	장 관
			신동익		(서명)	(서명)	전결			(서명)

외신과통제

0070

최고인민회의 결정

(92. 4. 10. 06:00. 중방)

" 조선민주주의인민공화국 최고인민회의 결정 "

핵무기전파방지조약에 따르는 담보적용에 관한 조선민주주의인민공화국 정부와 국제원자력기구 사이에 협정을 승인함에 대하여

조선민주주의인민공화국 최고인민회의는 핵무기전파방지조약에 따르는 담보적용에 관한 조선민주주의인민공화국 정부와 국제원자력기구 사이의 협정을 심의하고 다음과 같이 결정한다.

조선민주주의인민공화국 최고인민회의는 이 협정이 공화국 정부의 반핵 평화정책에 부합되며 조선반도의 비핵화를 실현하는데 크게 기여할 수 있으며 핵 에네르기 의 평화적 이용 분야에서 국제적 협조를 강화하는데 이바지 하리라고 인정하면서 핵무기전파방지조약 기탁국들 중 어느 한 나라도 조선반도에 핵무기를 전개하지 않으며 우리를 반대하여 핵 위협을 하지 않으리라는 것을 전제로 하면서 핵무기전파방지조약에 따르는 담보 적용에 관한 조선민주주의인민공화국 정부와 국제원자력기구 사이의 협정을 비준할데 대한 공화국 정부의 제안을 심의하고 이를 승인한다.

0071

조선민주주의인민공화국 최고인민회의 1992년 4월 9일 평 양

제202호

최고인민회의 제9기 제3차회의 진행(5)

- 핵안전협정 승인 및 헌법 일부 수정
('92.4.9 19:00 중방)

지금부터 조선민주주의인민공화국 최고인민회의 제9기 제3차회의 제2일 오후회의 소식을 보내 드리겠습니다.

회의에서는 셋째 의안 "조선민주주의인민공화국 정부와 국제원자력기구 사이에 맺은 핵무기전파방지조약에 따르는 담보협정을 비준할데 대한 제안심의에 대하여"에 대한 토의가 진행되었습니다.

회의에서는 원자력공업부장 최학근 대의원이 조선민주주의인민공화국 정부와 국제원자력기구 사이에 맺은 핵무기전파방지조약에 따르는 담보협정을 비준할데 대한 제안심의 보고를 했습니다.

대의원 동지들!

공화국 정부는 지난 1월 30일 국제원자력기구가 핵무기전파방지조약에 따르는 담보적용에 관한 조선민주주의인민공화국 정부와 국제원자력기구 사이의 협정에 서명하고 이를 최고인민회의 상설회의 심의에 제기하였습니다.

0072

- 1 -

이 제의에 따라 지난 2월 18일에 진행된 최고인민회의 상설회의 제9기 제16차 회의에서는 공화국 정부가 핵담보협정을 체결한데 대하여 검토하고 문제의 성격에 비추어 이를 최고인민회의 제9기 제3차 회의 심의에 제출하였습니다.

나는 위임에 의하여 우리 공화국 정부가 대외관계에서 가장 첨예한 문제의 하나로 제기되었던 핵담보협정 문제의 공정한 해결을 위하여 기울여온 성의있는 노력과 원칙적 입장에 대하여 보고하려 합니다.

조선민주주의인민공화국 정부는 1985년 12월 12일에 핵무기전파방지조약에 가입하였습니다. 공화국 정부가 이 조약에 가입한 것은 핵에네르기를 오직 평화적 목적에 이용하며 핵무기를 개발하지 않는다는 확고한 입장을 내외에 선언한 것으로서 우리당의 일관한 반핵평화정책으로부터 출발한 정당한 조치였습니다.

공화국 정부는 창건된 첫날부터 대외관계분야에서 반핵평화정책을 변함없이 실시하여 왔습니다. 우리당과 공화국 정부의 반핵평화정책은 세상에서 사람을 가장 귀중한 존재로 여기는 주체사상의 근본원리에 기초를 두고 있으며, 자주·평화·친선을 기본이념으로 하는 공화국 대외정책의 중요한 구성부분을 이루고 있습니다.

우리 당과 공화국 정부의 반핵평화정책은 인민대중 중심의 우리식 사회주의의 본질적 요구로부터 출발하고 있으며, 국가와 사회의 주인이며 자기 운명의 주인인 우리인민의 자주적인 요구와 평화의지를 반영하고 있습니다.

공화국 정부는 핵군비경쟁을 막고 핵무기를 철폐하기 위하여 적극 투쟁하여 왔으며 핵에네르기를 평화적 목적에 이용하기 위한 과학연구사업을 꾸준히 진행하여 왔습니다.

공화국 정부는 무엇보다 먼저 남조선에서 미국 핵무기를 철수시키고 조선반도의 비핵화를 실현하기 위하여 시종일관 노력하여 왔습니다.

위대한 수령 김일성 동지께서는 다음과 같이 교시하셨습니다.

조선반도를 비핵지대로 만드는 것은 조선의 평화를 유지 공고화하며, 나아가서 아세아와 세계의 평화를 보장하는데서 매우 절실한 문제로 나섭니다.

우리는 오랜세월 자기에게 가해진 핵위협을 제거하는 것을 민족의 생사존망과 관련한 중대한 문제로 보고 반핵투쟁을 잠시도 중단하지 않았습니다. 우리는 일찌기 1956년 11월 조선민주주의인민공화국 최고인민회의 제7차 회의에서 남조선에서의 원자무기 도입을 반대하는 공식입장을 천명한데 뒤이어 남조선이 미국의 핵기지로 전변되는 것을 허용하지 말데 대하여 거듭 주장하였습니다.

- 3 -

0074

우리는 1960년대와 1970년대에도 최고인민회의 회의들에서나 남북조절위원회와 군사정전위원회의 회의들에서 그리고 여러 기회에 남조선의 핵기지화를 반대하는 우리당과 공화국 정부의 정당한 입장을 거듭 천명하였습니다. 우리의 반핵투쟁은 핵시험전쟁인 팀스피리트합동군사연습이 거듭되어 조선반도에서 열핵전쟁의 위험이 더욱 커진 1980년대에 이르러 한층 강화되었으며, 그것은 조선반도와 동북아세아지역의 비핵지대화를 위한 투쟁으로 심화되었습니다.

우리 공화국 정부는 1980년대 조선반도에서 날로 증대되는 핵전쟁의 위험을 막기 위한 획기적인 조치로서 조선반도를 비핵지대로 만들고 군축을 실현할데 대한 일련의 제안들을 내놓았으며, 지난해에는 세계적인 군축추세에 맞게 조선반도에서도 군축을 실현하기 위하여 우선 북과 남이 협상을 진행할데 대한 제안을 내놓았습니다.

공화국 정부는 지난해 핵대국들이 핵군축의 실현과 핵전쟁 방지에 대한 문제에서 원칙적 합의를 이룩하였을 때에도 미국이 진정 평화를 원한다면 남조선에 있는 자기의 핵무기를 철수하고 조선반도를 비핵지대, 평화지대로 만드는데 응해 나설 것을 촉구하였습니다. 우리의 이러한 원칙적인 제안들은 조선반도에서 핵무기전파방지조약을 공정하게 이행함으로써 지구상에서 가장 위험한 핵전쟁 발원지를 없애고 조선반도에서 긴장상태를 완화하며, 아세아와 세계의 평화위업에 기여하려는 공화국 정부의 확고한 입장과 의지를 그대로 보여주었습니다.

공화국 정부는 또한 주체적이며 자립적인 핵동력 개발계획을 세우고 핵에네르기를 사회주의 경제건설에 이용하기 위한 연구사업에 심화시켜 왔습니다. 우리 공화국 정부는 원자력공업을 발전시킬데 대한 조선노동당 제4차 대회 결정에 따라 방사선과 방사선 동위원소를 인민경제의 여러 부문에 널리 이용하는 한편 자체의 힘으로 핵동력 개발을 위한 과학연구사업을 전망성 있게 진행하여 왔습니다.

우리는 화력과 수력자원에 의거하는 발전소 건설을 기본으로 하면서 늘어나는 인민경제의 전력수요를 원만히 보장하기 위하여 핵동력 개발에 큰 의의를 부여하고 오래전부터 우리의 자본, 우리의 기술, 우리의 힘으로 핵동력 개발사업을 꾸준히 진행하여 왔습니다.

공화국 정부는 주체적인 핵동력 개발계획에 따라 영변지구에 핵연구중심을 꾸려 놓고 원자력의 평화적 이용을 위한 연구사업을 진행하여 왔습니다. 우리의 과학자·기술자들은 자력갱생의 혁명정신을 가지고 간고분투하면서 핵에네르기 이용분야에서 귀중한 경험을 쌓게 되었으며, 자체로 원자력발전소를 건설하고 운영하는데 필요한 기술과 지식을 가질 수 있게 되었습니다.

이것은 핵에네르기의 평화적 이용에서 우리인민들이 이룩한 자랑찬 성과이며 핵동력공업을 전망성 있게 전개하여 나아갈 수 있는 고귀한 밑천입니다. 우리나라에서 핵에네르기의 평화적 이용을 위한 모든 활동의 법적 기초는 최고인민회의 상설회의가 1974년 1월 23일에 심의 결정하고 최고인민회의 제5기 제3차 회의의 승인을 받은 조선민주주의인민공화국 원자력법입니다.

- 5 -

0076

원자력법은 핵에네르기를 평화적 목적에 이용하기 위한 연구와 개발을 진행하여 나라의 과학과 경제를 급속히 발전시키고 인민들의 물질문화생활을 향상시키는데 이바지하여야 한다는 원자력 연구개발 목적을 밝혔습니다.

우리나라에서 자체의 힘과 기술에 의한 핵동력의 성과적인 개발, 방사선과 방사선 동위원소의 광범한 이용은 바로 원자력법이 규정한 이 목적을 달성하기 위한 투쟁과정에서 이룩된 결실들입니다. 우리는 앞으로도 핵동력공업 건설을 기본으로 하는 원자력의 평화적 이용을 위한 원자력 개발사업을 적극 추진시켜 나아갈 것입니다.

우리는 지금 운영하고 있는 전기출력이 5천Kw인 현 원자력발전소를 정상적으로 돌리는 한편, 건설중에 있는 전기출력 5만Kw 원자력발전소와 20만Kw원자력발전소 건설을 힘있게 추진하여 1990년대 중엽에 조업할 것입니다. 그리고 출력이 더 큰 새로운 원자력발전소를 년차별로 계속 건설하여 전력에 대한 늘어나는 인민경제의 수요를 보다 원만히 보장하는데 이바지할 것입니다.

또한 원자력법은 핵에네르기의 평화적 이용분야에서 다른 나라들과 평등·호혜의 원칙에서 교류와 기술적 협조를 진행하며, 국제원자력기구를 비롯한 국제기구와의 협조를 강화할데 대한 문제도 규정하고 있습니다. 핵에네르기의 군사적 이용분야에서 우리와 국제원자력기구와의 협조관계도 날을 따라 발전하고 있습니다.

국제원자력기구가 정상적으로 보내주고 있는 원자력의 평화적 이용을 위한 기술자료들과 각종 참고자료들은 우리의 핵동력 개발 연구사업과 동위원소의 이용, 방사선 보호와 핵안전 및 담보체계를 세우는데 효과적으로 이용되고 있습니다.

국제원자력기구가 제공하는 기술협조도 날을 따라 강화되고 있으며, 기구 성원국들인 구라파 및 아세아 나라들과의 협조관계도 좋게 발전하고 있습니다. 우리는 앞으로 원자력의 평화적 이용분야에서 국제원자력기구와 다른 나라들과의 과학기술협조를 강화하여 나아갈 것입니다.

대의원 동지들!

공화국 정부가 핵무기전파방지조약에 가입한 주되는 목적은 핵에네르기의 평화적 이용분야에서 국제적 협조를 강화하며 조선반도에서 미국의 핵무기를 철수시키고 우리에 대한 핵위협을 제거하며, 나아가서 한반도를 비핵지대로 만들려는데 있었습니다.

핵무기전파방지조약에 의하면 비핵 체약국들이 핵무기와 기타 핵폭발 장치들을 생산, 접수, 보유하지 않을데 대한 의무를 지니는 동시에 핵에네르기를 평화적 목적을 위해 개발하는 권리를 가지며, 핵무기 소유 체약국들은 비핵국가들에 대한 핵위협을 하지 않으며 안전을 담보할 의무를 지니고 있습니다.

미국의 핵위협을 항시적으로 받고 있는 우리인민들에게 있어서 조선반도에서 핵전쟁 위험을 막고 평화를 보장하는 것은 가장 절박한 문제로 제기되고 있습니다. 이것은 전적으로 미국이 핵무기를 가지고 우리인민을 반대하는 핵공갈정책을 실시하고 있는 것과 관련되어 있습니다.

미국은 1950년대 후반기에 정전협정을 위반하고 남조선에 핵무기를 비법적으로 끌어 들여 전개하기 시작하였으며, 조선반도를 핵전쟁의 위험한 발원지로 전변시켰습니다. 자료에 의하면 이미 1976년도 국방예산을 심의하는 회의에서 남조선에 1천여개의 핵무기와 54대의 핵적재기가 배치된 사실들이 공식적으로 밝혀졌습니다.

핵화약고로 된 남조선은 근 40년간 각양각색의 핵무기의 반입 배치로 하여 문자 그대로 극동지역의 미국 핵저장고로 되었습니다. 이리하여 남조선에서의 핵무기 배비밀도는 100평방Km당 1개로서 15개 나라가 망라된 나토보다 4배나 조밀하게 되고 그 총 폭발력은 13,000 K.t으로서 1945년 8월 일본 히로시마에 투하된 원자탄의 일천배 이상에 달하게 되었습니다.

1976년 이래 16년 동안이나 우리 공화국을 반대하는 핵시험전쟁인 팀스피리트합동군사연습이 거듭되고 이 전쟁연습에서 B-52 핵전략폭격기로부터 F-16 전술핵전투폭격기에 이르기까지 그리고 중거리랜스핵미사일로부터 푸른베레모 특공대의 핵배낭에 이르기까지의 모든 핵무기들이 우리 공화국을 겨냥하여 기동하였습니다.

미국의 고위 군사당국자들 속에서 입버릇처럼 한 우리에 대한 핵위협과 핵공갈 폭언은 사태를 엄중하게 하였습니다.

남조선의 핵기지화와 핵전쟁 시험장화는 조선반도뿐 아니라 아세아와 세계평화에 대한 엄중한 위협으로 되였습니다. 그것은 남조선에 전개된 핵무기의 엄청난 숫자와 남조선에서 벌어진 핵전쟁 연습들에 버금되곤 하였던 핵전략 및 전술폭격기들이 조선반도의 범위를 훨씬 벗어난 작전반경을 가지고 있는데서도 잘 알 수 있습니다. 특히 팀스피리트합동군사연습의 핵전쟁 촬영기인 E4B 기까지 출동시킨 사실은 이 훈련이 조선반도뿐 아니라 세계적인 전략속에서 연습을 진행하였다는 것을 보여줍니다.

남조선에 대한 미국 핵무기의 전개와 핵전쟁 연습의 강화는 우리나라의 자주권에 대한 난폭한 유린이였으며, 우리인민의 자주위업을 가로막는 최대의 장애물이였습니다. 이리하여 조선반도에서 핵전쟁의 위험을 막고 평화를 보장하는 것은 우리민족의 운명과 관련되는 사활적인 문제로 국제정치에서 해결을 기다리는 초미의 문제로 제기되게 되었습니다.

공화국 정부는 핵무기전파방지조약에 가입하게 되면서 미국이 핵무기의 보유국으로서 응당 비핵국가인 우리나라를 핵무기로 위협하지 않으며, 핵무기전파방지조약에 의하여 지닌 자기의 의무를 이행하리라고 기대하였습니다. 그러나 미국은 우리의 인내성있는 노력에도 불구하고 남조선에 핵무기를 계속 끌어 들이고 우리에 대한 핵위협을 더욱 강화하였으며, 있지도 않은 우리의 핵무기 개발설을 들고 나와 세계 여론을 오도하면서 우리에 대한 일방적인 핵사찰 압력소동을 벌였습니다.

미국의 일방적인 핵사찰 압력은 우리의 자존심에 대한 모독으로서 추호도 접수될 수 없는 것이였습니다. 자주권을 생명보다 귀중히 여기고 있는 우리 공화국 정부는 핵사찰 문제가 공정하게 해결되려면 우선 미국이 남조선에 배치한 핵무기를 완전히 철거하고 우리에 대한 핵위협을 제거하며, 우리에게 법적인 담보를 공약하고 남조선에 있는 미국의 핵무기와 핵기지에 대해서도 동시사찰을 수행해야 한다는 것을 주장하였습니다.

우리는 또한 핵전쟁 수단들이 동원된 대규모의 팀스피리트합동군사연습을 그만둘데 대해서도 주장하였습니다. 핵사찰 문제와 관련하여 우리 공화국 정부가 취한 입장은 매우 공명정대하였습니다. 우리의 정당한 요구와 세계의 광범한 사회여론을 더는 외면할 수 없게된 미국은 지난해에 전술핵무기 철수제안을 내놓고 남조선에 배치된 자기의 핵무기 존재를 간접적으로나마 시인하고 남조선으로부터 핵무기를 철수하겠다고 하였으며, 팀스피리트합동군사연습도 중지하겠다고 하였습니다.

또한 우리의 동시핵사찰 제의를 접수하고 조·미 고위급회담에도 응해 나오게 되었습니다. 남조선 당국자들도 우리의 정당한 요구를 무시할 수 없게 되자 마침내 핵부재선언을 발표하고 우리와 조선반도의 비핵화 선언을 합의하는데 이르게 되었습니다.

이리하여 남조선으로부터의 미국 핵무기 철거와 관련한 우리 공화국의 일관한 노력에 의하여 우리의 핵담보협정 서명에 제동을 걸던 근본장애들이 제거되게 되었으며, 핵담보협정 체결 문제를 해결할 수 있는 전제가 마련되게 되었습니다.

공화국 정부는 우리의 요구와 주장대로 조선반도에서 핵담보협정 체결 문제의 공정한 해결을 위한 환경과 조건이 마련된 상황에서 지난 1월말에 대표단을 오지리에 파견하여 핵무기전파방지조약에 따르는 담보적용에 의한 조선민주주의인민공화국 정부와 국제원자력기구 사이의 협정에 서명하였습니다.

이것은 우리 공화국 정부가 핵무기전파방지조약의 사명에 맞게 핵담보협정 문제를 해결하기 위하여 견지하여 온 시종일관한 노력의 결실이며, 남조선으로부터의 미국 핵무기 철거와 핵전쟁 위협을 제거하는 것을 민족의 자주권을 수호하기 위한 원칙적인 문제로 제기하고 꾸준하게 투쟁하여 온 결과에 이룩된 커다란 승리입니다.

결코 핵사찰문제는 그어떤 압력이나 힘의 방법으로는 해결될 수 없습니다. 지금 우리인민과 세계 광범한 사회계는 조선반도의 비핵화가 실현되게 되고 핵무기전파방지조약을 공정하게 이행하기 위한 환경이 성숙되고 있는데 대하여 환영하고 있습니다.

세계의 이목은 지구상에서 최대의 열전지역의 하나로 되고 있는 조선반도에서 일어나고 있는 이러한 긍정적인 사태 발생에 집중되고 있습니다. 이상의 제반사실들은 우리나라에서 핵사찰 문제를 평등의 원칙에서 공정하게 해결할 수 있는 원칙적 요구들이 기본적으로 해결되어 가고 있다는 것을 보여주고 있습니다.

우리 공화국의 적극적인 노력과 주동적인 조치들에 의하여 마침내 담보협정이 체결되고 핵사찰 문제가 공정성의 원칙에서 해결될 수 있는 전망이 열리게 되였습니다.

우리 공화국이 핵무기전파방지조약에 가입한 때로부터 오늘에 이르는 전과정은 핵사찰문제와 관련하여 우리 공화국이 견지하여온 입장과 주장이 매우 정당하다는 것을 그대로 보여주고 있습니다.

대의원 동지들!

나는 이번 최고인민회의 제9기 제3차 회의에서 우리의 핵담보협정이 심의되고 승인되면 국제원자력기구와 합의되는 실무적 절차에 따라 지체없이 핵사찰을 받을 것이라는 공화국 정부의 입장을 다시한번 내외에 천명합니다.

지난 2월 오지리의 수도 윈에서 진행된 국제원자력기구 2월 관리이사회 회의에서 우리 대표단은 우리의 핵담보협정이 최고인민회의 제9기 제3차 회의에서 심의되고 승인되는데 따라 국제원자력기구의 핵사찰을 받기 위한 실무적 조치들을 곧 취할 것이라는 것을 명백히 밝혔습니다.

회의에 참가한 절대 다수의 나라들은 핵담보협정의 비준절차와 관련한 우리의 이러한 일정계획에 대하여 환영하였습니다. 이것은 핵담보협정 비준절차와 관련한 우리의 주동적인 계획들이 국제적인 인정을 받았다는 것을 보여주고 있습니다.

이번 최고인민회의에서 우리의 핵담보협정에 대한 심의가 성과적으로 결속되면 우리는 핵사찰에 필요한 문건들과 자료들을 제때에 국제원자력기구에 제출할 것이며, 모든 핵물질과 핵시설들을 사찰을 위하여 보장함으로써 핵무기전파방지조약에 따르는 자기의 의무를 성실히 이행하여 나아갈 것입니다.

우리는 이미 우리에게 핵무기가 없으며 그것을 만들 의사도 능력도 없으며, 또 만들 필요도 없다는데 대하여 여러차례 밝힌 바 있습니다. 우리는 주변의 큰 나라들과 핵대결을 할 생각이 없으며, 단지 동족을 멸살시킬 수 있는 핵무기를 개발한다는 것은 도저히 상상도 할 수 없는 일입니다. 이에 대해서는 누구도 의심을 가지지 않아도 될 것입니다. 미국도 우리의 핵사찰 문제가 순조롭게 해결될 수 있도록 우리의 자주적 입장을 존중하고 신의를 보여주어야 할 것이며, 핵무기전파방지조약에 따라 지닌 의무를 성실히 이행하여야 할 것입니다.

나는 이상과 같이 핵사찰 문제와 관련하여 공화국 정부가 견지하여 온 입장과 앞으로의 활동에 대하여 보고하면서 본 회의가 국제원자력기구와 체결한 핵담보협정을 승인할데 대한 공화국 정부의 제안을 찬동해 주리라는 확신을 표명합니다.

먼저 현준극 대의원이 토론했습니다. (※ 이하 각 대의원 토론 생략)

회의에서는 핵무기전파방지조약에 따르는 관계 배경에 관한 조선민주주의인민공화국 정부와 국제원자력기구 사이의 협정을 승인함에 대한 조선민주주의인민공화국 최고인민회의 결정초안이 낭독되었습니다.

『조선민주주의인민공화국 최고인민회의 결정초안』

" 핵무기전파방지조약에 따르는 담보적용에 관한 조선민주주의인민공화국 정부와 국제원자력기구 사이의 협정을 승인함에 대하여 조선민주주의인민공화국 최고인민회의는 핵무기전파방지조약에 따르는 담보적용에 관한 조선민주주의인민공화국 정부와 국제원자력기구 사이의 협정을 승인하고 다음과 같이 결정한다.

조선민주주의인민공화국 최고인민회의는 이 협정이 공화국 정부의 반핵평화정책에 부합되며 조선반도의 비핵화를 실현하는데 크게 기여할 수 있으며 핵에네르기의 평화적 이용분야에서 국제적 협조를 도모하는데 이바지하리라고 인정하면서 핵무기전파방지조약 기탁국들중 어느 한 나라도 조선반도의 핵무기를 전개하지 않으며 우리를 반대하여 핵위협을 하지 않으리라는 것을 전제로 하면서 핵무기전파방지조약에 따르는 담보적용에 관한 조선민주주의인민공화국 정부와 국제원자력기구 사이의 협정을 비준할데 대한 공화국 정부의 제안을 심의하고 이를 승인한다. "

회의에서는 핵무기전파방지조약에 따르는 담보적용에 관한 조선민주주의인민공화국 정부와 원자력기구 사이의 협정을 승인함에 대한 조선민주주의인민공화국 최고인민회의 결정이 대의원들의 전원일치로 채택되었습니다.

회의에서는 넷째 의안 조선민주주의인민공화국 사회주의의 헌법을 일부 수정·보충함에 대하여 토의가 있었습니다.

회의에서는 조선민주주의인민공화국 사회주의 헌법이 발표된 때로부터 20년이 된다고 하면서 우리나라 사회주의 헌법이 채택공표된 이후 위대한 수령 김일성 동지와 우리당이 새롭게 제시한 사상과 이념들, 당과 수령의 현명한 영도밑에 우리 인민이 혁명과 건설에서 이룩한 성과들을 반영하여 헌법을 일부 수정 보충했다고 지적했습니다.

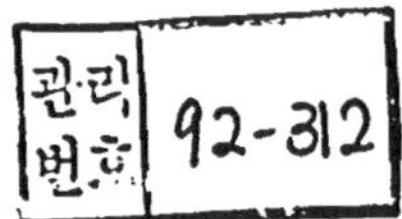

長 官 報 告 事 項

報 告 畢

1992. 4. 10.
國際機構局
國際機構課(25)

題 目 : 북한 최고인민회의의 핵안전협정 비준 동의 관련사항

1. 4.9.(목) 최학근 원자력 공업부장의 비준제안 주요내용

o 북한정부는 핵동력개발 계획에 따라 영변지구에 핵연구 센타를 설치하고 연구 사업을 진행한 결과, 자체힘으로 원자력 발전소를 건설하고 운영 하는데 필요한 기술과 지식을 가질수 있게 됨.

* 1974. 1월 최고인민회의가 '북한 원자력법' 승인

o 북한은 전기출력이 5MW인 현 원자력발전소를 정상적으로 가동시키는 한편, 전기 출력 50MW급과 200MW급 원자력 발전소 건설을 추진하여 1990년 중엽에 가동계획

- 상기 5MW급은 그간 알려진 30MW급 원자로(제2원자로)를 의미하는것으로 추정

* 통상 전기출력은 열출력의 20-30% 정도

o 북한정부가 핵무기 비확산조약(NPT)에 가입한 주요목적 은 핵 에너지의 평화적 이용을 위한 국제적 협조를 강화하고, 미국의 핵무기를 철수시켜 한반도를 비 핵지대로 만들려는데 있음

o 미국의 일방적 핵사찰 압력은 북한의 자존심에 대한 모독이며, 핵사찰문제 해결을 위해 북한은 미국에 대해 핵위협제거를 위한 법적인 보장 을 공약하고, 남한내 미국의 핵무기와 기지에 대해 동시사찰 을 수행해야 함을 주장 해옴

0087

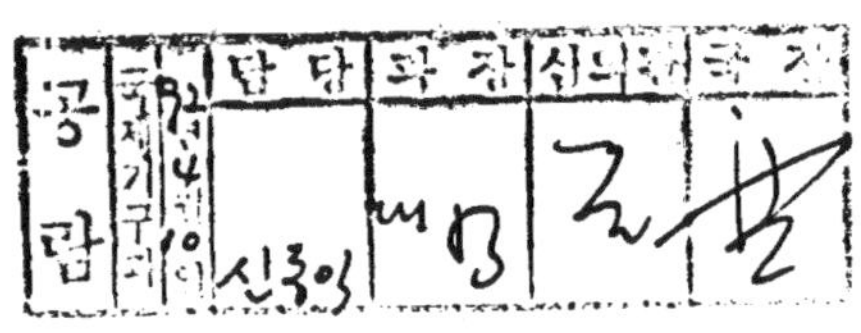

- 이에따라 미국은 동시 핵사찰 제의를 수락하고 미-북한 고위급 회담에 응하였으며, 남한은 「핵부재선언」을 발표하였음. 또한 남북한은 「한반도 비핵화 공동선언」에 합의

- 이와같이 핵안전협정 체결에 제동이 되었던 근본장애들이 제거됨으로써 핵사찰문제 해결의 전제가 마련됨

o 금번 최고인민회의에서 핵안전협정이 심의되고 승인되면 IAEA와 합의되는 실무적 절차에 따라 지체없이 핵사찰을 받을것 이라는 북한 정부 입장을 대내외적으로 천명

2. 일본정부 반응

o '한반도에 핵무기를 배치하거나 북한에 핵 위협을 초래하지 않는다는 것을 전제로 핵안전협정 비준'한다는 것은 북한의 또다른 지연작전으로 볼수도 있음

o 일본은 금번 북한의 조치에 대해 담화를 발표하지 않고, 북한이 IAEA에 비준통지를 하게되면 북한이 협정에 비준했음을 의미하는 것이기 때문에 이를 평가한다는 담화를 발표할 예정 임.

3. 북한의 협정비준 동의관련 특기사항 및 조치내용

가. 특기사항

o 4.9. 주비엔나 북한대표부 윤호진 참사관 은 아국대사관에 전화 로 '협정비준 사실의 IAEA 통고는 곧 지시를 보낼테니 기다리라는 평양의 지시가 있었다'고 통보 해옴

o 4.9. IAEA 섭외국장에 확인한 결과 현재까지 북한측으로부터 협정 비준에 관한 통보는 없었다함

나. 조치내용

o 4.9. 북한최고인민회의의 핵안전조치 협정비준 동의에 대한 외무부 당국자 반응 을 외무부 출입기자들에게 배포

o 4.9자 북한 방송문내용을 6개 주요공관에 fax 송부

4. 미측 Talking Points에 대한 아국입장을 주오스트리아대사에게 통보 (4.10. 미국무성 Kenndedy 대사의 IAEA 사무총장 면담용)

o 북한 이 4월중 비준, 발효 및 5월말 최초보고서 제출의 일정을 지키지 않을 경우 IAEA 특별이사회 소집 에 대해 이의 없음.

o Blix 사무총장 이 북한의 최초보고서가 접수된 이후에 방북하는것이 좋다 는데 의견 일치

미국의희망과는달리

o 북한 이 ~~시설 정보제출~~ 최초보고서에 재처리시설 관련 정보를 포함시키지 않을 경우 미국 이 고려하고 있는 대처방안 문의. 끝.

예고: 92. 6. 30

0089

長 官 報 告 事 項

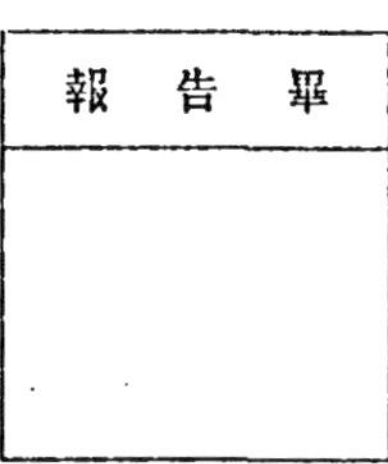

1992. 4. 10.
國際機構局
國際機構課(25)

題 目 : 북한 최고인민회의의 핵안전협정 비준 동의 관련사항

1. 4.9.(목) 최학근 원자력 공업부장의 비준제안 주요내용

   o 북한정부는 핵동력개발 계획에 따라 영변지구에 핵연구 센타를 설치하고 연구 사업을 진행한 결과, 자체힘으로 원자력 발전소를 건설하고 운영 하는데 필요한 기술과 지식을 가질수 있게 됨.

   * 1974. 1월 최고인민회의가 '북한 원자력법' 승인

   o 북한은 전기출력이 5MW인 현 원자력발전소를 정상적으로 가동시키는 한편, 전기 출력 50MW급과 200MW급 원자력 발전소 건설을 추진하여 1990년 중엽에 가동계획

   - 상기 5MW급은 그간 알려진 30MW급 원자로(제2원자로)를 의미하는것으로 추정

     * 통상 전기출력은 열출력의 20-30% 정도

   o 북한정부가 핵무기 비확산조약(NPT)에 가입한 주요목적 은 핵 에너지의 평화적 이용을 위한 국제적 협조를 강화하고, 미국의 핵무기를 철수시켜 한반도를 비핵지대로 만들려는데 있음

   o 미국의 일방적 핵사찰 압력은 북한의 자존심에 대한 모독이며, 핵사찰문제 해결을 위해 북한은 미국에 대해 핵위협제거를 위한 법적인 보장 을 공약하고, 남한내 미국의 핵무기와 기지에 대해 동시사찰 을 수행해야 함을 주장 해옴

- 1 -

0090

- 이에따라 미국은 동시 핵사찰 제의를 수락하고 미-북한 고위급 회담에 응하였으며, 남한은 「핵부재선언」을 발표하였음. 또한 남북한은 「한반도 비핵화 공동선언」에 합의

- 이와같이 핵안전협정 체결에 제동이 되었던 근본장애들이 제거됨으로써 핵 사찰문제 해결의 전제가 마련됨

o 금번 최고인민회의에서 핵안전협정이 심의되고 승인되면 IAEA와 합의되는 실무적 절차에 따라 지체없이 핵사찰을 받을것 이라는 북한 정부 입장을 대내외적으로 천명

2. 일본정부 반응

o '한반도에 핵무기를 배치하거나 북한에 핵 위협을 초래하지 않는다는 것을 전제로 핵안전협정 비준'한다는 것은 북한의 또다른 지연작전으로 볼수도 있음

o 일본은 금번 북한의 조치에 대해 담화를 발표하지 않고, 북한이 IAEA에 비준 통지를 하게되면 북한이 협정에 비준했음을 의미하는 것이기 때문에 이를 평가한다는 담화를 발표할 예정 임.

3. 북한의 협정비준 동의관련 특기사항 및 조치내용

가. 특기사항

o 4.9. 주비엔나 북한대표부 윤호진 참사관 은 아국대사관에 전화 로 '협정 비준 사실의 IAEA 통고는 곧 지시를 보낼테니 기다리라는 평양의 지시가 있었다'고 통보 해옴

o 4.9. IAEA 섭외국장에 확인한 결과 현재까지 북한측으로부터 협정 비준에 관한 통보는 없었다함

나. 조치내용

o 4.9. 북한최고인민회의의 핵안전조치 협정비준 동의에 대한 외무부 당국자 반응 을 외무부 출입기자들에게 배포

o 4.9자 북한 방송문내용을 6개 주요공관에 fax 송부

4. 미측 Talking Points에 대한 아국입장을 주오스트리아대사에게 통보 (4.10. 미국무성 Kenndedy 대사의 IAEA 사무총장 면담용)

o 북한 이 4월중 비준, 발효 및 5월말 최초보고서 제출의 일정을 지키지 않을 경우 IAEA 특별이사회 소집 에 대해 이의 없음.

o Blix 사무총장 이 북한의 최초보고서가 접수된 이후에 방북하는것이 좋다 는데 의견 일치

o 미국의 희망과는 달리 북한 이 최초보고서에 재처리시설 관련 정보를 포함시키지 않을 경우 미국 이 고려하고 있는 대처방안 문의. 끝.

원 본

외 무 부

종 별 :

번 호 : JAW-2096 일 시 : 92 0410 1359

수 신 : 장 관(국기,정특,아일)

발 신 : 주 일 대사(일정)

제 목 : 북한 핵안전협정 비준

작 4.9.(목) 조선 중앙통신의 북한 핵안전 협정 비준보도와 관련, 금 4.10.(금) 당지주요언론(조간)의 분석요지를 하기 보고함

1. 아사히 신문('여전히 냉엄한 국제여론' 제하)

-북한의 일본.미국과의 대화를 진전시키기 위하여 IAEA 사찰을 수락키로 결단을내린 것으로 보임

-그러나 북한에 대한 국제여론은 여전히 냉엄함. 설사 IAEA 사찰을 통해 '핵무기 개발의 용의점이 없다'는 결론이 나온다 해도, 미국은 걸프전쟁시 이라크의 경험등에 비추어, 북한이 신고하지 않은 핵물질에 대하여도 사찰이 가능한 '특별 사찰'실시를 IAEA 에 요구할 가능성이 매우 높음

-북한으로서는 핵사찰 수락에 대한 댓가로서, 주한미군 핵무기 철수의 확인을 강력히 요구할 자세를 보이고 있어, '핵카드'를 사용한 외교전술은 금후로도 계속될것같음

2. 일본 경제신문(사설: '핵안전협정 비준후의 북한에 바란다' 제하)

-북한이 핵안전협정을 승인함으로써 오랜현안이 일단락된것은 나름대로 의미가 있으나, 북한의 핵의 혹이 실질적으로 해소되기까지 많은 문제가 남아 있다는 점에는변화가 없음. 북한이 성실히 사찰에 응하여 불안감이 불식될수 있기를 기대함

-미국은 경우에 따라 북한에 대한 경제 봉쇄, 유엔 안보리 결의에 의거한 강제사찰 및 무력을 포함한 강경수단까지도 검토하고 있는 바, 이러한 수단은 국제적 긴장을 고조시키는 것이므로 바람직하지 않음. 북한은 핵문제를 한국, 미국등으로 부터양보를 얻어내기 위한 카드로서 충분히 활용하려 하는것 같으나, 핵은 그러한 흥정의 재료로 하기에는 너무나 중대한 영향력을 갖고 있음

-북한의 핵무장은 한국은 물론 일본을 포함한 동북아시아 전역에 커다란

국기국 아주국 외정실 1차보

92.04.10 15:02 WH

외신 1과 통제관

충격을가져오게 될것임. 미국은 이를 경계하고 있음

3. 일본 경제신문('한.미, 완전사찰에 압력 ' 제하)

-금번 조치로 북한의 핵사찰 실현에 필요한 한가지 절차가 완료된것은 틀림없음. 그러나 사찰대상 및 방법등 구체적 내용은 여전히 불투명함

-북한으로서는 협정 비준으로써 국제적 압력을 회피하는 동시에, 미.북한 관계 개선의 돌파구로 삼고자 하는 의도인 것으로 보임

-만일 북한이 금후, 실제 사찰수락을 지연시킬경우, 미국은 유엔 안보리를 통한문제해결등 한층 강경한 자세를 취할 공산이 큼. 그러나 남북한 당사자간의 핵문제해결을 지향하는 한국이 북한에 양보함으로써 한.미간의 공동보조가 무너질 가능성을 지적하는 의견도 있음

4. 요미우리 신문('사찰실현에는 여전히 곡절' 제하)

-금후 북한이 영변등 관련시설을 신고하지 않을경우, IAEA 의 '특별 사찰' 제1호가 될 가능성이 있는등, 사찰실현에 이르기까지는 여전히 곡절이 예상됨

5. 마이니치 신문('핵사찰, 더욱 현실감' 제하)

-금번 비준조치로 인해 북한의 핵시설에 대한 사찰실시는, 한층 현실감을 갖게 되었으나, 실제 사찰에 이르기까지는 곡절이 예상됨

-북한은 협정비준을 대미관계 개선의 카드로서 활용할 것인바, 이에 대해 한.미양국정부는 지금까지의 북한측의 대응에 깊은 불신감을 갖고 있음

-한.미 양국이 설정한 시한인 6월까지 북한의 핵사찰이 실현될것인지는 극히 유동적임. 만일 이때까지 사찰이 실현되지 않을 경우, 미국정부는 유엔안보리에 문제를제기할 방침을 굳히고 있음

6. 동경 신문('상호사찰 촛점에' 제하)

-금번 비준조치는 핵사찰을 위한 한단계에 불과하며, 남은 절차과정에서 여전히파란이 예상됨

-한국정부는 IAEA 사찰과는 별도로 남북상호사찰에서 활로를 찾으려 하고 있는 바, 북한의 핵문제는 남북한의 직접 교섭추이에 달려있음

7. 산케이 신문('영변의 시설신고 주시' 제하)

-정부는 지금까지 '북한에 핵 재처리 시설이 존재할 가능성이 높다'고 하여, 일.북 교섭에서 동시설의 폐기를 요구해 왔는 바, 북한은 그존재를 부정하고 있어, 모두보고에서도(재 처리시설)신고하지 않을 가능성이 높음. 끝

PAGE 2

0094

(대사 오재희-국장)

PAGE 3

0095

관리번호	92-314

3 원 본

외 무 부

종 별 : 긴 급

번 호 : AVW-0569 일 시 : 92 0410 1230

수 신 : 장 관(국기,정특,미이)

발 신 : 주 오스트리아 대사

제 목 : 북한 핵안전 협정 비준 통보

대:WAV-0489

1. IAEA 사무국 담당관 KELTSCH 에 의하면 당지 북한 대표부는 금 4.10(금) 오후중 핵안전협정 비준 국내절차가 완료되었다는 대표부 명의 공한을 수교하기로 하였다 함(당지 북한 대표부 대사는 금일 오후중 BLIX 사무총장 면담신청을 하였으나, BLIX 사무총장 부재중이라 시간이 확정되지 않았다 하며, 면담시간을 BLIX 총장이 오후 2 시에 집무실에 나온후 결정될 것이라 함.

2. 또한 북한측은 상기 대표부 공한에 이어 협정 비준절차 완료에 관한 외교부장 명의 서한을 보내겠다고 하였다 하며, IAEA 측은 대표부 공한만으로 협정발효에 필요한 조건이 충족 되는것으로 본다함. 끝.

(대사 이시영-국장)

예 고:92.6.30 일반.

일반문서로 재분류 (1992.6.30.)

검토필 (1992.6.30.)

국기국	장관	차관	1차보	미주국	상황실	외정실	분석관	청와대
안기부								

PAGE 1

92.04.10 19:47

외신 2과 통제관 BS

0096

관리번호	92-316

원 본

외 무 부

종 별 : 긴 급

번 호 : AVW-0575 일 시 : 92 0410 1610

수 신 : 장 관(국기,정특,미이,기정)

발 신 : 주 오스트리아 대사

제 목 : 북한의 핵안전 협정 비준 통보

연:AVW-0569

1. 금 4.10 오후 3.30 시 본직은 BLIX 사무총장과의 통화를 통하여 당지 북한 전인찬대사가 금일 오후 3 시경 동 사무총장을 방문하여 북한의 IAEA 와의 핵안전 협정 비준에 필요한 대내 절차가 종료되었음을 통보하며 이로써 금일자로 동 협정의 효력이 발생한다는 내용의 공한을 동 사무총장에게 전달했음을 확인하였음.

2. 동 사무총장은 본직 문의에 대하여 북한으로 부터 5 월 15 일 이전에 최초보고서를 제출하게 될것이라는 시사(INDICATION)를 받은바 있다고 말하였음.

3. 동 사무총장은 금일 북한대사가 동 사무총장에대한 5 월중 방북 초청을 확인했다 하며, 따라서 동 총장으로서는 북한의 최초 보고서를 받은후 방북하게 될것으로 기대하고 있다고 말하였음.

4.IAEA 사무국은 곧 북한측의 상기 통보사실을 공표 할것이라고 하며, 북한측 공한 텍스트는 곧 추보하겠음.

5. 상기 2,3 항 내용에 관하여 BLIX 총장은 대외적으로 공표하지 않을 것이므로 협조 해줄것으로 요망했으니 유념해 주시기 바람. 끝.

(대사 이시영-국장)

예고:92.6.30 일반.

일반문서로 재분류 (92.6.30.)

국기국	장관	차관	1차보	미주국	상황실	외정실	분석관	청와대
안기부								

PAGE 1

92.04.11 00:02

외신 2과 통제관 DV

0097

원 본

외 무 부

암호수신

종 별 :

번 호 : AVW-0577 일 시 : 92 0410 1900

수 신 : 장 관(국기,정특,과기처)

발 신 : 주 오스트리아 대사

제 목 : 북한 핵안전 협정 비준통보

연:AVW-0575,0569

연호 당지 북한 대표부의 핵안전협정 비준 통보와 관련한 IAEA 사무국의 보도자료(FAX 1)와 비준 통보 공한 본문내용(FAX 2)를 별전 송부함.

별첨:AVW(F)-062 2 매.끝.

(대사 이시영-국장)

국기국 장관 차관 1차보 외정실 분석관 과기처

PAGE 1

92.04.11 05:18

외신 2과 통제관 DV

0098

3

EMBASSY OF THE REPUBLIC OF KOREA

Praterstrasse 31, Vienna
Austria 1020 (FAX : 2163438)

No : AVW(F) - 062	Date : 20410 1900
To : 장 관(국기, 정특, 과기처) (FAX No :)	
Subject : 첨 부	

표지포함 3 매

Total Number of Page :

0099

1[illegible]ril 1992
P[illegible]/20
FOR IMMEDIATED RELEASE

FAX 1

DEMOCRATIC PEOPLE'S REPUBLIC OF KOREA RATIFIES
IAEA NUCLEAR SAFEGUARDS AGREEMENT

The Resident Representative of the Democratic People's Republic of Korea (DPRK) to the International Atomic Energy Agency in Vienna, Ambassador Chon in Chan, today informed the Director General of the International Atomic Energy Agency, Dr. Hans Blix, of his country's ratification of its safeguards Agreement with the IAEA.

The Agreement, which was signed in Vienna, on 30 January 1992, was ratified by the Supreme People's Assembly of the DPRK on 9 April. The Director General was informed that this constitutes the DPRK's statutory and constitutional requirements for entry into force of the Agreement. The Agreement thus enters into force today.

The DPRK, under the safeguards Agreement, is to submit to the Agency its Initial Report of all nuclear materials subject to the Agreement and their location before May 31 1992. It is expected that the Agency inspection visits will begin in June.

* * * * *

Doc. 8510x
1992-04-10
DKyd/sch/1271

0100

가 FAX 2

The Permanent Mission of the Democratic People's Republic of Korea to the International Organizations in Vienna is authorized to inform herewith the International Atomic Energy Agency that by the ratification at the Supreme People's Assembly of the Democratic People's Republic of Korea on 9 April 1992 of the Agreement between the Government of the Democratic People's Republic of Korea and the International Atomic Energy Agency for the Application of Safeguards in connection with the Treaty on the Non-Proliferation of Nuclear Weapons the stutory and constitutional requirements for the entry into force of the Agreement has been met.

0101

관리 번호 92-199

외 무 부

종 별 :

번 호 : AVW-0582 일 시 : 92 0410 1930

수 신 : 장 관(국기,아이,정특,미이,구이)

발 신 : 주 오스트리아 대사

제 목 : 예방보고

1. 본직은 4.9 당지 KUME 일본 국제기구대사및 CHEN 중국 국제기구대사를 각각 예방하고 환담하였음.

2. 중국대사는 이례적으로 동국대표부 접견실에서 정식으로 본직을 영접하고 약 1시간에 걸쳐 북한 핵문제, 한중관계등 광범위하게 의견 교환하였는바 주요 요지 아래와 같음.

-북한은 구소련의 붕괴 이전까지만 해도 핵개발을 구체적으로 추진할 의사가 있었던 것으로 알고 있으며, 다만 소련 붕괴후 러시아로부터 핵분야 협력을 기대할수 없게되고,중국으로부터는 핵 협력이 없었으므로 이제는 핵개발을 진전시킴에 있어 어느 외국으로 부터도 협조를 얻을수 없는 상황이 조성됨에 따라 결국 비핵화 방향으로 선회하게 된것으로 보고 있음. 따라서 조만간 안전협정비준과 사찰 수락의 절차를 밟을 것으로 봄.

-한.중 관계는 그간의 착실한 실질관계 증진에 비추어 조만간 정상화 될것으로 보며, 이상옥 장관의 금번 방중이 그 중요한 한 단계가 될것으로 기대함.

-당지 북한 대사와는 별로 접촉이 없는 편이며 양국대표부간 협조 관계도 미미함.

-앞으로 양국대사간 및 실무진간 긴밀한 협조를 다짐함. 끝.

(대사 이시영-국장)

예 고:92.12.31 까지.

검토필(1992. 6 . 30.)

92.12.31

국기국	장관	차관	1차보	2차보	아주국	미주국	구주국	외정실
분석관								

0102

PAGE 1 92.04.11 04:31

외신 2과 통제관 DV

관리번호 92-315

원 본

외 무 부

종 별 : 지 급

번 호 : JAW-2124 일 시 : 92 0410 2255

수 신 : 장 관(국기,아일,정특)

발 신 : 주 일 대사(일정)

제 목 : 북한의 IAEA 핵안전협정 비준문제

연: JAW-2085

1. 연호, 금 4.10(금) 외무성 사다오까 원자력과장은 당관 김영소 정무과장에게 표제관련, 담화발표대신 기자들의 질문에 대비 대외응답 요령으로서 외무성이 준비한 내용을 아래와 같이 알려왔음.

0 4.9. 북한 최고인민회의가 IAEA 와의 핵안전협정의 비준을 결정하였다는 내용이 보도된 것으로 알고 있음. 그러나 비준의 승인에 'NPT 체약국이 한반도에의 핵의 배치 및 위협을 가져오지 않는다'는 전제가 붙어있다 하는바, 금번결정이 북한의 비준행위의 완료를 의미하는 지는 불명함.

0 이것이 북한으로서의 비준을 의미하는 것이라면, 북한이 갖는 NPT 조약상의 의무의 이행이라는 오랜 현안의 해결을 향하여 일본전진한 것으로서 평가할수있음.

0 정부로서는 북한이 본건협정의 발효후, 협정상의 의무인 사찰의 수락등을 조기에 그리고 무조건적으로 완전 이행하고, 또한 재처리.농축시설을 보유하지 않을것을 포함한 '한반도 비핵화에 관한 공동선언'의 내용을 성실히 실행에 옮김으로써, 핵무기 개발에 관한 국제적 우려를 조기에 해소할 것을 계속 강력히 요구해 나가고자 함.

2. 한편, 김과장이 금 4.10 무또 북동아과장과 면담시 표제건 타진한바, 동과장은 '혹시나 하고 생각했으나, 북한측이 또다시 전제를 달고 나와 금후 전망을 하기가 힘들다'고 하면서, '북한내 군부의 의견등도 있을 것이므로 내부조정 하는데 어려움이 있는 것이 아닐까 생각한다'는 반응이었음. (동과장은 내부 애기라고 하면서 당초 북동아과로서는 절차에 따른 북한측의 조치에 대해 일일히 평가한다는 담화등을 발표할 필요는 없을것이라고 생각, 1.30 북한의 핵안전협정 서명시와 마찬가지로 기자질의에 대비한 응답요령으로 족하다는 의견을 제시하였으나, IAEA 를 담당하는 원자력과가 비준은 중요한 의미가 있으므로 격을 높여 외무보도관의 환영담화를

국기국 장관 차관 1차보 아주국 외정실 분석관 청와대 안기부

PAGE 1

92.04.11 00:36

외신 2과 통제관 DV

0103

발표하자고 하여 환영담화를 발표키로 내부 조정이 되었으나, 북한측이 전제를 제시함으로써 결국 응답요령 작성으로 결정되었다는 경위를 알려주었음)끝

(대사 오재희-국장)

예고:92.12.31.일반

공 란

공 란

공　　　　란

공 란

공　　　란

제 208 호

외교부대변인, 핵안전협정 승인관련 발언

- 중앙통신사와의 회견 통해

(92. 4. 11. 09:30. 중 방)

조선민주주의인민공화국 최고인민회의 제9기 제3차 회의에서 공화국 정부와 국제원자력기구 사이에 체결된 핵담보협정이 심의.승인 된것과 관련하여 어제 조선민주주의인민공화국 외교부 대변인은 조선중앙통신사 기자가 제기한 질문에 다음과 같이 대답했습니다.

이미 보도된바와 같이 조선민주주의인민공화국 최고인민회의 제9기 제3차 회의에서는 핵무기전파방지조약에 따라 조선민주주의인민공화국 정부와 국제원자력기구 사이에 체결된 핵담보협정을 비준할데 대한 제안을 심의하고 만장일치로 승인하는 역사적 결정을 채택하였다.

이것은 지구상에서 핵전쟁의 위협을 근본적으로 제거하고 공고한 평화와 안전을 보장하기 위하여 반핵평화정책을 내놓고 그 실현을 위하여 일관하게 투쟁하여온 우리 공화국정부의 노력에 대한 빛나는 승리로 된다.

지금 전체 조선인민은 조선반도에서 핵문제가 자기의 지향과 요구에 맞게 공정하게 해결될 수 있게 되어 마침내 최고인민회의 제9기 제3차 회의에서 핵담보협정이 심의.승인 된것을 열렬히 환영하고 있다.

이번에 핵담보협정이 최고인민회의에서 심의.승인 된것은, 우리 공화국정부가 이미 천명한 바와 같이 "한다고하면 하는것이지 결코 빈말을 하지 않는

- 1 -

0110

다고 한 우리의 시종일관한 입장의 진실성을 말로서만 아니라 실천행동으로 보여준 논박할 수 없는 증거로 된다.

우리 공화국정부는 핵무기전파방지조약에 가입한 첫날부터 핵전쟁을 방지하고 공고한 평화를 보장하며 조약의 숭고한 목적과 사명이 공정하게 이행되도록 하기 위하여 적극 노력하여 왔다.

공화국정부는 핵담보협정체결을 위한 환경조성과 관련하여 우리측이 일관하게 주장하여온 조건들이 성숙되어감에 따라 지체함이 없이 주동적으로 지난 1월30일 국제원자력기구와 핵담보협정에 서명하고 국내법적 절차에 따라 해당기관들에서 심의하였으며, 이번에 진행된 최고인민회의 제9기 제3차회의 심의에 제출하였던 것이다.

우리는 이번 최고인민회의에서 핵담보협정이 승인된 이상 협정에 따라 국제원자력기구에 의한 핵사찰을 허심하게 받을 것이며, 앞으로도 핵무기전파방지 조약에 의하여 지닌 자기의 의무를 성실히 이행할 것이다.

이와 관련하여 우리는 핵담보협정에 규정된 대로 인차 핵시설설계 통보와 초기 핵물질 재고량 보고서를 국제원자력기구에 제출할것이며 기구와 부서회칙 작성 등 사찰이행에 필요한 실무적 문제들을 협의하여 핵사찰이 순조롭게 진행되도록 모든 노력을 다할것이다.

핵무기전파방지 조약이 지닌 자기의 의무를 성실히 이행하려는 우리 공화국정부의 일관한 입장에는 변함이 없다.

조선민주주의인민공화국 최고인민회의가 우리 공화국정부와 국제원자력기구 사이에 서명된 핵담보협정을 승인한 것과 관련하여 지금 세계여러나들에서 긍정적인 반향들이 연이어 일어나고 있으며, 우리에 대한 국제적인 신뢰감이 더욱 높아가고 있다.

그러나 유감스럽게도 오늘 세계가 조선반도에서 핵문제가 순조롭게 해결되어 가고 있는데 대하여 기뻐하고 환영하고 있는 때에 아직도 이것을 못마땅하게 여기면서 어떻게 해서든지 여기에 빗장을 가로 지르려고 애쓰는 일부 계층들도 없지 않다.

미중앙정보국을 비롯한 미국의 일부 계층의 사람들은 우리의 이른바 핵무기개발에 대한 여론을 유포시키면서 국제원자력기구에 의한 핵사찰이 실시된 후에도 북조선의 핵관련시설에 대한 공중폭격등의 대응조치를 고려하고 있다느니 뭐니하면서 우리에게 천만부당한 압력을 계속가하고 있다.

이것은 인위적인 장애를 조성하여 우리로 하여금 국제원자력기구에 의한 핵사찰 자체를 받지못하게 하고 그 책임을 우리에게 넘겨 씌우며 또한 미군이 남조선에 계속 비법적으로 주둔해있을 그 어떤 구실을 찾자는 불순한 정치적 목적에서 발상된 권모술수에 지나지 않는다.

지금까지 우리의 핵무기개발설을 떠들면서 「국제원자력기구의 사찰」을 빨리 받으라고 매번 간섭적인 압력을 가하던 사람들이 갑자기 국제원자력기구에 의한 사찰만으로는 미덥지 못하다는설을 들고나와 독자적인 사찰의 필요성까지 운운하고 있는데 대하여 세상사람들이 그들의 진의도에 대한 의혹을 가지는 것은 너무도 응당하다.

일부 사람들이 제아무리 우리를 모해하려고 열을 올리고 위협하여도 국제원자력기구에 의한 핵사찰을 통하여 이른바 핵무기개발설의 허위성은

- 3 -

0112

명백히 들어나게될 것이며 그들의 음모는 쓰디찬 참패만을 보게될 것이다.

우리 공화국정부는 지난날과 마찬가지로 앞으로도 핵무기전파방지조약에 의하여 지닌 자기의 숭고한 의무를 철저히 이행함으로써 조선반도의 비핵화를 반드시 실현할 것이다.

북한의 핵안전조치 협정 발효에 대한 외무부 대변인 논평

92. 4. 11.

1. 북한이 국제원자력기구(IAEA)와 지난 1월 30일 서명한 핵 안전조치 협정을 92년4월10일자로 발효시킨것을 환영한다.

2. 우리는 북한이 핵 안전조치 협정에 규정된 절차에 따라 보유하고 있는 모든 핵물질과 시설 내용을 국제원자력기구(IAEA)에 성실히 신고하고 조속히 핵 사찰을 수락함으로써 핵 비확산 조약(NPT) 당사국으로서의 의무를 완전 이행 할것을 기대한다. 끝.

0114

〈보도 참고자료〉

1. 북한의 핵 안전조치협정 서명,비준 및 발효 경위

o 85.12. 북한, 핵 비확산조약(NPT) 가입

o 89.12 -90 7. 북한, 3차에 걸쳐 IAEA와 협정체결 교섭
   - 북한은 한반도내 핵무기 철거와 미국의 북한에 대한 개별적 핵 선제 불사용보장(NSA)을 협정체결 전재조건으로 주장

o 91.7.16. 북한, IAEA와 협정문안을 최종 확정, 91. 9월 이사회 승인을 득함

o 91.9.12. IAEA 이사회, 북한에 대해 동 협정의 조속한 서명, 비준 및 이행을 촉구하는 결의 채택

o 91.9.27. 「부쉬」 미국대통령의 핵감축 선언과 11. 8. 노대통령의 「한반도 비핵화」 선언

o 91.11.27. 북한, 남한에서 핵무기 철수가 개시될 경우 핵사찰에 응하겠다는 외교부 성명 발표

o 91.12.18. 노대통령, 「한국내 핵부재」 선언

o 91.12.31. 핵문제 협의를 위한 제3차 남북 판문점회담에서 남북한은 「한반도 비핵화에 관한 공동선언」 채택

o 92.1.1. 김일성, 신년사에서 북한은 공정성이 보장되는 조건에서 핵사찰 수락할 것임을 밝힘

o 92.1.7. 북한, 92.1월말 협정서명후 적절한 절차에 따라 가장 빠른 시기내에 비준및 발효, IAEA와 합의하는 시기에 사찰수락 계획 발표

o 92.1.30. 북한, IAEA와 핵안전협정서명

o 92.2.19. 제6차 남북 고위급회담에서 「남북한 기본합의서」와 「한반도 비핵화 공동선언」을 발효시킴

o 92.2.25. 오창림 북한 순회대사, 4월초 예정된 최고인민회의에서 핵 안전 협정을 비준, 빠르면 6월중 북한내 핵시설 및 관계 연구단지 공개 계획 발표

o 92.3.19. 남북한간 「남북 핵 통제 공동위원회」 발족

o 92.3.30. 한시해 북한 조평통 부위원장, 4월8일 개최되는 최고인민회의에서 핵 안전 협정을 비준후 이를 즉시 IAEA에 통보할것임을 밝힘

o 92.3.31. 김일성, 4월8일 개최되는 최고인민회의에서 협정이 비준되면 핵사찰은 정해진 순서에 따라 해결될것이라고 언급

o 92.4.4. 황장엽 북한 노동당서기, 북한의 핵사찰 협정 비준과 관련 4.9일 최고인민회의에서 결정을 내릴것이라고 언급

o 92.4.9. 북한최고인민회의, 핵 안전조치 협정 비준 동의

o 92.4.10. 북한, IAEA에 핵안전 협정비준 사실 통보(협정 발효)

2. 북한의 핵안전협정 발효이후 사찰 실시까지의 절차

가. 협정 발효

o 핵안전 협정 발효를 위한 헌법상 요건이 충족되었다는 북한 정부의 서면 통고(written notification)를 IAEA가 접수한 일자에 협정 발효

나. 보조약정 체결 및 보고서 제출

o 북한은 핵안전협정에 규정된 절차의 시행방법과 사찰대상 시설을 구체적으로 명시하는 보조약정(subsidiay arrangement)을 안전조치협정 발효후 90일 이내 발효시켜야 함

o 사찰대상이 될 모든 핵물질 에 관한 최초 보고서 (initial report)는 협정 발효 해당월의 마지막날로부터 30일 이내에 IAEA에 제출

o 기존 핵시설에 관한 설계정보 는 보조약정 체결 협의기간중(협정 발효후 90일이내) IAEA에 제출

- IAEA는 제출받은 각 시설별 설계정보 설문서(Design Information Questionnaire) 내용을 확인후 보조약정 시설부록(Facility Attachment)을 작성

다. 임시사찰(ad hoc inspection)

o 핵물질에 관한 최초보고서에 포함된 정보내용을 검증하기 위해 IAEA는 임시사찰 실시

- 임시 사찰을 위한 사찰관 임명은 가능한한 핵안전협정 발효후 30일이내 완결

- 북한은 사찰관 임명수락 요청을 받은후 30일이내에 사무총장에게 결과 통보

- IAEA는 사찰관 수락회보 접수후 최소한 1주일전 북한에 통보후 사찰관 파견

o 보조약정 체결전 제출된 핵시설 설계정보의 검증을 위해서도 IAEA는 사찰 실시 가능

- 상기 임시사찰과 유사한 절차를 거쳐 사찰관 파견

라. IAEA 사찰관 임명 및일반 사찰(routine inspection) 실시

o IAEA 사무총장은 북한에 대해 IAEA 사찰관 임명에 대한 동의를 서면으로 요청

o 북한은 사찰관임명 동의 요청 접수후 30일 이내에 수락여부를 사무총장에게 통보

o IAEA는 북한에 사전통보(24시간 내지 1주일전)후 사찰관을 파견함으로써 일반사찰 실시 시작

3. 핵 안전 조치협정 주요내용

가. 안전조치대상 핵물질 및 시설(전문 및 98조)

o 핵물질 : 풀루토늄, 우라늄, 토리움 등

o 핵시설 : 원자로, 전환공장, 가공공장, 재처리공장 등으로서 정량 1kg 이상의 핵물질이 통상 사용되는 장소

나. 핵물질에 대한 기록유지 및 보고(제51-69조)

o 기록유지의 대상, 국제적 측정기준 및 보관기간(최소 5년) 설정

o 핵물질 계량 기록 보고(계량, 특별 및 추가 보고서등)

다. 핵시설 설계에 대한 정보(제42-50조)

o 검증의 편의를 위해 안전조치 관계시설 및 핵물질 형태의 보고

o 신규시설은 핵물질 반입 전 가능한한 조속히 보고

o 설계정보내용
- 시설의 일반적 특성, 목적, 명목, 용량 및 지리적 위치등
- 핵물질의 형태, 위치 및 유통 현황등

라. 안전조치의 기점, 종료 및 면제(제11-14조, 제33-38조)

o 핵물질의 국내수입시부터 안전조치적용

o 핵물질의 소모, 희석으로 더 이상 이용 불가능하거나 회수 불가능시 (IAEA와 협의) 또는 당사국 밖으로 핵물질 이전시(IAEA에 사전 통보) 종료

마. 핵물질의 국제이동(제91-97조)

o 당사국 밖으로 핵물질 반출시 IAEA에 사전 통고

- 반출 핵물질의 책임 수령일로부터 3개월 이내 동 물질의 이전 확인 및 약정 조치 필요

o 당사국내로 핵물질 반입시 IAEA에 보고

- 안전조치 대상 핵물질 반입시 반입량, 양도지점 및 도착일시등 보고

바. 안전조치 사찰(제70조-제90조)

o 임시사찰(ad hoc inspection)

- 최초 보고서에 포함된 정보 검증

- 최초 보고일자 이후에 발생한 상황변화에 대한 검증

o 일반사찰(routine inspection)

- 핵 안전협정의 내용에 따른 정기사찰

- 보고서 내용과 기록과의 일치 여부에 대한 통상적 사찰

o 특별사찰(special inspection)

- 특별보고서상의 정보를 검증할 필요가 있을 때나(특별보고서는 돌발적인 사고, 상황으로 인한 핵물질 손실 발생시에 협정 당사국이 IAEA에 제출)

- 일반사찰 정보와 당사국 제공 정보가 책임이행에 충분치 못하다고 판단되는 경우에 특별사찰. 끝.

북한의 핵 안전조치협정 발효후 IAEA 사찰실시 과정 도표

92.4.11. 국제기구과

1. 협정의 발효 o 발효일은 협정 비준 사실에 대한 북한정부의 서면 통고를 IAEA가 접수한 일자	92.4.10발효 ☆ 이하 4.10.발효 따른 각단계별 최대한 일자
2. 사찰대상 모든 핵 물질에 대한 최초 보고서 (initial report) 를 IAEA에 제출 o 발효 해당월의 최종일로 부터 30일 이내	92.5.31 까지 제출
3. 최초보고서 내용에 대한 IAEA의 임시사찰 (ad hoc inspection) 실시	92.6월16일경 실시 가능
o 임시사찰을 위한 사찰관 임명은 가능한한 안전조치협정 발효후 30일 이내 완결	- 92.5월10일경
o 북한은 상기 IAEA 사찰관 임명 수락 여부를 제의받은 후 30일 이내에 사무총장에게 통보	- 92.6월9일경
o IAEA는 사찰관 수락회보 접수후 최소한 1주일전 북한에 통보후 사찰관 파견	- 92.6월16일경
4. 보조약정서(하기 5항) 체결 협의기간중 기존 핵시설 관련 설계정보 (design information)를 IAEA에 제출 o 설계정보는 재처리시설 관련 정보도 포함하여 각 시설별 설계정보 설문서(Design Information Questionnaire)형식으로 제출	92.4.10-7.9 사이

0120

o 제출된 설계정보 검증을 위해 IAEA는 북한에 사찰관 파견 (임시사찰과 같은 절차를 거쳐 파견)	
o IAEA는 상기 설계정보내용 확인후 시설부록 (Facility Attachment)을 작성 보조약정서에 첨부	
5. <u>보조약정서</u> (subsidiary arrangement) <u>체결 및 발효</u>	92.7.9까지
o 협정에 규정된 안전조치 절차와 시행방법을 구체적으로 명시하는 보조약정서를 IAEA와 체결	
o 보조약정서는 안전조치협정 발효후 90일이내에 체결 및 발효 시키도록 노력	
6. <u>사찰관 임명</u> 을 위한 사전 협의	
o 사무총장은 북한에 대해 IAEA 사찰관 임명에 대한 동의를 서면으로 요청	
o 북한은 임명동의 요청 접수후 30일 이내에 수락여부를 사무총장에게 통고	92.8.8 경
* 사무총장은 필요에 따라 보조약정 체결전이라도 북한에 사찰관 임명 동의 요청 가능	
* 일단 임명동의를 받은 사찰관들은 향후 사찰을 위해 북한 재입국시 임명동의 재요청 불필요	
7. <u>일반사찰</u> (routine inspection) 실시	
o IAEA는 사찰관 임명동의 접수후 사찰실시 1주일전 북한에 사찰관 파견 사전통보	
o 사찰관 북한 입국, 일반사찰 실시	92.8.15 경
8. <u>특별사찰</u> (special inspection) 실시	일반사찰 실시후 필요시
o 특별사찰은 일반사찰을 통해 획득한 정보가 협정에 따른 책임 이행에 충분치 못하다고 판단될 때 실시	

0121

o 따라서 북한의 미신고 핵물질 및 시설에 대한 의혹이 있을 경우 IAEA 이사회 결정에 따라 특별사찰 실시가능

* 92.2월 IAEA이사회는 IAEA가 상기 핵관련 추가정보를 입수하여 관련장소를 조사할수 있는 권한을 갖고 있음을 재확인

o 쌍방 합의후 가능한한 빠른 시일내 사찰관 파견 사전 통보후 실시

끝.

0122

	분류번호	보존기간

발 신 전 보

번 호 : EM-0010 920411 1007 ED 종별 : ~~암호송신~~

수 신 : 주 수신처 참조 대사. 총영사

발 신 : 장 관 (국기)

제 목 : 북한의 핵안전협정 발효

1. 4.10(금) 오후 북한의 전인찬 주비엔나 국제기구담당대사가 IAEA 사무총장을 방문, 북한의 IAEA와의 핵안전조치 협정비준에 필요한 국내절차가 완료되었음을 공식통보함으로써 4.10자로 동 협정의 효력이 북한에 대해 발생하게 되었음

2. 이와관련 본부는 금일(4.11) 북한의 협정 발효에 대한 대변인 논평을 아래와 같이 발표하였으니 참고바람.

가. 북한이 국제원자력기구(IAEA)와 지난 1월 30일 서명한 핵 안전조치 협정을 92년4월10일자로 발효시킨것을 환영한다.

나. 우리는 북한이 핵 안전조치 협정에 규정된 절차에 따라 보유하고 있는 모든 핵물질과 시설 내용을 국제원자력기구(IAEA)에 성실히 신고하고 조속히 핵사찰을 수락함으로써 핵 비확산 조약(NPT) 당사국으로서의 의무를 완전 이행할것을 기대한다. 끝.

(국제기구국장 김 재 섭)

수신처 : 전대사 주재공관장 (주카이로 총영사 포함)

보안 통제	B

앙 고 재	92년 4월 11일	국제기구 과	기안자 성명		과 장	심의관	국 장		차 관	장 관
			신동익		(서명)	(서명)	전결 (서명)			(서명)

외신과통제

0123

공 란

공 란

공 란

공 란

北核협정 발효…美国의 対北정책

북한이 10일부터 국제원자력기구와 핵안전협정을 정식 발효시킴에 따라 미국의 対북한 정책에도 상당한 변화가 뒤따를 것으로 보인다. 국무부를 통한 논평에서 미국은 북한의 핵안전협정 비준을 환영했다. 그러나 북한에대한 미국의「核嫌疑」가 완전히 벗겨질것 같지는 않다.

위기상존-낙관, 국방-국무부 異見

「핵협의」아직안벗겨져

우선 미국 정부의 정부-국방 사이드와 외교 사이드는 지금까지 북한핵에 대한 미국의 정책 및 対한반도 정책에서 이견을 빚고 있는 것으로 나타나고 있다.

이것은 정확하게 CIA-국방부의 강경론 내지는 위기론 그리고 국무부의 낙관론 내지 신중론으로 대별되는 현상이다. 아직 분명하지 않은 것은 미국 정부가 국방관계자나 정보책임자의 입을 통해 강경론을 표현하면서 한편으로 신중한 낙관론을 펴고 있는 것인지, 아니면 실제로 정부내의 이견과 갈등이 표출되고 있는지에 대한 판단이다.

말하자면 부시행정부가 포괄적인 전략하에 당근과 채찍을 번갈아 구사하고있는 것인지 아니면 정부내 부처별로 정보 판단 차이의 골이 깊어 그것이 걸러지지 못한 상태로 노출되고 있는 것인지 분명하지 않다는 것이다. 물론 이같은 현상은 앞으로 북한의 핵사찰수용태도에 따라 정리될것이다.

이달들어 미국의 칼 포드 국방차관보는 1일 하원 군사위 청문회에 나와 『북한의 핵무기 개발이 아시아의 안정에 가장 중대한 위협이 되고있다』고 강조하면서, 미국의 対북한 핵정책의 목표가「총체적인 핵능력의 영구적인 저지」에 있음을 분명히 하고 있다. 포드의 증언은 북한핵의 위협정도를 부각시키면서, 그에대한 강경 대응을 강조한 것이다.

核능력 영구저지 위해 강력대응 해야 국방
6월 사찰기대… 관계개선 뜻비치기도 국무

情報차이·당근과 채찍說

◇제임스 릴리

◇콜린 파월

◇리처드 솔로몬

◇로버트 게이츠

그러나 같은날 美국무부의 리처드 솔로몬 東亞太담 담차관보는 상원 외교위에서 한반도 상황에 「몇가지 희망적인 조짐」들을 진단하면서, 6월로 약속된 북한의 핵사찰에 대해 기대를 표명했다. 솔로몬 차관보가 밝힌 美국무부의 입장은 북한이 4월에 핵안전협정에 비준하고, 5월에 국제원자력기구에 핵시설의 명세서를 낸뒤, 6월에 핵사찰을 받아들이겠다고 약속한 것에 기대를 실으면서 북한의 성실한 약속이행을 기다려 보자는 것이다. 솔로몬은 이에따라 한반도의 비핵화 정착은 물론, 美-북한의 관계개선에도 희망을 걸고 있음을 드러내고 있다.

이와함께 북한의 金容淳 국제부장이 3월17일 북경 창구를통해 캔터국무차관에게 보내온 관계개선 요구에 대해서도 美국무부는 지난주 다분히 유화적인답변을 보낸것으로 알려지고 있다. 『핵문제를 해결할경우』라는 단서가 붙어있긴 하지만, 국무부의 입장은 『상호주의에 바탕을 두어 외교관 접촉을격상하고, 점진적으로 관계를 개선하겠다』는 것이다.

"전쟁 아직 안끝났다"

그러나 美국방부의 고위 관리들은 한결같이 북한의 핵문제에 대해 국무부보다는굳어있는표정들이다. 3월27일 제임스 릴리국방부 국제안보담당차관보도회견을통해 『대규모 군사력을 갖추고있는 북한이 아시아 지역에 중대한 위협이되고 있다』는 위기론을 제시하고있다. 릴리 차관보의 입장은 『한반도에서 전쟁은 아직 끝나지 않았다』는것을 강조하는 것이다.

美중앙정보부의 판단도 대략 국방부와 궤를 같이 하고 있는 것으로 보인다. 로버트게이츠 CIA국장은 릴리차관보의 회견이 있던 지난달 27일 하원 군사위 청문회에서 북한의 군사전략가들이 남한에 대한 재래식 무기의 전략적 우위를 상실하기 전에 남침감행을 제안할 가능성에 대비, 韓-美 양국군은 경계태세를 늦추지 않아야 한다고 말했다. 게이츠의 발언도 북한의 남침 가능성을 부각시키는 것이다.

게이츠는 지난 2월말 의회증언에서 북한이 핵무기를 보유하는데는 『플루토늄을 축적한후 수개월에서 1~2년 정도의 기간』이 필요할 것이라고 말했다가, 다시 3월12일에는 한 세미나에서 『북한이 영변에 플루토늄을 추출하는 제3의 원자로 건설을 완료했다』고 말하고, 북한이 핵장치를 갖는데는 몇개월에서 2년정도의 기간이 걸릴 것이라고 밝힌 바 있다.

이러한 방향의 진단은 3월23일 콜린 파월 美합참의장이 해병특수전투비행단 주요 작전지휘관회의에서 『미국 해병은 북한의 핵사용에 대비, 3주째 신속 침투및 방어훈련을 실시중』이라고 밝힌것이나, 스티븐 솔라즈 美하원 亞太小委 위원장이 3월12일 『미국은 북한의 핵개발을 저지하기 위해 북한에 대한 양보를 중단해야하며, 유엔 안보리를 통해 북한에 대한 경제제재를 취하고 무력사용도 검토해야한다』고 주장한것등과 맥을 같이하고 있다.

이에앞서 파월은 3월5일 『북한이 남침할 경우 미국은 저지 및 방어의 단계를넘어 축출 (eject)까지 하겠다』고 발언, 미국의 対북한 방위가적극적 방어개념에서 적극적공세 개념으로 전환 했음을 처음으로 확인하기도 했고, 솔라즈는 이날짜 한 주간지에 실린 기고문에서 북한 핵문제와 관련, 북한에 좀더 압력을 가하자는 결연한 대응을 촉구 하기도 했다.

파월, "남침 가능성"

이러한 태도는 북한 대흥호가 스커드미사일을 싣고 중동을 향해하는 사건이 진행중이던 3월7일 美해군이「명령만 떨어지면」(if ordered)대흥호를정선시키겠다고 결의를 다지던것, 그리고 그에앞서 2월24일 서울을 방문한 더글러스 팔 백악관 亞洲담당선임보좌관이 金宗輝 청와대외교안보수석비서관을 만난 자리에서 북한의 핵문제가 해결되기 전까지는 남북의 경제협력이 바람직하지 않다는 입장을 밝힌 것과도 연결돼 있다.

그러나 이러한 과정에서도 美국무부의 판단은 조금 다른쪽으로 흐르고 있었다. 국무부의 솔로몬 차관보는 3월19일 『북한에 대한 핵사찰이실현되면…』이라는 희망적인 전제하에 『미국은 미-북한간 고위급협의를 상설화할 방침』이라고 밝힌 바 있고, 이보다 한달쯤 앞선 2월16일 로널드 레먼 美국무부 군축국장도 한 기고문에서 『한국에서의 핵위협을 감소시키기 위해 한국과 미국은 중요한 단계를 밟아왔고, 이에따라 북한은 몇가지 정책을 완화시켜왔다』고 분석한뒤, 『우리는 이같은 발전을 환영한다』고 말했었다.

〈金佾日기자〉

0128

'92 4/15

관리번호	92-321

원 본

외 무 부

종 별 : 지 급

번 호 : JAW-2147 일 시 : 92 0413 1104

수 신 : 장관(국기,아일,정특)

발 신 : 주 일 대사(일정)

제 목 : 북한의 핵안전협정 발효

연 : JAW-2085,2124

대 : EM-0010

대호, 4.10 자로 북한의 핵안전협정이 효력을 발생하게 됨에따라, 일 외무성은 연호와 같이 외무보도관 담화를 발표한바, 동담화 전문은 아래와 같음.

0 금번 북한과 IAEA 와의 핵안전협정이 발효된 것은, 북한이 갖는 NPT 조약상의 의무를 이행하라고 하는 오랜 현안의 해결을 향하여 일보 전진한 것으로서 평가함.

0 정부로서는, 북한이 본건 협정상의 의무인 사찰수락등을 조기에 그리고 무조건적으로 완전히 이행하며, 또한 재처리.농축 시설을 보유하지 않음을 포함하는 '한반도의 비핵화에 관한 공동선언'의 내용을 성실히 실행에 옮김으로써, 핵무기개발에 관한 국제적 우려를 조기에 해소할 것을 계속 하여 강력히 요구해 나가고자함. 끝

(대사 오재희-국장)

예고:92.12.31. 일반

검토필 (1992. 6. 30.)

국기국 차관 1차보 아주국 외정실 분석관 청와대 안기부

PAGE 1

92.04.13 11:35

외신 2과 통제관 BN

0129

원 본

외 무 부

종 별 :

번 호 : UNW-1084 일 시 : 92 0413 1900

수 신 : 장 관(연일,미이,정특,기정)

발 신 : 주 유엔 대사

제 목 : 북한핵 관련기사

북한의 IAEA 안전협정비준 조치관련, 금 4.13자 NYT 지 사설 및 OP-ED 난 기고문을 별첨 FAX송부함

(대사 유종하-국장)

첨부: UNW(F)-0381

국기국 1차보 미주국 외정실 분석관 청와대 안기부

PAGE 1 92.04.14 09:34 FE

외신 1과 통제관

0130

UNW(F)-0 [illegible] 20413 1900

NYT 92. 4. 13.

UNW-1084의 첨부

3-2

North Korea, Almost Nuclear-Free

Nuclear renegade. That's what many feared North Korea would become — a nation capable of producing a nuclear bomb, yet so isolated and paranoid that it would not listen to the world's pleas for sanity.

For months, however, North Korea has been moving steadily in sanity's direction. If it can be persuaded to keep going, peaceful coexistence may yet replace years of hardened hostility on the Korean peninsula. North Korea's one-time enemies can do much to achieve that objective.

[illegible] ing it[illegible] Thursday, when its National Assembly ratified a safeguards accord with the International Atomic Energy Agency. But the agreement calls for one more crucial step: North Korea must open all suspected nuclear sites to international inspection within 90 days.

It is more likely to do so if it receives assurances that such inspections will be followed, in short order, by normal diplomatic relations with Japan and the U.S. and increased trade and investment. The U.S., Japan and South Korea are not obliged to provide such assurances; yet each has a large stake in a nuclear-free Korean peninsula, and persuasive cards to play.

Washington can tell Pyongyang it's ready to establish diplomatic relations once inspections are under way. Seoul can now propose mutual arms cuts. That would allow North Korea to reduce its own defense budget, which absorbs a prohibitively large portion of its gross national product and saps its economic growth.

Japan can pledge essential aid and investment to be delivered once North Korea allows inspections. Pyongyang would be free to claim that the aid was reparations for the grievous suffering Japan caused Korea during decades of occupation.

But before any of these promises can be carried out, North Korea needs to fulfill its obligations both to I.A.E.A. and to South Korea to allow nuclear inspections by July.

Any list provided to the I.A.E.A. should include sites like the suspected reprocessing plant at Yongbyon. South Korea would also be allowed to inspect all the facilities at Yongbyon and at 20-odd other suspect sites in the North. In return, Pyongyang would be entitled to inspect military and other sites in the South that, it thinks, once housed U.S. nuclear arms and related equipment.

Frequent, timely and reciprocal inspections are essential to end decades of hostility and suspicion between North and South. Washington, Seoul and Tokyo can speed this process by assuring North Korea that it will be welcomed back into the family of nations.

381-2-1

0131

THE NEW YORK TIMES OP-ED MONDAY, APRIL 13, 1992

Defusing North Korea's Nuclear Notions

By William J. Taylor
and Michael Mazarr

WASHINGTON

Cold war thinking is alive and unveiled in Seoul and Washington. It goes this way: We cannot trust North Korea. Kim Il Sung has been stalling for time on accepting inspections of nuclear facilities, with a clear goal of acquiring nuclear weapons. If he continues, the military option — hit them before they hit us — is our last-ditch means of stopping the development of an atomic bomb.

Last week, the North Korean Parliament ratified the North's agreement to nuclear inspections, but administrative barriers and North Korean bickering may delay them for some time. The temptation may grow to give up on diplomacy and turn to sanctions or military strikes. This approach would be disastrous.

For two years, the U.S. and South Korea have pursued a carrots-and-stick policy toward North Korea aimed at ending its suspected nuclear weapons program, blocking its missile sales, halting its use and support of terrorism, and promoting arms control and progress toward reunification with the South.

The sticks have been the strong U.S.-South Korean defense relationship and continued economic and political isolation of the North. But North Korea never responds favorably to demands. So, since 1990 South Korean, U.S. and Japanese officials have held out the promise of expanded economic and political contacts if the North chooses moderation.

To encourage agreement on nuclear inspections, the U.S. has removed its nuclear weapons from South Korea and held its highest level talks ever with North Korea. The U.S. and the South have suspended annual joint military exercises. North Korea has responded favorably partly because it is obsessed with economic development. It desperately needs hard currency to import oil and food and, in the long term, for capital, technology and management help to develop industries and promote growth.

A military strike isn't the answer.

The only way to build these foreign ties is to resolve the nuclear issue, and skillful U.S. and South Korean diplomacy has nudged the North well down that path. That's why the growing drumbeat in the media and among academic analysts in support of striking the North's military sites is wrongheaded. An attack would lead to a second Korean war, which Washington and Seoul might have to fight alone.

Without inspection teams on the ground, we do not know the right targets. Even if we knew what to hit, reports suggest the North Koreans have dug shelters, deep into rock, that are impervious to most precision weapons. In the gulf war, 40 days of air strikes did not halt Iraq's nuclear program, and Kim Il Sung's labs are dug far deeper than Saddam Hussein's.

Advocates of the military option appear to seek a guarantee that there will be no bomb. But the only way to be completely confident that the North has ended work on nuclear arms would be to conquer and occupy most of it. An embargo to force it to accept inspections would be fruitless, for the economy is in trouble, but not in crisis. Once an embargo is put in place, hope for negotiations will be lost.

Yes, the world faces a risk that North Korea is assembling an atomic bomb. The best way to deal with that risk is to continue the policy of economic and political contacts, which would provide leverage to demand inspections and a ban on North Korean's exporting its nuclear know-how. As for military action, forget it. □

William J. Taylor is vice president for international security programs at the Center for Strategic and International Studies. Michael Mazarr is a senior fellow at the center.

0132

장관보고사항

92.4.14. 국제기구과

북한의 핵안전 협정 발효에 대한 일본 및 미국 논평(4.13)

1. 일본 외무성

   o 북한-IAEA간 핵안전협정이 발효된것은 북한의 NPT 조약상 의무이행이라는 오랜 현안의 해결을 향한 일보 전진으로 평가

   o 북한이 핵안전 협정상 의무인 사찰수락등을 조기에 그리고 무조건적으로 완전히 이행하며, 재처리·농축시설을 보유하지 않기로한 「한반도 비핵화 공동선언」 내용을 성실히 이행함으로써 핵무기 개발에 대한 국제적 우려를 조기에 해소할것을 강력히 요구

2. 미국무부

   o 북한의 협정 발효조치를 환영하며, 북한이 완전하고도 조속히 핵물질 및 설계정보를 제출하여 IAEA 사찰을 수락할것을 촉구

   o 남북한이 상호사찰을 위한 협상을 조속히 완료하여 한반도내 핵 확산 위협제거에 대한 상호확신을 갖도록 촉구 끝.

0133

4/15 신
3

4. 北韓의 核安全協定 發效 관련 主要國 反應

o 4.10 北韓의 核安全協定 發效에 대한 主要國 反應은 아래임.

(美 國務部 代辯人, 4.13)

- 北韓의 核安全協定 發效 措置를 歡迎하나, 이와관련 對北韓 接觸水準 格上에 대해서는 아직 論議된 것이 없음.

(日 外務省 代辯人, 4.11)

- 금번 北韓의 核安全協定 批准 發效는 北韓의 核擴散禁止 條約上의 義務履行이라는 오랜 懸案 解決을 향한 一步 前進으로 평가함.

- 日 政府는 北韓이 IAEA 核査察 受諾등을 조속히 無條件的으로 完全히 履行하고 韓半島 非核化 共同宣言의 내용을 誠實히 實行함으로써, 核武器 開發에 대한 國際的 憂慮를 早期에 解消할 것을 계속 강력히 要求해 나가고자 함.

(EC 會員國 外務部 亞洲局長會議, 4.10)

- 북한의 IAEA 核査察 早期受容 희망 입장을 北韓側에 전달키로 함. (駐美, 駐日, 駐EC大使 報告) 끝.

0134

	분류번호	보존기간

발 신 전 보

번 호 : WAV-0581 920423 1759 FO 종별 :

수 신 : 주 오스트리아 대사. ~~총영사~~

발 신 : 장 관 (국기)

제 목 : IAEA 2월이사회 회의록

대 : 오스트리아 20332-337 (4.16)

대호 표제관련문서에 2.24및 26자 토의요약이 누락되어 있는바, IAEA 사무국에 확인후 추가 송부 바람.

(국제기구국장 김 재 섭)

보안통제	

앙고재	92년 4월 23일	국제기구과	기안자 성명		과 장	심의관	국 장		차 관	장 관
			신종이				전결			

외신과통제

0135

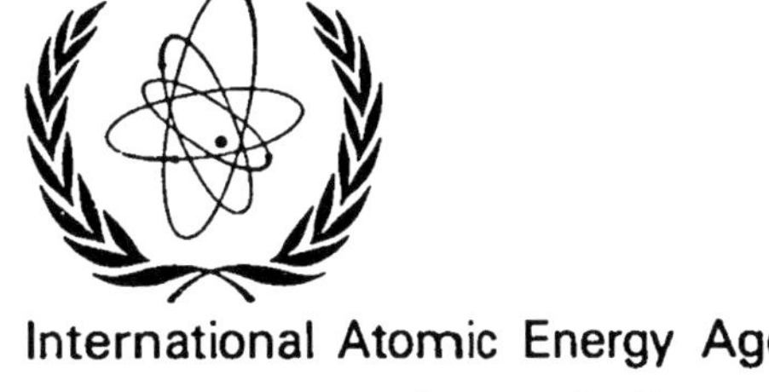

International Atomic Energy Agency

BOARD OF GOVERNORS

GOV/OR.775
15 April 1992

RESTRICTED Distr.

ENGLISH
Original: ENGLISH and FRENCH

For official use only

RECORD OF THE SEVEN HUNDRED AND SEVENTY-FIFTH MEETING

Held at Headquarters, Vienna,
on Tuesday, 25 February 1992, at 10.15 a.m.

CONTENTS

[*] GOV/2575.

9516e/882e
92-00730

0136

Attendance

(The list below gives, for each delegation, the name of the senior member who participated in the meeting and that of any other member whose statement is summarized in this record.)

Mr. MONDINO	Chairman (Argentina)

Mr. LAMAMRA	Algeria
Mr. ORNSTEIN	Argentina
Mr. WILSON) Mr. HOGG)	Australia
Mr. PREUSCHEN	Austria
Mr. VILAIN XIIII	Belgium
Mr. SANTANA CARVALHO) Ms. MACHADO QUINTELLA)	Brazil
Mr. GEORGIEV	Bulgaria
Mr. LEE	Canada
Mr. CHEN) Mr. PENG)	China
Mr. ROSALES ARIAS) Mr. GUZMAN MARTINEZ)	Cuba
Mr. PAREJA CUCALON	Ecuador
Mr. ONSY	Egypt
Mr. de LA FORTELLE	France
Mr. LOOSCH	Germany
Mr. IKOSSIPENTARCHOS	Greece
Mr. BAKSHI	India
Mr. AHIMSA) Mr. RAZAK)	Indonesia
Mr. AMROLLAHI	Iran, Islamic Republic of
Mr. ENDO	Japan
Mr. LEE	Korea, Republic of
Mr. ANGUIANO	Mexico
Mr. FASSI FIHRI	Morocco
Mr. AAMODT	Norway
Mr. AHMAD	Pakistan
Mr. ARY dos SANTOS	Portugal
Mr. BALANESCU	Romania
Mr. RYZHOV) Mr. MAYORSKI) Mr. KUCHINOV)	Russian Federation
Mr. SANGIAMBUT	Thailand
Mr. KOSTENKO	Ukraine
Mr. WALKER	United Kingdom of Great Britain and Northern Ireland
Mr. KENNEDY	United States of America
Mr. RIET ALVARIZA	Uruguay
Mr. TA NGUYEN	Viet Nam
Mr. GHONDA	Zaire

0137

Attendance
(contd.)

Mr. BLIX	Director General
Mr. JENNEKENS	Deputy Director General, Department of Safeguards
Mr. ELBARADEI	Director, Division of External Relations
Mr. STURMS	Director, Legal Division
Mr. SANMUGANATHAN	Secretary of the Board

Representatives of the following Member States attended the meeting:

Belarus, Bolivia, Chile, Costa Rica, Czechoslovakia, Democratic People's Republic of Korea, Finland, Holy See, Hungary, Iraq, Ireland, Israel, Italy, Kuwait, Lebanon, Libyan Arab Jamahiriya, Luxembourg, Malaysia, Netherlands, Nigeria, Peru, Philippines, Qatar, Saudi Arabia, South Africa, Spain, Sudan, Sweden, Switzerland, Syrian Arab Republic, Tunisia, Turkey, Venezuela, Yugoslavia.

Abbreviations used in this record

ASSET	Analysis of Safety Significant Events Team
DPRK	Democratic People's Republic of Korea
INSAG	International Nuclear Safety Advisory Group
INWAC	International Radioactive Waste Management Advisory Committee
NPT	Treaty on the Non-Proliferation of Nuclear Weapons
NUSSAG	Nuclear Safety Standards Advisory Group
OSART	Operational Safety Review Team

0138

SAFEGUARDS

(c) REPORT ON THE STATUS OF IMPLEMENTATION OF THE SAFEGUARDS AGREEMENT WITH THE DEMOCRATIC PEOPLE'S REPUBLIC OF KOREA (continued)

1. Mr. GHONDA (Zaire) welcomed the safeguards agreement concluded on 30 January 1992 between the Democratic People's Republic of Korea and the Agency, and also the Joint Declaration of the North and the South, which had shown the clear intention to transform that part of the world into a nuclear-weapon-free zone. While his delegation was gratified to note the new spirit of peace prevailing in the Korean Peninsula, it nevertheless regretted that ratification of the safeguards agreement was not proceeding with the same speed as had been shown in the case of the North and South Agreement on Reconciliation, Non-Aggression, and Co-operation and Exchange. His country therefore urged the DPRK to ratify the safeguards agreement at the earliest possible opportunity.

2. Mr. TA NGUYEN (Viet Nam) welcomed the signing of the safeguards agreement between the DPRK and the Agency and the DPRK's intention to turn the Korean Peninsula into a nuclear-weapon-free zone, which would contribute greatly to peace in that region. His delegation looked forward to hearing from the Director General that ratification of the safeguards agreement had taken place as expected in April.

3. Mr. PENG (China) thanked the Director General for his report on the status of the safeguards agreement with the DPRK. He welcomed the signing of that agreement in January, and also the Joint Declaration of the North and the South according to which both countries would use nuclear energy for peaceful purposes only and would not test, manufacture, produce, accept, possess, store, deploy or use nuclear weapons. The safeguards agreement would be conducive to the relaxation of tension not only in the Korean Peninsula, but throughout Asia and the world.

4. He noted that the Standing Committee of the Supreme People's Assembly of the DPRK had approved the Joint Declaration in a timely manner, and hoped that ratification of the full-scope safeguards agreement would soon follow and that both would come into effect at the earliest possible date.

0139

5. Mr. ONSY (Egypt) noted with satisfaction the conclusion of the safeguards agreement with the DPRK, which represented a step forward for the DPRK towards meeting its international obligations. He hoped that the agreement would be ratified and implemented as soon as possible, and trusted that, together with the Joint Declaration, it would have a positive effect on the Korean Peninsula and on Asia as a whole.

6. Mr. ROSALES ARIAS (Cuba) said that the latest developments in the Korean Peninsula showed that there were ways to resolve differences which might arise in the international arena other than the use of force and political pressure. He was pleased that the safeguards agreement between the DPRK and the Agency had been concluded on terms favourable to both parties, highlighting the political will of the DPRK to fulfil its international obligations and demonstrating its commitment to world peace. He welcomed the news from the Government of the DPRK and the Director General that the safeguards agreement would shortly be ratified following the enactment of internal legislation. An international organization should respect such processes, and he hoped that Board members would show the necessary understanding and refrain from passing any judgement liable to harm the deliberations taking place.

7. Mr. RAZAK (Indonesia), too, welcomed the signing of the safeguards agreement which clearly indicated that positive developments were taking place on the Korean Peninsula. His delegation looked forward to hearing from the Director General at the Board's meetings in June that the agreement had been speedily ratified and brought into effect.

8. Mr. GEORGIEV (Bulgaria) hoped that the safeguards agreement, together with the North-South Agreement, would contribute to world peace and security. His country had always supported the creation of nuclear-free zones and considered the North-South Agreement a good example for other regions to follow.

9. While noting that the safeguards agreement had been forwarded to the Supreme People's Assembly of the DPRK, he nevertheless regretted that ratification and implementation had not yet taken place in accordance with the resolution contained in document GOV/2543 and adopted by the Board the previous September. He urged the DPRK to take prompt action to put the

0140

agreement into effect, and looked forward to the Agency's inspectors being able to start their work at the earliest possible date thereafter. He trusted that the Director General would take the necessary steps to apply Agency safeguards to all materials and facilities under DPRK jurisdiction and inform the Board concerning the results.

10. Mr. LOOSCH (Germany) associated himself with the remarks made by the Governor from Portugal on behalf of the European Community and its Member States, but wished to add that the long-awaited signature of a full-scope safeguards agreement by the DPRK fulfilled only one part of that country's international obligations under Article III of the NPT. He looked forward to the rapid entry into force of that agreement, and meanwhile appealed to the DPRK to provide the Agency immediately with all relevant information concerning its nuclear installations and nuclear material inventory and to permit the Agency to start carrying out verification activities forthwith. That would not only create confidence in the intentions of the DPRK with regard to non-proliferation, but would also correspond to international treaty law, which provided for measures to be taken in support of the objectives of an international agreement from signature onwards, even if the formal entry into force of the agreement was still dependent upon the completion of internal procedures. At all events, he trusted that the Director General would continue to keep the Board informed regarding progress in the matter.

11. Mr. EL FASSI (Morocco) warmly welcomed the recent initiatives aimed at reducing tension within the Korean Peninsula, including notably the signing of a safeguards agreement between the DPRK and the Agency pursuant to Article III of the NPT, of which that country was a signatory.

12. His delegation had noted the statement by the Director General to the effect that ratification of the agreement would take place in April. However, the representative of the DPRK had failed to confirm that date in his statement. Morocco therefore urged the DPRK to ratify and implement its agreement fully as soon as possible. Moreover, it was highly desirable that the DPRK should respond to the offer made by the Director General regarding the submission of all useful information such as the initial inventory of nuclear installations and materials. He looked forward to hearing the

Director General report to the Board at its meetings in June on developments concerning the application of the safeguards agreement with the DPRK.

13. Mr. BAKSHI (India) said he understood the concerns expressed by several Governors, but wished to emphasize that the implementation of safeguards by Member States was entirely voluntary. Nevertheless, his country firmly believed that all States should discharge their international obligations in a timely manner.

14. Mr. MAYORSKI (Russian Federation) expressed his delegation's satisfaction at the signing of the safeguards agreement between the DPRK and the Agency. It hoped that the DPRK would soon complete the constitutional procedures necessary for implementing its agreement, and thus enable the Agency to commence its inspection activities on that country's territory.

15. In conclusion, he wished to express his country's regret with regard to certain irrelevant comparisons which the Governor from the Republic of Korea had made in his statement the previous day.

16. Mr. KENNEDY (United States of America) joined other delegations in welcoming the long-delayed step towards meeting its international obligations under the NPT taken by the DPRK in signing its safeguards agreement, implementation of which would help dispel world-wide concerns regarding the DPRK's nuclear programme. However, he noted with regret that no specific date had been given by the DPRK for ratifying the agreement or bringing it into effect - it had merely been passed on to parliament for "consideration". Previous statements by the DPRK had indicated that the agreement might be ratified by the time of the present meeting, but once again, that hope had been disappointed.

17. The United States delegation therefore strongly urged the DPRK to take prompt action to ratify its safeguards agreement and bring it into force without any preconditions and without further delay, in fulfilment of its obligations and of the resolution adopted by an overwhelming majority of Board members in September 1991. Further delays in taking practical measures to implement safeguards could only deepen international concern and suspicion about the ultimate intentions of the DPRK.

18. His delegation expected that, as early as possible after ratification and entry into force of the agreement, Agency safeguards would be applied to all materials and facilities within the territory of the DPRK or under its jurisdiction or control, including the facilities at Yongbyon. Moreover, the DPRK would do well to respond positively to the Director General's offer, made during the most recent session of the General Conference, expressing his readiness to receive any relevant information, such as the initial inventory of facilities and materials, even before the agreement between the DPRK and the Agency had entered into force.

19. Finally, he called on the Director General to keep Board members informed of any progress in the immediate future towards ratification and, subsequently, implementation of the agreement. His delegation shared the views expressed by the Governors from France and Australia concerning the expectation that the Board would receive a full report by the Director General in June, and looked forward to hearing the DPRK's response to the questions raised in the present debate by the Republic of Korea and Japan.

20. Mr. WALKER (United Kingdom) said that the Governor from Portugal had already welcomed, on behalf of the United Kingdom and its European Community partners, the signing of the safeguards agreement between the DPRK and the Agency. However, in order not to undermine what little progress had been made, it was important that there should be early ratification and full implementation of that agreement, and his delegation was gratified that the Agency wished to begin the process of verifying the nuclear materials initially declared by the DPRK and inspecting its nuclear facilities as soon as possible. Further delays in ratification and implementation would only fuel international suspicions, and he hoped the Director General would be able to report on concrete progress at the Board's meetings in June.

21. Mr. LEE (Canada) regretted that once again the Board was required to address the long-standing question of the safeguards agreement with the DPRK. While it was gratifying to note that the DPRK had finally signed the agreement, truly substantive and meaningful action on the part of that country's Government unfortunately still remained to be taken.

22. His delegation was encouraged by the growing rapprochement between the Governments of the two countries on the Korean Peninsula. However, such

constructive developments had not been matched by equivalent progress in the DPRK's multilateral agreements, and consequently the question of ratification and implementation of the safeguards agreement remained open.

23. The signing of an international agreement gave rise to expectations that the signatory State would act in accordance with its provisions. Therefore, his delegation expected that, as a gesture of good will, the DPRK would take whatever steps were necessary to reaffirm its commitment to the NPT and to reassure other States which were concerned about its lack of progress in achieving the goal of full implementation. Such concerns had been expressed by numerous delegations at the previous September's Board meetings, and his delegation felt that the DPRK had an obligation to respond positively.

24. One way of meeting those concerns would be to accept the offer made by the Director General at the most recent session of the General Conference concerning the provision to the Agency of relevant information, such as an inventory of facilities and material, or design information, even before the safeguards agreement entered into force. There was nothing to prevent the DPRK from taking such a course. As another indication of good faith, the DPRK could also permit ad hoc inspections. Thus, pending the outcome of constitutional ratification and implementation in the DPRK, there were a number of positive steps that country might take to reinforce its commitments under the NPT and to dispel doubts and concerns that had arisen in the minds of others.

25. In conclusion, he urged the DPRK to spare no effort in expediting the ratification and implementation process so that safeguards could be applied as soon as possible to all materials and facilities anywhere within its jurisdiction or control. His delegation hoped that by the Board's meetings in June, the ratification process would be complete and implementation well under way so that the item could finally be removed from the Board's agenda. In the meantime, his delegation joined others in requesting the Director General to keep Board members informed of any progress made towards achieving those aims.

26. Mr. AHMAD (Pakistan), noting that the DPRK had complied with its stated intention to sign its safeguards agreement by the end of January 1992, but that the matter of ratification had been referred to the April 1992

0144

session of the DPRK Supreme People's Assembly, urged the DPRK to strive to achieve ratification and implementation in the shortest possible time consistent with national legislative requirements, in view of the great international attention and interest in the issue.

27. His delegation hoped that the developments in the Korean Peninsula during recent months would advance nuclear non-proliferation and facilitate the lessening of tension in the region. His own country had long advocated regional arrangements as an effective means of expanding the nuclear non-proliferation regime.

28. Mr. ANGUIANO (Mexico) urged all countries not parties to the NPT to accede to it, and all those countries which had signed it also to sign and ratify their safeguards agreements with the Agency and ensure full implementation thereof as soon as possible.

29. Mr. KOSTENKO (Ukraine) said that the signing of the safeguards agreement under discussion had been an important step towards stabilizing the situation in the Korean Peninsula. He noted with interest that the agreement was being examined by the competent authorities within the DPRK and hoped that it would be ratified, and the process of its implementation commenced, in time for the Board's June meetings.

30. Mr. RIET ALVARIZA (Uruguay) welcomed the signing of the safeguards agreement and the Joint Declaration concerning the establishment of a nuclear-weapon-free zone on the Korean Peninsula. However, he noted with concern that the DPRK had not yet completed the internal formalities required for bringing the agreement into force. He therefore urged that country to ratify the agreement as soon as possible and bring to an end what had already been an over-long process.

31. Mr. PAREJA CUCALON (Ecuador), commending the DPRK on the signing of its safeguards agreement, said that détente in the Korean Peninsula would be a cornerstone of world peace. His country's foreign policy had always been based on the universality of the NPT and so he looked forward to hearing soon from the Director General that ratification of the agreement had taken place. In addition, he hoped the DPRK would hand over to the Agency all relevant information concerning inventories of nuclear installations and material.

0145

32. Ms. MACHADO QUINTELLA (Brazil), too, welcomed the signing of the safeguards agreement and the news that the process of ratification was under way. Her delegation looked forward to early and full implementation of the agreement.

33. Mr. RIHA (Czechoslovakia)[*], speaking on behalf of the Central European States of Hungary, Poland and the Czechoslovakia, expressed their satisfaction and relief that after six years of negotiations a safeguards agreement between the DPRK and the Agency had finally been signed in January. That important first step should now be followed at the earliest possible opportunity by ratification and full implementation of the safeguards agreement, as requested in the Board resolution adopted in September 1991, which meant that a complete inventory of all nuclear installations and facilities on the territory of the DPRK would have to be declared.

34. The latest developments on the Korean Peninsula were highly promising, and the efforts aimed at making that area nuclear-free should be encouraged as a potentially significant contribution to the strengthening of the global non-proliferation regime.

35. Mr. BALANESCU (Romania) said that given the complexity of the ratification procedures still to be completed within the DPRK, he called upon the representative of that country to make a firm and unqualified statement on behalf of his Government to the effect that the DPRK would soon communicate to the Agency a complete list of nuclear materials and facilities together with their locations and that it would accept inspection by the Agency at all its sites prior to ratification of its safeguards agreement.

36. Mr. CONSTENLA (Costa Rica)[*] said that the statement made by the President of the Republic of Korea on 18 December 1991 concerning the non-existence of nuclear weapons in the Republic of Korea had been received with satisfaction by his own country's Government, which hoped that real progress could be made towards guaranteeing the non-existence of nuclear weapons in the DPRK also. Consequently, his Government very much welcomed that country's signature of a safeguards agreement with the Agency on 30 January.

---

[*] Member States not members of the Board of Governors are indicated by an asterisk.

0146

37. His Government urged the DPRK to ratify that agreement as soon as possible in accordance with the Board resolution adopted in September 1991. The DPRK would thereby dispel the international community's suspicions regarding the purpose of its nuclear activities. His delegation also urged that country to collaborate with the international community in ensuring that all its nuclear materials, installations and facilities were placed under the international system of inspections without further delay and in a complete manner permitting total verifiability. Such collaboration would represent an effective contribution towards the peace efforts in the Korean Peninsula.

38. Finally, he requested the Director General to keep the Board informed of any developments relating to the ratification and implementation of the safeguards agreement by the DPRK, as well as any delay or difficulty that might arise.

39. Mr. O (Democratic People's Republic of Korea)[*], responding to previous speakers' demands that his country should swiftly ratify the safeguards agreement with the Agency, and even before doing so should submit an inventory list of nuclear materials, said that the DPRK would not fail to ratify the agreement at the earliest possible date in accordance with its national legal procedures and would indeed submit the initial inventory report and design information to the Agency. He expressed surprise at the statement made by the Governor from the Republic of Korea the previous day, but could not avoid the conclusion that that statement must reflect the position of the Government of the Republic of Korea, despite the doubt it cast on that Government's attitude towards the recently adopted historic North-South Agreement. At a time when the entire Korean people were looking forward to the faithful implementation of the Agreement, and to its ultimate goal of national reunification, and only one week after the entry into force of the Joint Declaration of the North and the South on the Denuclearization of the Korean Peninsula, the serious slander and accusations levelled at his delegation by that of the Republic of Korea seemed particularly inappropriate. After all, the Agreement was clearly directed towards achieving reconciliation, non-aggression, co-operation and exchange between the two countries. More specifically, it stipulated that the two countries should recognize and respect each other's systems, not interfere in each other's

internal affairs, cease to abuse and slander each other, and co-operate rather than compete by making concerted efforts for the sake of national dignity and their joint interests in the international arena.

40. In that context, the remarks made by the Governor from the Republic of Korea to the effect that no progress had been made since the Joint Declaration had been adopted were clearly unreasonable and out of touch with reality. That Declaration and the North-South Agreement had entered into force as a result of high-level talks in Pyongyang on 19 February. One of the decisions contained in the Joint Declaration had been to establish a Joint Committee on Nuclear Control which would start its work within a period of one month, conducting inspections in both countries and taking practical action to denuclearize the Korean Peninsula.

41. Thus, notwithstanding the assertions by the Governor from the Republic of Korea to the contrary, he could assure the Board that the forthcoming session of the Supreme People's Assembly would ratify the safeguards agreement in accordance with its own legal procedures. As to that Governor's unreasonable and unsubstantiated remarks to the effect that the DPRK was attempting to reunify North and South Korea by means of nuclear weapons, he could only say that such remarks merely served to impede the implementation of the North-South Agreement and should be viewed with the utmost concern.

42. Mr. AYATOLLAHI (Islamic Republic of Iran) said that his delegation welcomed the signature of the safeguards agreement between the DPRK and the Agency and, having always supported the principle of nuclear-weapon-free zones, hoped that such a zone could eventually be established in the Korean Peninsula. It also hoped that the ratification process could be concluded as soon as possible.

43. Mr. LEE (Republic of Korea) said that he would refrain from commenting on the remarks by the representative of the DPRK since the Agency's Board of Governors was not a political forum. He would confine himself to urging that country not to propagate the inter-Korean drama as a means of burying the nuclear issue, but instead to ratify the safeguards agreement immediately, implement it faithfully and honestly, and respond to the requests made by many Governors the previous day and during the present meeting.

0148

44. Mr. O (Democratic People's Republic of Korea) wished to clarify his country's position once again, namely that it had every intention to ratify the safeguards agreement with the Agency as soon as possible, most probably by the beginning of April.

45. The CHAIRMAN, summing up the discussion, said that many speakers had expressed satisfaction that the safeguards agreement required under the NPT had been signed by the DPRK. The fact had been stressed, however, that the Government of the DPRK still had the important and urgent task of bringing the agreement into force and ensuring its full implementation without further delay. In that connection, many speakers had noted the statement by the representative of the DPRK that the Standing Committee of the Supreme People's Assembly had reviewed the safeguards agreement and had decided to submit it to the Assembly for consideration at its forthcoming session in April. The Board hoped that that was the only outstanding formality to be completed before the entry into force and full implementation of the agreement by the DPRK and urged the Government of the DPRK to have the agreement brought into force without delay and to co-operate with the Agency in the meantime by providing the requisite initial information.

46. He took it, therefore, that the Board wished to request the Director General to keep in close contact with the authorities of the DPRK and report to the Board in June on developments in the ratification and implementation of the safeguards agreement with that country.

47. It was so agreed.

(d) THE STAFF OF THE DEPARTMENT OF SAFEGUARDS TO BE USED AS INSPECTORS (GOV/2566, Note to Governors of 14 January 1992)

48. The CHAIRMAN recalled that the Secretariat's proposals concerning the present item were contained in document GOV/2566 and that the curricula vitae of the four Professional staff members whom the Director General proposed to use as safeguards inspectors had been circulated to members of the Board by the Secretariat under cover of a letter dated 14 January 1992. A summary, by nationality, of the staff of the Department of Safeguards to be used as inspectors, reflecting the information contained in document GOV/2566, had also been circulated under cover of a note dated 14 January.

0149

49. He had gathered from consultations prior to the present meeting that Governors would agree to giving the Director General the requested authorization.

50. Mr. AL TAIFI (Saudi Arabia)[*] said that, having carefully examined document GOV/2566, his delegation felt that there was an imbalance in the staffing of the Department of Safeguards which could be corrected if the Agency intensified its training courses for nationals of developing countries, and in particular from the Middle East. The Agency had demonstrated in the past that it was capable of responding to the legitimate request that a greater proportion of its staff be drawn from such countries, for example by organizing courses to train young people as inspectors. Opening up competition for posts in the Department of Safeguards by creating more opportunities for all countries was in keeping with the General Conference's resolutions on recruitment policy and could only benefit the Agency through the increase in the number of candidates thus achieved.

51. Mr. JENNEKENS (Deputy Director General, Head of the Department of Safeguards) concurred that, whereas normally the Department of Safeguards conducted two training courses per year, in 1991 it had only conducted one such course. Furthermore, of the four proposed new safeguards inspectors, only one was a new staff member, the others having already served in the Department's Support Divisions for some time. In 1992 again, it was expected that the Department of Safeguards would continue to fulfil its functions despite keeping a number of posts vacant. That was partly because of the 13% cut affecting the entire Agency - one result of which for the Department of Safeguards was that only one of the two introductory courses on Agency safeguards would be held in 1992 - and partly because it had been found possible to manage with a slightly reduced staff owing to various unforeseen economies.

52. On the other hand, he wished to draw the Board's attention to the fact that, of all the Agency's Departments, the Department of Safeguards had the largest number of nationalities represented on its staff - 67 at the last count.

0150

53. The CHAIRMAN assumed that the Board wished to take the action requested in paragraph 5 of document GOV/2566 and to authorize the Director General to use the four Professional staff members referred to in paragraphs 2 and 3 of that document as safeguards inspectors.

54. It was so decided.

IMPLEMENTATION OF GENERAL CONFERENCE RESOLUTION GC(XXXV)/RES/553 ON "MEASURES TO STRENGTHEN INTERNATIONAL CO-OPERATION IN MATTERS RELATING TO NUCLEAR SAFETY AND RADIOLOGICAL PROTECTION": OUTLINE OF THE POSSIBLE ELEMENTS OF A NUCLEAR SAFETY CONVENTION (GOV/2567 and Corr.1)

55. The CHAIRMAN recalled that the item was on the agenda pursuant to operative paragraph 4 of resolution GC(XXXV)/RES/553, in which the General Conference had invited the Director General

> "to prepare, for the Board's consideration in February 1992, an outline of the possible elements of a nuclear safety convention, taking into account the activities and roles of relevant international and intergovernmental bodies and drawing on the advice of standing groups like INSAG, NUSSAG and INWAC, and also on expertise made available by Member States and competent international organizations".

56. For that purpose, the Director General had convened a group of experts which had met in December 1991, and the Board now had before it document GOV/2567 (with a Corrigendum) containing a report in which the Director General summarized the conclusions reached by the expert group and stated his own views. The full report of the expert group had been made available on request.

57. In paragraph 12 of his report, the Director General requested the Board to authorize him to set up an open-ended working group with the task of carrying out the necessary substantive preparations for a nuclear safety convention, it being understood that he would report to the Board periodically on the progress of the group's work. Board members would recall that at the Secretariat briefing on 5 February, the Director General had made a statement in which he had provided additional information and clarification with regard to the term "framework convention" which was used in document GOV/2567.

58. Mr. ARY dos SANTOS (Portugal), speaking on behalf of the European Community and its 12 Member States, said that they continued to attach great importance to progress towards a nuclear safety convention, which they,

0151

incidentally, had been the first to propose. They had taken note of the Director General's report contained in document GOV/2567 and the ideas put forward by the group of experts in their report of December 1991. With regard to paragraph 12 of document GOV/2567, the Twelve understood that the working group to be set up would build upon and develop further the work which had been done by the group of experts and other relevant work being done within the Agency, and they hoped that the group would make quick progress.

59. Mr. LEE (Canada) said that his delegation supported the development of a nuclear safety convention, as requested by General Conference resolution GC(XXXV)/RES/553. He recognized the importance to the international community of ensuring that all nuclear facilities were safe, well-regulated and environmentally sound, and that effective practices were in place for the safe management and disposal of all categories of radioactive waste. He agreed with the establishment of a working group to carry out the preparations for a nuclear safety convention, as recommended in document GOV/2567.

60. In his view, the safety convention should be based on safety principles or fundamentals rather than on prescribed detailed requirements, which could be taken care of in technical annexes elaborated over time. Nuclear safety was the responsibility of national authorities and the safety convention should not dilute or confuse the accountability and authority of sovereign States in that regard. With that in mind, the safety convention should be clearly constructed to avoid being interpreted as constituting an international regulatory regime.

61. The positive impact of the safety convention must be assured in order to enhance nuclear safety internationally and, in particular, to increase public confidence in nuclear power. He therefore believed that reporting safety performance on a regular basis for peer review was a key element for the success of such a convention. The reports should include data on items such as the release of radioactive materials and incidents rated at a severity level of 3 and above on the International Nuclear Event Scale. If the Board of Governors approved the establishment of the working group, his country would welcome the opportunity to participate in that group and to contribute to the early implementation of a nuclear safety convention.

0152

62. Mr. ANGUIANO (Mexico) first of all thanked the Director General for the report he had presented in document GOV/2567 and Corr.1. Mexico was in favour of holding informal meetings of the open-ended working group of technical and legal experts which was to have the task of carrying out preparations for a nuclear safety convention. Given the lack of financial resources, the group would not be able to progress formally since that would mean that the meetings would need to have simultaneous interpretation in all the working languages.

63. With regard to the convention, his country believed that emphasis should be placed on general principles and procedures rather than on technical details regarding nuclear safety; for example, criteria such as those recommended by NUSSAG could be used, which were considered appropriate for all types of installation in the civil nuclear fuel cycle and not just power plants. Likewise, the convention could include binding annexes (protocols) on the basic standards for radiation protection, regulations for the transport of radioactive materials, notification of accidents for public information purposes, and the transboundary movement of radioactive waste, as indicated in paragraph 8 of document GOV/2567.

64. The nuclear safety convention should not affect the rights and responsibilities of sovereign countries, and so should allow for some form of international verification which did not constitute real intervention, since primarily the responsibility for nuclear safety must remain with the country owning the nuclear installations. Such verification could be based on something like his own country's commitment to adopt Agency safety standards and to demonstrate compliance with them, for example, through OSART and ASSET missions as well as other similar Agency services which his country had used.

65. Finally, he believed that if one of the objectives was to foster the confidence of international public opinion in reactor safety then the coverage by a possible nuclear safety convention of reactors used for other than purely commercial or civil purposes should not, at the Board's request, be excluded from the outset. Recalling that in the Convention on Early Notification of a Nuclear Accident it was stipulated that information relating to accidents occurring in non-civil installations could be communicated if the State party

0153

concerned so wished, he suggested that that precedent might well serve as a basis for defining the scope of application of an international instrument on nuclear safety.

66. Mr. KOSTENKO (Ukraine) said that the work done by the group of experts had been very useful and that it was now clearer how the problems involved could be dealt with. His country supported the proposal to set up an open-ended working group. With regard to the structure of such a convention, a point which was raised in paragraph 4 of document GOV/2567, his country felt it would be advisable to opt for a framework convention with technical annexes or protocols, some of which could be adopted simultaneously with the convention while others could be added at a later date.

67. Mr. WALKER (United Kingdom) endorsed the statement made by the Governor from Portugal on behalf of the European Community and its 12 Member States, and thanked the group of experts convened by the Director General for the detailed study they had made of the problems of developing a possible international nuclear safety convention, adding that it would have been useful to have the full text of the group's report included in the documentation presented to the Board. The Director General's report contained a number of specific recommendations on the scope and structure of a possible convention and also on the way in which work might proceed. He regretted that the Director General, in his report, had not accepted all the recommendations of the group of experts.

68. Nevertheless, the two reports still showed that there was a sufficient consensus to undertake preparations for an international convention setting out the fundamental principles of nuclear reactor safety, an area of major international concern in which rapid progress was essential to improve safety in real terms and to reassure the public. In his view, agreement on such a convention could only be reached if it were based on principles which had already found broad acceptance. No progress would be made if efforts were directed towards the establishment of safety standards with too much restrictive technical detail or if too wide a scope were addressed prematurely.

0154

69. Similarly, care should be taken not to detract from the principle of national responsibility for nuclear safety regulation. His country was not in favour of establishing an international regulatory regime, but endorsed the experts' proposal that the convention should be based on the draft Agency document on safety fundamentals and that it should be limited, at the present stage, to power reactor safety. It would oppose a convention stipulating an obligation on the part of the States parties to meet dubious and vague commitments, which would certainly present difficulties for many Member States. He hoped, however, that allowance would be made for broadening the scope of the convention once consensus had been reached in other areas such as waste management. To that end, a clause could be included providing for a review of the convention by the parties after three or four years. Given that the Member States parties to the convention would be committed through their own regulations to achieving high levels of safety, regular meetings of the parties would be an effective way of exercising pressure on any country failing to observe the principles laid down in the convention.

70. He shared the opinion that work should start quickly. He was surprised, however, by the suggestion made in the Director General's report that the convention should not include a protocol on nuclear safety but limit itself to two or three other matters. He felt that that would not help to build up confidence in nuclear safety. A nuclear safety convention should certainly include concrete provisions on nuclear safety and constitute progress beyond the current international situation.

71. His country agreed to the Director General's recommendation that the Board should convene a working group, consisting if possible of technical and legal experts, who would be given the express task of reworking the document on safety fundamentals into elements which could be incorporated into a convention or into protocols to such a convention. The group should also be given a fixed deadline for completion of its work. He proposed that a text be submitted to the Board in good time for approval and submission to the General Conference in September 1993.

72. Mr. ORNSTEIN (Argentina) said that his country had always contributed substantially to the Agency's nuclear safety activities and had also participated actively in the group of experts convened by the Director General to advise on the structure and content of the possible elements of an

0155

international convention on that matter. Consequently, he was able to give his overall support to the conclusions reached by the group of experts, as given in their report and as summarized in document GOV/2567.

73. He also endorsed the Director General's request in paragraph 12 of document GOV/2567 that he be authorized to set up an open-ended working group with the task of carrying out the necessary substantive preparations for a future convention. Clearly, though, in view of the serious financial crisis affecting the Agency, the impact on the budget of the working group's activities must be kept to a minimum.

74. With regard to the main issue at hand, his delegation favoured an international convention of a reference framework type limited initially to nuclear power plants and research reactors, leaving aside for the time being nuclear fuel cycle facilities, both because there would be major difficulties in reaching a consensus owing to the particular complexity of those facilities and because they did not present such a great risk as nuclear power plants and research reactors.

75. He also, in principle, would prefer the convention to give ample opportunity for peer discussions on safety aspects of the construction and operation of such facilities - which could take place at regular meetings organized by the Agency at no major additional cost - rather than having obligatory international inspections of those facilities.

76. Mr. de LA FORTELLE (France) said that he had taken note of the Director General's report on the implementation of General Conference resolution GC(XXXV)/RES/553 and thanked the Secretariat for having acted so swiftly in response to that resolution. The meeting of the group of experts convened by the Agency in December 1991 to give advice on the structure and content of possible elements of an international convention on nuclear safety had identified a number of problems and put forward suggestions for resolving them. That meeting was a starting point for further Agency action in the months to come.

77. His country attached the greatest importance to strengthening nuclear safety all over the world and supported the activities undertaken by the Agency to that end, as far as they lay within its competence and mandate. It seemed both desirable and expedient to establish an international safety

0156

system for all civil nuclear facilities and activities which would uphold the principle that the primary responsibility for safety lay with national authorities. France considered that the Agency, supported by experts from Member States and using the experience acquired by its teams in the various fields of nuclear safety, possessed the know-how and necessary resources to play an important role in the development of such a system.

78. On the whole, his delegation's analysis of the conclusions drawn by the group of experts which had met in Vienna in December 1991 was in agreement with the Director General's views as stated in document GOV/2567. The first stage of the process should be the formulation of a framework text defining the commitments and obligations to be taken on voluntarily by States parties and setting out the fundamental safety principles relevant to all civil nuclear facilities and activities. That text could be progressively supplemented with technical annexes detailing the fundamental principles applying to various types of facilities and activities with no essential modification of the commitments and obligations undertaken by the States parties.

79. A first draft, including an annex on nuclear power plants, could be submitted to the Board of Governors in September 1992 and then to the thirty-sixth session of the General Conference. Following any necessary revisions, that draft could be submitted to an intergovernmental conference and adopted by the States which were in favour. It would then be the responsibility of States parties to the convention to organize regular conferences of the parties to assess the measures adopted and the compliance of the various States parties with the fundamental principles, and to publish the results of that assessment. The conference of the parties could also, if need arose, put pressure on States which had not honoured their commitments to take the steps required to remedy the situation. The conference of the parties could draw upon Agency infrastructures and services to assist it in its tasks. An agreement between the Agency and the conference of the parties would set out the modalities of that co-operation and define the nature and scope of the actions to be taken by the Agency on behalf of the conference of parties.

80. In conclusion, he approved of the approach suggested by the Director General in document GOV/2567 regarding the Agency's further activities in connection with the development of an international safety system. The tasks for 1992 should not involve any significant financial cost and could therefore be included in the 1992 programme, despite the present financial difficulties.

81. Mr. PENG (China) thanked the group of experts for their advice with regard to the structure and content of possible elements of a nuclear safety convention. In its report, the group had made a very exhaustive analysis of matters which should be covered by that convention and had thereby provided a solid basis for the future work of the Secretariat and of the Board. With regard to preparations for the convention, he had several comments to make.

82. Firstly, as his delegation had indicated at the Board meetings in December 1991, his country supported measures to strengthen international co-operation in nuclear safety and radiation protection. It also favoured the step-by-step development of an international convention on nuclear safety.

83. Secondly, China endorsed the view that the responsibility for nuclear safety lay first and foremost with States. That was already a broadly accepted principle in the international community and should be taken into account in the convention.

84. Thirdly, his delegation supported the view that the convention should focus on general principles and procedures rather than on technical details.

85. Fourthly, it felt that the tentative list of eight obligations provided by the group of experts could serve as the basis for further discussions.

86. Finally, his delegation agreed to the Board's authorizing the Director General to set up an open-ended working group with the task of carrying out the necessary substantive preparations for a nuclear safety convention. His delegation was prepared to participate in the drafting of the convention and in the working group.

87. Mr. ROSALES ARIAS (Cuba) said that his delegation's position on the development of a nuclear safety convention had been outlined at the thirty-fifth session of the General Conference and at the various Board meetings which had dealt with that matter.

0158

88. First of all, he wished to reiterate, for the record, that in order to attain satisfactory levels of nuclear safety on a world scale, the first thing to be done was to ensure a good climate of international co-operation based on mutual confidence between neighbouring States, for legally binding standards alone would not suffice if the desired objective as stated in resolution GC(XXXV)/RES/553 were to be attained.

89. In the same spirit, he felt that if a consensus were reached on the framework convention on nuclear safety, it must remain clear that the Agency should not overstep its role as adviser and forum for safety matters. In other words, his country would not accept a convention which provided for verification or supervision activities that would be an additional financial burden to the Agency.

90. With regard to document GOV/2567, he considered that the scope of the convention should correspond to the clearly stated objectives of preambular paragraph (d) and operative paragraphs 3 and 8 of resolution GC(XXXV)/RES/553 and consequently encompass military and other installations.

91. Paragraph 6 of document GOV/2567 only listed obligations which seemed obvious. The first task should be to establish the general principles for defining the obligations of parties to the convention. It could be stated, inter alia, that it was recognized that nuclear safety was primarily the responsibility of national regulatory bodies and that co-operation between States parties was necessary. He did not rule out the possibility of giving a regional dimension to the global nuclear safety framework convention, meaning that regional arrangements could be included in it.

92. Finally, he agreed that an open-ended working group could be set up to carry out the preparations for the future nuclear safety convention. However, in view of the subject matter and the complex legal questions which could arise, he felt that appropriate language services would need to be provided; otherwise the work should be deferred to 1993 and sufficient financial provision made for it within the framework of the Agency's Regular Budget.

93. In conclusion, he took note of document GOV/2567, on the understanding that his comments would be taken into account.

94. Mr. SANGIAMBUT (Thailand) supported the Secretariat's proposal to set up an open-ended working group with the task of carrying out preparations for a nuclear safety convention, which was very important for the security of mankind. He hoped that the working group would be set up as soon as possible.

95. Mr. AAMODT (Norway) recalled that his country had on many occasions stressed the importance of the Agency's regulatory functions and had always given its full support to the safety programme. He commended the Director General on his decision to convene the group of experts, which had put forward very constructive proposals regarding the possible elements of a nuclear safety convention. He supported the setting up of an open-ended working group to make preparations for such a convention. As to the substance of its work, he felt that the best approach would be to establish a framework convention containing basic safety principles; more specific documents dealing with the various technology areas and reflecting widely agreed views on nuclear safety in a more concrete way could be annexed at a later date. The convention would make a major contribution to the further strengthening of nuclear safety. He hoped, therefore, that the work would be actively pursued.

96. Mr. LOOSCH (Germany) associated himself with the views expressed by the Governor from Portugal on behalf of the European Community. The German Government had a keen interest in the development of an international safety convention, hoping thereby to achieve the highest possible safety standards, not only in nuclear power plants and reactors, but also in other facilities. He thanked the European Community, the Member States of the Agency and the Director General for encouraging that initiative. He fully supported the proposal to set up a working group, which should represent the best expertise available in Member States while remaining as limited as possible in numbers. The reasons for that were essentially twofold: the Agency's financial difficulties on the one hand, and a desire for efficiency on the other, since a small working group would be better able to prepare a draft convention quickly for submission to and adoption by an international conference. As for the timetable to be established for the activities, he agreed with the Governor from France that the first results should be ready by autumn 1992. As far as financing was concerned, he had full confidence in the co-operation

0160

of the experts who would make up the working group and in the Secretariat's capacity to complete the work swiftly, despite the Agency's financial difficulties.

97. Mr. VILAIN XIIII (Belgium) said that his country's position on the subject essentially corresponded to that expressed by the Governor from Portugal in his statement on behalf of the European Community. Belgium was basically in favour of the elaboration of a nuclear safety convention. The sometimes very precarious situations which had come to light recently in certain European countries in relation to nuclear safety had amply demonstrated the need for an international instrument to which the competent national authorities could refer. Of course, the application of the regulations and fulfilment of obligations relating to nuclear safety lay, and always would lie, exclusively within the competence of national authorities.

98. His delegation welcomed the valuable work done by the group of experts, which would form a good basis for further efforts to draft a convention. Without wishing to give a final opinion on the procedure to be followed by an open-ended working group, he would not exclude the possibility of a smaller group of experts on nuclear safety and/or international law continuing to meet in order to make the preparatory work for the convention more efficient in certain specific areas. Care must also be taken to ensure that the working group's activities were not prolonged needlessly. The report of the group of experts also showed that a consensus had already emerged on the main elements to be included in a convention. It should be possible to obtain some tangible results within a reasonable period of time, preferably during the first half of 1993.

99. He agreed with the Director General that the convention's structure was an issue which should be looked into from the very outset of the preparatory work. As for the choice between a framework convention and a single convention, Belgium was firmly in favour of the latter option, i.e. the adoption of any protocols and annexes simultaneously with the convention. Continued discussion within the Agency on amendments or annexes to a framework convention would prove an excessive burden both for the Agency and for the national services concerned and would not make for greater public confidence in the safety of the nuclear industry. The group of experts had concluded,

moreover, that the convention should concentrate on general principles and procedures rather than technical details relating to nuclear safety. The States parties should undertake to apply conscientiously the provisions of the convention in their facilities, while remaining free to stipulate additional regulations or technical standards pertaining specifically to such facilities.

100. With regard to the possible scope of a convention, his delegation had no wish to rule out a text on the entire fuel cycle provided that the issues raised by nuclear power plants were fully covered. The public was entirely justified in being most immediately concerned at present about the worrying state of certain Member States' nuclear power plants.

101. The Agency's important role in safety matters had to be recognized. No other institution enabled regulatory authorities and experts to meet at the world level and to exchange information and experience. It was to be hoped that the activities undertaken would be continued with due regard to developments in the safety field throughout the world and to the necessity of concentrating on those areas in which the Agency was called upon to play a role. His delegation did not consider it desirable to set up an international regime to verify the implementation of the convention and, accordingly, was opposed to the Agency's assuming an institutional role in that regard. On the other hand, it would be in favour of more detailed definition of the concept of "peer review", which it felt should be included in the nuclear safety convention.

102. Mr. BALANESCU (Romania) said that his country, too, attached great importance to nuclear safety and was in favour of preparing an international convention on the subject. It was also willing to make an active contribution at all stages of the preparatory work, which should be started as soon as possible. His delegation felt that at the present stage the convention should be confined to questions related to the safety of nuclear power plants, which was the most urgent issue and one of universal concern. There seemed to be some consensus regarding the elements necessary to ensure the safety of commercial plants, and that would facilitate the drafting of the international convention. Consensus on the other stages of the nuclear fuel cycle, however, was still a long way off.

103. There were a number of points which needed to be underlined. Firstly, responsibility for nuclear safety rested primarily with national authorities. An international convention would undoubtedly help countries to take more effective action in discharging that responsibility, but it did not seem expedient to transfer it to an international body. His delegation therefore agreed with those who favoured a single convention.

104. As for the elements to be included in such a convention, obligations to take appropriate action in the following areas might be envisaged: the safety of facilities in terms of design, siting, construction, commissioning and decommissioning; the safe operation and maintenance of facilities; the requirement of continuous surveillance of the safety of facilities and additional periodic reassessments; the safe management and disposal of radioactive wastes; the sharing of certain types of information; the training of manpower; and the provision of emergency plans for responding to accident situations.

105. If the convention attracted wide adherence, it would help to raise safety standards in nuclear plants and to bolster public confidence in nuclear energy. Moreover, the adoption of a system of periodic reviews of the practical implementation of the convention would provide the best guarantee that the parties were abiding by the principles set forth in it.

106. Mr. LAMAMRA (Algeria) said that his country supported the strengthening of international co-operation in the sphere of nuclear safety and radiation protection. It approved the Director General's suggestion that an open-ended working group be entrusted with the task of preparing legal instruments designed to strengthen international co-operation through a framework convention establishing general principles as well as the obligations of States to ensure the safe operation and maintenance of nuclear facilities and, more particularly, commercial nuclear power plants, which posed the most urgent safety problems for the international community.

107. The convention could also cover the institutional mechanisms and procedures and specific technical provisions relating to international obligations, in particular regarding the adoption of basic radiation protection standards and safety regulations applicable to nuclear facilities,

together with regulations governing the management and disposal of radioactive waste. For reasons of efficiency, his delegation believed it preferable that technical provisions relating to the convention should be the subject of protocols and annexes to be adopted, if possible, at the same time as the framework convention itself. Although an international safety convention encompassing nuclear power plants would unquestionably help to improve operating conditions throughout the world and to encourage public acceptance of nuclear energy, it should nevertheless be emphasized that such an international legal instrument could be no substitute for States' obligations with regard to nuclear safety. Such obligations concerned, in particular, the safe operation of facilities, personnel qualifications, the adoption of satisfactory measures for continuous surveillance and emergency preparedness for accident situations, and the adoption of appropriate measures for the management and disposal of radioactive waste.

108. Regarding the functioning of the proposed working group, his delegation shared the view that it should be provided with linguistic services.

109. Mr. HOGG (Australia) recalled that one of the main results of the International Safety Conference held in September 1991 had been the recommendation that steps be taken to establish an international nuclear safety convention. The December meeting of the group of experts who had assembled to draw up an outline of the possible elements of such a convention had yielded a useful exchange of ideas on what such an instrument might contain and how it might be implemented. His delegation was pleased with the progress made to date towards the elaboration of the convention. It had already stated, and remained convinced, that any activity undertaken in pursuance of the General Conference resolution should be carried out within the Agency's existing Regular Budget or through extrabudgetary resources.

110. His delegation supported the conclusions of the group of experts and favoured a convention encompassing all nuclear facilities and activities of the civil nuclear fuel cycle. A framework convention of that type, even if it called for more time and effort, would be the best solution, as it could be easily modified if necessary and would prove to be the most workable approach in the long term. That issue warranted further discussion by the Board.

0164

111. His delegation supported the establishment of an open-ended working group entrusted with the task of carrying out the necessary substantive preparations for a nuclear safety convention and noted that no Regular Budget resources were to be made available for the meetings involved.

112. Mr. RAZAK (Indonesia) was in favour of setting up an open-ended working group as proposed in document GOV/2567. His delegation sincerely hoped that such a working group would be able to reach agreement on the principles to be incorporated in a nuclear safety convention. A convention of that kind would certainly help to strengthen public confidence in the safety of nuclear technology.

113. Mr. GHONDA (Zaire) said that recent experience demonstrated the importance and necessity of an international instrument on nuclear safety. In view of the complexity of the factors involved in the elaboration of such an international instrument, his delegation supported the proposal to set up an open-ended working group, which it felt should include legal as well as technical experts. In the light of past practice, the envisaged international convention would take the form of either a framework convention with attached annexes or protocols on technical questions or a single convention incorporating the technical annexes or protocols. It should be stressed, however, that even if an international convention were adopted, there would be no derogation of States' responsibility.

114. Given the importance of the tasks to be undertaken by the working group, it was deplorable that the Agency's financial difficulties prevented it from releasing the funds necessary for organizing meetings with adequate interpretation and translation services. That being said, he approved the proposal set forth in paragraph 12 of document GOV/2567.

115. Mr. KUCHINOV (Russian Federation) said he had taken note of the Director General's report on the implementation of resolution GC(XXXV)/RES/553 and the proposal of the group of experts, which had met in December 1991, and had concluded that there was a need for an international instrument on nuclear safety and recommended that preparatory work for the establishment of such an instrument begin as soon as possible. It was hard to imagine how it might be possible to expand nuclear energy without strengthening international

co-operation in the field of safety. The best solution would probably be to draw up a single convention together with technical annexes relating, for instance, to the safety aspects of nuclear power plants, but that might prove to be time-consuming and impracticable. Another option might therefore be worth considering, namely the establishment of a framework convention setting forth general obligations with regard to civil nuclear facilities and defining the procedures and mechanisms required for the adoption of annexes containing specific technical provisions.

116. His delegation recognized the need for such a convention, provided the fundamental principle of States' responsibility for nuclear safety matters was not thereby weakened. He was also in favour of setting up in 1992 an open-ended working group with the task of carrying out the preparatory work necessary for the speedy adoption of the convention, on the understanding that it would report to the Board periodically on the progress of its work. The Russian Federation was willing to participate in such work, whether or not linguistic services were made available.

117. Mr. ENDO (Japan) stressed that in order to improve nuclear safety - an essential element in promoting the peaceful uses of nuclear energy - it was necessary to strengthen international co-operation. His country had acquired extensive experience in the management and operation of nuclear facilities and was prepared to continue its co-operation in the field of nuclear safety, inter alia, by providing experts.

118. In order to ensure the effectiveness of the nuclear safety measures envisaged, some basic principles should be borne in mind. Firstly, nuclear safety was primarily a question of States' responsibility. Unless each country made the necessary efforts to establish its own national safety culture, co-operation between the Agency and Member States with broad experience in safety matters would not yield tangible results.

119. Secondly, the future convention should be acceptable to all countries. In that regard, the report prepared by the group of experts which had met in December 1991 was very constructive, reflecting as it did the ideas of many experts from various regions and organizations. However, the Secretariat's document diverged somewhat from the experts' report where the content of a

0166

possible convention were concerned. In the end, it was desirable that the provisions of the convention should be based less on the Agency's ideas than on the expectations of countries, as expressed in the discussions of the working group consisting of Member States' representatives; that was the only way of ensuring wide acceptance and efficacy of the new convention.

120. It was up to the newly created working group to explore those questions in detail. Japan, for its part, considered that the future convention should concentrate on general principles and that the Agency should not be given any new institutional role with regard to the safety of nuclear installations; that was, moreover, the view taken by most of the experts at the December meeting.

121. In conclusion, his delegation supported the measures proposed in document GOV/2567 and was fully prepared to co-operate in preparing the convention.

122. Mr. KENNEDY (United States of America) supported the negotiation of an international nuclear safety convention. Such a convention must be carefully crafted to provide substantive benefits to the parties while at the same time attracting early and wide agreement. To that end, the future convention should incorporate a number of basic principles.

123. The first principle was that of the sovereign responsibility of each State with respect to nuclear safety; any attempt to dilute that responsibility would run counter to the objectives set. Secondly, the scope of the convention should, at the present stage, be confined to commercial nuclear power plants. Attempts to cover the entire nuclear fuel cycle could delay implementation of the convention, especially in the area of most immediate concern, namely the safe operation of commercial reactors. Thirdly, the convention should not seek to establish an international inspection regime. A system of peer reviews, possibly in the form of periodic conferences of the parties to the convention, would provide assurances that its provisions were being observed without any dilution of the concept of States' responsibility. Such a system would also foster a sense of each country's responsibility for nuclear safety without infringing upon national sovereignty. Fourthly, the convention should seek to establish basic safety

principles such as those contained in the draft IAEA document on the safety of nuclear installations. It would not be realistic to include detailed and binding technical standards in view of the variety of reactor types, sites, legal systems and regulations in the future States parties to the convention. In the fifth place, it would be wisest to opt for a single document in order to increase the likelihood of early implementation and to keep negotiations focused on the essential purpose of the convention, which was to ensure that basic reactor safety principles were routinely respected by all nations. An open-ended negotiation on an unlimited series of protocols could only delay proceedings and broaden the instrument's scope beyond what was acceptable to the majority of the States likely to adhere to the convention.

124. The United States endorsed the Director General's recommendation that the Board authorize the establishment of an open-ended working group to carry out the preparatory work for a nuclear safety convention and hoped that the group thus established would remain small enough to work effectively.

125. Mr. PREUSCHEN (Austria) said that his country wholeheartedly supported the Director General's request in paragraph 12 of document GOV/2567. The inadequacy of safety measures in certain nuclear facilities was a source of concern for the entire international community, given the major transboundary damage which could result from deficiencies in that area. The issue of nuclear safety should have been dealt with long ago in international instruments obliging States to maintain the highest possible safety standards within their territories.

126. Austria had repeatedly urged that binding international safety standards be laid down for nuclear installations. With the technical safety of various installations now being called into question - certain national standards evidently being less rigorous than the internationally accepted ones - it would appear that his country's appeals had been fully justified. He therefore sincerely hoped that a future nuclear safety convention would provide for legally binding safety standards for nuclear installations, which he believed could be achieved if the convention emphasized general principles and procedures rather than technical details.

127. It was argued that a single set of binding international standards could not encompass all the differences between countries in terms of plant design, site, operating philosophy and legal and regulatory systems. Austria maintained that such diversities were already taken into account in the non-binding safety standards currently applied by the Agency, and that their transformation into binding standards should not be impossible.

128. The preparatory work for the elaboration of the new convention should commence without delay. If interpretation and translation services were not available initially, it should be possible to organize informal meetings. The usefulness of such meetings had been demonstrated by the intersessionary work of the Standing Committee on Liability for Nuclear Damage. Discussions on the structure of the future convention should not delay substantive work on its content. The main issue to be tackled was the technical safety of commercial nuclear power plants which, because of their size, number and location, posed the greatest threat of transboundary damage. A related question, that of the technical safety of spent fuel repositories, should also be examined.

129. Finally, if a decision was taken in favour of a framework convention accompanied by annexes or technical protocols, priority should be given to the issues of the safety of nuclear power plants and spent fuel repositories. Also, a subsidiary instrument should perhaps be elaborated and negotiated at the same time as the framework convention.

130. Mr. AHMAD (Pakistan) said he had read document GOV/2567 and the report of the group of experts with great interest. The idea of a convention encompassing nuclear power plants as well as the nuclear fuel cycle seemed attractive, but it should be remembered that it was nuclear power plants that posed the greatest threat of transboundary releases, far greater than that posed by other activities such as mining, fuel fabrication, enrichment, research reactor operation and even fuel reprocessing. The best course might therefore be to prepare a framework convention, setting forth basic safety principles and placing special emphasis on nuclear power plants. Subsequently, other provisions relating to radioactive waste disposal and the rest of the fuel cycle could be added. In that connection, Pakistan shared

the view expressed, among others, by the Governors from China and the United States that responsibility for nuclear safety lay primarily with national authorities.

131. In conclusion, he supported the establishment of an open-ended working group with the task of preparing a draft framework convention giving emphasis to general principles and procedures. He wished, finally, to stress that the future convention should not serve as yet another pretext for denying nuclear technology to Third World countries.

The meeting rose at 12.50 p.m.

정 리 보 존 문 서 목 록					
기록물종류	일반공문서철	등록번호	2021060052	등록일자	2021-06-10
분류번호	726.62	국가코드	UN	보존기간	영구
명 칭	북한 핵문제 : 유엔에서의 토의 및 동향, 1992				
생 산 과	국제연합1과/북미2과	생산년도	1992~1992	담당그룹	
내용목차	* 第46차 유엔총회에서의 북한 핵문제 포함				

0001

외 무 부

종 별 :

번 호 : UNW-0059 일 시 : 92 0108 1900

수 신 : 장 관 (미이,정특,해기,연일,기정)

발 신 : 주 유엔대사

제 목 : 북한 PRESS RELEASE

당지 북한대표부는 1.7.자 핵사찰 관련 북한외교부 대변인 성명을 PRESS RELEASE로 제작 배포한바 별전 보고함. 끝

(대사 노창희-해공관장)

첨부: FAX(UNW(F)-0026)

미주국 1차보 국기국 외정실 분석관 청와대 안기부 공보처

PAGE 1 92.01.09 09:34 WH

외신 1과 통제관

0002

Democratic People's Republic of Korea

PERMANENT MISSION TO THE UNITED NATIONS

225 East 86th Street, New York, N.Y. 10028

TEL (212) 722-3536 FAX (212) 534-3612

Press Release

No.2
January 7, 1992

DPRK FOREIGN MINISTRY SPOKESMAN ISSUES STATEMENT ON NUCLEAR INSPECTION PROBLEM

A spokesman for the Foreign Ministry of the Democratic People's Republic of Korea on January 7 published a statement regarding the problem of nuclear inspection.

Following is the statement:

The Government of the Democratic People's Republic of Korea, proceeding from the noble mission and idea of the Nuclear Non-Proliferation Treaty, put forward a proposal for the conversion of the Korean peninsula into a denuclearized zone and has made tireless efforts for its realization.

It has been the principled stand consistently maintained by us over the nuclear inspection problem to get the U.S. nuclear weapons completely withdrawn from south Korea and remove the very source of its nuclear threat to us.

When the ardent desire of the entire Korean nation for the denuclearization of the Korean peninsula was growing fiercer, the south Korean authorities some time ago published a "Declaration on the Absence of Nuclear Weapons" and then responded at last to the adoption of a "Joint Declaration on the Denuclearization of the Korean Peninsula" which we had proposed long ago.

When the world people were lifting up louder voices demanding the complete withdrawal of the U.S. nuclear weapons from south Korea, the United States recently expressed welcome to the south Korean authorities' "Declaration on the Absence of Nuclear Weapons" through various channels.

Not only the entire Korean people but the world's peace-loving people are now genuinely rejoiced over the fact that it has become possible to solve the nuclear problem on the Korean peninsula on an equitable basis at last thanks to our principled stand and painstaking efforts.

0003

This proves once again that our principled stand toward the nuclear inspection problem was entirely just.

Now that circumstances and conditions have been brought to maturity for a fair solution of the nuclear problem on the Korean peninsula the Government of our Republic decided to sign the Nuclear Safeguards Accord in the near future and have it ratified through legal procedures at the earliest possible date and accept an inspection at a time agreed upon with the International Atomic Energy Agency (IAEA).

The Government of our Republic has decided to formally inform the IAEA of this stand of ours.

The DPRK Government will, in the future, too, faithfully fulfil its obligations under the Nuclear Non-Proliferation Treaty and thus make an active contribution to the cause of completely eliminating nuclear weapons from the globe and defending peace and security in Asia and the rest of the world.

관리 번호	92-80

외 무 부

종 별 :

번 호 : UNW-0163 일 시 : 92 0117 1900

수 신 : 장 관(연일,미이)

발 신 : 주 유엔 대사

제 목 : 안보리정상회의

대:WUN-0121

연:UNW-53,57,107

1. 당관 원참사관이 그간 관련대표부 담당관들로 부터 탐문한 표제회의 추진 관련 주요동향을 아래보고함.

가. 회의 진행개요(안)

1)92.1.31(금) 오전회의(11:00-13:00) , 사무총장 주최오찬, 오후회의(15:00-17:00) 순으로 진행

2)의장인 J.MAJOR 영국수상소개로 B.BOUROS-GHALI 사무총장 연설(20 분정도), 이어 이사국대표들 연설(각국당 15 분정도)

3)미국(G.BUSH 대통령)은 이사국들중 제일먼저 연설하기를 강하게 희망하고있다고 하며, 각국 연설순서는 국명 알파벳순 기준 가능성 큼.

4)J.MAJOR 영수상이 의장으로서 제일 마지막 연설하게 될 것으로 보이며, 의장명의 선언문은 회의말미에 발표하게 된다함.

5)상임이사국 5 개국을 포함한 대부분 이사국의 정상참석 전망(표제회의 참석기회를 이용, 회의를 전후한 각정상간 개별접촉예상)

나. 의제

1)현재 확정된 의제(안)은 없음. (단, 연호 보고및 하기 선언문 골자참조)

2)정상들이 연설하는 의식적인 성격이 강한 회의인 만큼 각국은 의제를 존중하되 비교적 자유롭게 자국 관심사를 언급하게 될것이므로 형식적인 의제는 큰 의미가 없을것이라고함.

다. 의장명의 선언문

1)의장국인 영국측은 동 선언문(STATEMENT) 에 기본적으로 포함시킬 사항을

국기국 장관 차관 1차보 2차보 미주국 외정실 분석관 청와대
안기부

PAGE 1 92.01.18 09:42

외신 2과 통제관 BS

46-1

0005

이사국들에게 제시하고 현재 이에대한 각국의 의견을 요청중이라고 함.

2)상기 영국측이 제시한 선언문 골격및 기본포함사항(ESSENTIALS) 은 다음과 같음.

가)회의 의의및 목적

I) 안보리의 첫 정상회의임과 신임사무총장의 취임 첫달에 개최됨을 언급

II) 본건회의 목적, 국제적인 변혁기, 유엔의 새로운 방향설정을 위한 적기

나)집단안보

I) 국제관계에서 법의 지배를 위한 안보리의 지지입장 재확인

II) 국제집단 안보체제 강화. 평화위협에 대한 효과적 대처. 필요시 침략행위 격퇴를위한 결의, 안보리의 쿠웨이트 침공격퇴 역할언급

다)분쟁의 평화적 해결

유엔의 주요 법기관인 ICJ 를 포함하여 분쟁의 평화적 해결을 위한 기존의 제반수단 활용역설

라)지역분쟁

I) 캄보디아, 엘살바돌 사태를 비롯한 장기적 지역분쟁 해결진척

II) 안보리에 계류중인 여타 분쟁해결을 위한 안보리의 노력약속

마)국제평화.안전대책

I) 국제평화. 안전에의 위협에 대한 유엔의 대응이 가능하도록 필요한 제도발전 노력

II) 예방외교. 분쟁해결. 평화유지 분야에서 유엔및 사무총장의 대응노력 제고필요

III) 사무총장의 주선.헌장 99 조상의 권한(국제평화 안전 위협사안 안보리제기) 행사증대

바)군축

I) 군비통제. 축소와핵무기를 포함한 대량파괴 무기의 확산방지의 중요성강조

II) START.CFE 조약의 비준을 비롯하여 기존 군비통제합의에 참여및 이행의 중요성 재확인

III) 92 년 화학무기 협약체결등 국제및 지역수준의 군축추진. 대량살상 무기확산 방지. 재래식 무기이전 투명성.핵무기 기술확산 규제노력

IV) 핵무기 보유국을 포함한 일부 국가들의 NPT 가입결정 환영 및 미가입국의 가입촉구

사)인권

I) 인권.기본적 자유관련 각국의 의무이행 촉구및 헌장의 목적및 원칙강조

II) 선거감시. 인권감시와 관련한 유엔역할 증대언급

아)결어

국제평화 안전증진을 위한 적극적이고도 실제적인 진전을 위한 안보리의 계속적인 노력천명

3)영국측은 신임총장에 대한 안보리의 지원약속, 지역문제등도 구체적 문안작성시 적절히 추가보완시켜 나갈수있을 것으로 보고있다함.

4)영국측의 상기기본안은 금주초 이사국들에 제시되었다고 하는바, 각국의 본격적인 반응은 다음주에나 있을것으로 보인다고함.

I) 비동맹이사국(CAUCUS 6 개국) 들의 특기할 움직임은 포착되고 있지 않으나, 지난 1.10 비동맹 조정위회의시 말련발언(UNW-0089) , 대호 모로코측 언급에비추어 남북문제등 재기가능성

II) 일본, 베네주엘라, 인도등 안보리 개편문제(상임이사국 증대)언급포함 요청가능성(일본담당관 시사)

PAGE 3

0007

3. 관련사항 수시 추보 위계임.

첨부: 1.17 WP 기사:UNW(F)-59 끝

(대사 노창희-국장)

예고:92.12.31. 일반

PAGE 4

0008

#번정 ⊫W(FR)-59 20117 1pc (연일. 이이) 총/44

Bush to Meet Chinese Premier at U.N.

By Don Oberdorfer
Washington Post Staff Writer

President Bush will hold a bilateral meeting with Chinese Premier Li Peng at the United Nations Jan. 31, White House press secretary Marlin Fitzwater said yesterday, disclosing plans for what will be the highest-level, Sino-American meeting since China's 1989 crackdown and an important step toward full normalization of relations.

The Bush-Li meeting is scheduled to coincide with a summit session of all members of the U.N. Security Council but comes amid continuing strain over China's position on the export of missile technology.

Administration officials revealed yesterday that the two nations are at loggerheads over a U.S. demand that China put in writing a verbal commitment given Secretary of State James A. Baker III last November to take a major step against missile proliferation.

Because of disagreements over what past Chinese nonproliferation promises have meant in practice, a senior administration official said that "another oral assurance taken to our Congress will not be satisfactory." The official also said there are hints that China is seeking to reopen anti-proliferation issues that Baker thought had been settled during his mid-November visit to Beijing.

Baker announced Nov. 17 after two days of negotiations that China intended to observe the "guidelines and parameters" of the Missile Technology Control Regime, an accord devised by the United States and other powers to limit the supply of ballistic missiles to Third World countries. "To us, this means that they will apply them to any exports of missiles and related technology," Baker said at the time.

Baker said he had gone over his announcement word for word with Chinese Foreign Minister Qian Qichen so there would be no misunderstanding. On returning to Washington, Baker described the missile technology accord as one of the most important results of his trip.

The Reagan administration came under sharp criticism in 1984 for relying on a vaguely worded dinner toast by then-Premier Zhao Ziyang, rather than a written commitment on nuclear nonproliferation, as the basis for a U.S.-China nuclear cooperation agreement.

After the New China News Agency initially reported the Chinese commitment to Baker in vague language, the Chinese Foreign Ministry at U.S. request said clearly on Nov. 21 that "China intends to observe guidelines and parameters" established by the missile technology accord.

"We want to make sure they knew what it was we felt they understood during those [Beijing] meetings," an administration official said. Previous Chinese verbal commitments not to supply advanced weapons to the Middle East have led to controversy over whether missile sales to Syria and Pakistan were nevertheless in the works.

Administration sources said they understand—and that it was made clear in Baker's meetings in Beijing—that the recent agreement barred among other things advanced missile sales to Iran. The sources indicated this was questioned by the Chinese in recent weeks.

China's commitment to abide by the missile technology export rules was made conditional on U.S. willingness to lift proliferation sanctions that were imposed on two Chinese companies in June. They have not yet been lifted, evidently because of the disagreement over China's nonproliferation commitment.

Staff writer John E. Yang contributed to this report.

1-1

0009

UNITED NATIONS

A S

General Assembly Security Council

Distr.
GENERAL

A/47/96
S/23645
26 February 1992

ORIGINAL: ENGLISH

GENERAL ASSEMBLY
Forty-seventh session
Items 61, 62 and 69 of the preliminary list*
GENERAL AND COMPLETE DISARMAMENT
REVIEW AND IMPLEMENTATION OF THE CONCLUDING DOCUMENT OF THE TWELFTH SPECIAL SESSION OF THE GENERAL ASSEMBLY
REVIEW OF THE IMPLEMENTATION OF THE DECLARATION ON THE STRENGTHENING OF INTERNATIONAL SECURITY

SECURITY COUNCIL
Forty-seventh year

Letter dated 26 February 1992 from the Permanent Representative of the Democratic People's Republic of Korea to the United Nations addressed to the Secretary-General

I have the honour to transmit to you the text of a statement made on 20 February 1992 by President Kim Il Sung of the Democratic People's Republic of Korea (see annex).

I should be grateful if the text of this letter and its annex could be circulated as an official document of the General Assembly, under items 61, 62, and 69 of the preliminary list, and of the Security Council.

(Signed) PAK Gil Yon
Ambassador
Permanent Representative

---

* A/47/50.

92-08760 3677a (E) 270292 /...

270292

1100

0010

ANNEX

Statement made on 20 February 1992 by the President of the Democratic People's Republic of Korea

I am glad today to meet you, the delegates of both sides, who have concluded the 6th north-south high-level talks with success.

I feel satisfied with and highly praise the joint efforts you have exerted for the "Agreement on Reconciliation, Non-aggression, Cooperation and Exchange between North and South" and the "Joint Declaration on the Denuclearization of the Korean Peninsula", which became effective at this time.

The coming into effect of these documents is an epoch-making event and a landmark on the way to realizing peace and reunification of the country.

With the north-south agreement and the joint declaration coming into effect, the north and south could break with the past full of mistrust and confrontation and make a new turning-point for reconciliation; further, they are able to eliminate the danger of war and are looking forward to the bright future of peace and peaceful reunification of the country.

The pledge of the north and south to reconcile themselves to and cooperate with each other without fighting and to advance towards reunification proved irrefutably that neither the outside forces nor the differences in ideology and system can split our nation, one and the same blood, which has lived for thousands of years.

Now, all the compatriots in the north and the south, as well as abroad, actively support and warmly welcome the success of your talks, regarding it as the common success of the nation and the historic victory of the national ideal.

With the 6th north-south high-level talks as a momentum, our fellow countrymen have taken a truly valuable first step forward towards the independent and peaceful reunification of the country. This step should not be stopped nor faltered; it must unfailingly be continued over to the reunification of the future.

To this end, the independent stand should be maintained before anything else.

The division of our country caused by outside forces should on all accounts be ended through the efforts of our nation itself.

If one side depends on foreign forces and tolerates foreign interference when the country is divided into the north and the south, it can be viewed as an attitude of confrontation, not an attitude of reunification.

0011 /...

Such an attitude will make it impossible to implement the north-south agreements properly and will make it difficult to conduct dialogues for which both sides bear responsibility and which is trusted by both sides.

Now that both sides have promised reconciliation, they must discard the idea of confrontation and trust their fellow countrymen and rely on the national force of independence instead of depending on foreign forces.

The north and the south must also direct primary attention to the settlement of the question of peace and take practical measures for ensuring peace in the country.

Since they have agreed on non-aggression, the north and the south must stop the arms race and realize disarmament.

Herein lie the most reliable guarantees for non-aggression and also the way to remove completely the apprehension of "invasion" from the north and invasion from the south.

Now there is no need for foreign troops to be in our country, nor is there any reason for foreign military bases to be kept there.

We consider that it is high time for us to make a decision on this problem.

The nuclear problem of the Korean peninsula should also be solved.

We do not know whether there are still nuclear weapons in south Korea or all of them have been withdrawn.

This state has not removed up to now the grave concern of those of us who have been exposed to a nuclear threat for more than 30 years.

So far as we are concerned, as we have already declared repeatedly, we do not make nuclear weapons nor do we have any need to do so, to say nothing of the fact that we do not have them.

We have no intention of nuclear confrontation with neighbouring big Powers and, moreover, it is unimaginable for us to develop nuclear weapons which can exterminate the same nation.

No one will have a doubt about this.

Promoting the great unity of the nation is the fundamental spirit of the north-south agreement.

If the north and south are to become reconciled and achieve reunification, they should in any case bring about great national unity, transcending differences in ideas and systems. Opposing each other and

/...

regarding the other as a heretic because ideologies and ideas differ, only produces the result of national disruption.

Everyone, being a Korean, should put the common interests of the nation to the fore, subordinate everything to it and unite on the basis of patriotism and the spirit of national independence.

We should destroy the barriers in ideology and system and pursue a policy oriented to great national unity of broad range and love of the country and the nation for uniting the whole nation.

The agreements which became effective at the 6th north-south high-level talks are a pledge made by the responsible authorities of the north and south to the nation.

The Government of our Republic regards these historic agreements as precious results of the efforts for the independent and peaceful reunification of the country and will make our every effort to implement them.

We are convinced that if the north and south build up mutual confidence by working on details, adhering to the principles of independence, peaceful reunification and great national unity they will be able to give our people greater pleasure in the future and achieve without fail the reunification of the country in the 1990s, which the entire nation desires.

In conclusion, I express my expectation that the north and the south will join efforts to open more forcefully the way to peace and the reunification of the country, and I wish the delegates of both sides greater successes in the future.

공 란

공 란

공 란

원 본

이명

외 무 부

종 별 :

번 호 : UNW-0667 일 시 : 92 0310 1930

수 신 : 장 관(연일,국기,미일,정특,기정)사본:유종하대사

발 신 : 주 유엔대사

제 목 : 북한 핵관련 기사

연: UNW-0655

북한 핵문제 관련 3.10.자 NYT 지 기사를 별첨 FAX 송부함. 끝

(대사대리 신기복-국장)

첨부: FAX (UNW(F)-237)

국기국 차관실 미주국 국기국 외정실 분석관 청와대 안기부

PAGE 1

92.03.11 10:11 WH

외신 1과 통제관

0017

UNW(F)-237 20310 1930
주유엔 UN—667
총1매

U.S. AGENCIES SPLIT OVER NORTH KOREA

State Dept. and C.I.A. Differ on Nuclear Predictions

By ELAINE SCIOLINO
Special to The New York Times

WASHINGTON, March 9 — The State Department is disputing the prediction by Robert M. Gates, the Director of Central Intelligence, that North Korea is on the verge of becoming a nuclear power, senior Administration officials said today.

The issue, which has been debated vigorously, but privately, for months, was publicly disclosed after Mr. Gates told the House Foreign Affairs Committee late last month that Pyongyang could have a nuclear weapon from within a few months to a couple of years. He made the same prediction in closed testimony before the committee, officials familiar with his testimony said.

Much of the State Department bureaucracy believes there is insufficient hard evidence to make such a prediction and that based on North Korea's industrial capability, it needs two years or more to build a nuclear bomb.

'A Classic Case'

A number of senior Administration officials said they were stunned and irritated that Mr. Gates took such a hard line at a particularly crucial diplomatic juncture. Both the White House and State Department have tried to use what officials call "diplomatic engagement" to press North Korea into following through with its accord with the South to ban nuclear-related installations on the peninsula and with its pledge to allow inspections by the International Atomic Energy Agency.

"This is a classic case where the C.I.A. and the State Department have very different perspectives," said an Administration official who follows arms issues. "The C.I.A. has to be absolutely certain that if anything bad happens they predicted it first, so that it cannot be accused of a repeat of what happened in Iraq. The State Department is responsible for solving the problem diplomatically, and the natural inclination is to say that there is still sufficient time to solve this problem."

A senior State Department official called Mr. Gates's prediction "the absolute worst-worst case analysis." He added, "The more reasonable, middle-of-the-road-assessment is that you're still talking about several years."

Pentagon officials are also divided, with the Defense Intelligence Agency generally sharing the C.I.A.'s view and some senior Pentagon officials calling Mr. Gates's prediction too harsh.

The New York Times

Robert M. Gates, the Director of Central Intelligence.

In a second area of concern to Washington, United States intelligence agencies have begun to track the Iranian-flagged Iran Salaam, which is suspected of carrying Scud-C missiles and equipment to build them from North Korea to Syria, Pentagon officials said.

The United States put another ship, the Dae Hung Ho, under surveillance after it left North Korea in early February; it is believed to be carrying Scud-C missiles and related production equipment. American warships are poised to intercept or board it as an intimidating gesture if it enters the Persian Gulf. Although such deliveries do not violate international law, under a United Nations blockade imposed on Iraq after it invaded Kuwait, American forces have legal authority to board the ship if it enters the Persian Gulf.

The Administration is still debating whether to take any action and has not given orders to board the Dae Hung Ho. American intelligence agencies originally said they believed that was headed for Bandar Abbas, Iran, although some reports suggested it was bound for the Iranian port of Busheir or Karachi, Pakistan.

But later tonight, a senior Administration official said United States intelligence agencies have lost track of the Dae Hung Ho, which has led Administration officials to believe that the ship may have changed course.

"We obviously have been monitoring the course of the ship and have no indication that it is proceeding along the path it was originally following," the official said. "As a result, we believe it has changed course."

A third North Korean ship, the Dae Hung Dan, which left port in February, is also being watched, although Administration officials said today that they do not believe Israeli intelligence reports that the ship is carrying manufacturing equipment for the missiles.

North Korea's shipment of missiles and missile technology to the Middle East and its continuing development of a nuclear program illustrate the difficulty the United States faces in trying to curb the spread of weapons.

The absence of clear evidence makes it extraordinarily difficult to draw conclusions about North Korea's nuclear capability with much accuracy. American intelligence officials describe the country as more impenetrable than Iraq, whose vast nuclear arms program was revealed only through intrusive United Nations inspections after Iraq's defeat in the Persian Gulf war.

With so little information, many Administration officials say that predicting when North Korea will have a nuclear weapon is a useless exercise. The State Department and the C.I.A., for example, are relying on the same data but drawing different conclusions.

Apparent Contradiction?

Even Mr. Gates appeared to contradict himself during his testimony on Feb. 25. His prepared remarks were rather muted, apparently because they had to be reviewed in advance by all Government intelligence agencies, including the State Department's Bureau of Intelligence and Research, which has taken a more cautious view.

"Even after North Korea accumulates enough plutonium, making a device would require several additional steps that could require months or even years," Mr. Gates said in his prepared testimony.

But in response to Representative Stephen J. Solarz, the New York Democrat, Mr. Gates was more decisive.

Assuming the North Koreans continue their nuclear weapons program, Mr. Solarz asked: "How long do you estimate it would take for them to produce a sufficient amount of fissile material to make a weapon? And how long would it take them to weaponize it?"

Mr. Gates said, "We think a few months to as much as a couple of years."

No Misunderstanding

Mr. Solarz asked, "A few months to produce the fissile material?" to which Mr. Gates answered, "To have a weapon."

"To have a weapon?" Mr. Solarz asked.

"To have a weapon," Mr. Gates replied.

A C.I.A. official told other Administration experts later that perhaps Mr. Gates had been misunderstood.

But today the C.I.A. said that there is no contradiction and that Mr. Gates stands by his tougher assessment.

"There should be no confusion," said a C.I.A. official familiar with the testimony. "We believe that the North Koreans are at a minimum a matter of months or at most a couple of years away from having a nuclear weapon whether or not they have already extracted the plutonium. The extraction process would itself take only a few months, which does not change Mr. Gates's statement that they are 'a few months to a couple of years away.'"

NYT. March 10, P2

0018

외 무 부

종 별 :

번 호 : UNW-0676 일 시 : 92 0311 1800

수 신 : 장 관(정특,연일,해기,기정)사본:유종하대사

발 신 : 주 유엔 대사대리

제 목 : 북한 PRESS RELEASE

당지 북한대표부는 3.11 제 9차 최고인민회의소집 (4.8)및 솔라즈 미하원 의원의 북한 핵개발관련 발언내용을 비방하는 PRESS RELEASE 를 각각 제작 배포했는바 별전보고함

(대사대리 신기복-해공관장)

첨부:UNW(F)-0240

외정실 차관실 1차보 국기국 안기부 공보처

PAGE 1

92.03.12 09:36 WG

외신 1과 통제관

0019

MAR 11 '92 17:22 KOREAN MISSION P.1

UNW-0240 20311 1800 UNW-0606 의 첨부

Democratic People's Republic of Korea

PERMANENT MISSION TO THE UNITED NATIONS

225 East 86th Street, New York, N.Y. 10028

TEL (212) 722-3536 FAX (212) 534-3612

Press Release

No.9

March 10, 1992

ON CONVOCATION OF DPRK SUPREME PEOPLE'S ASSEMBLY SESSION

The Third Session of the Ninth Supreme People's Assembly (SPA) of the Democratic People's Republic of Korea will be convened in Pyongyang on April 8, 1992, under the decision of the SPA Standing Committee dated March 7.

According to the announcement of the convocation of the SPA session of the DPRK, the agenda items of the session are as follows:

1. On the review of the fulfillment of the 1991 state budget of the DPRK and on the 1992 state budget,

2. On endorsing laws on which the SPA Standing Committee of the DPRK discussed and decided during the break of the SPA,

3. On the deliberation of the request for the ratification of the Safeguards Accords under the Non-Proliferation Treaty signed between the DPRK Government and the International Atomic Energy Agency.

240-3-1

0020

Democratic People's Republic of Korea
PERMANENT MISSION TO THE UNITED NATIONS
225 East 86th Street, New York, N.Y. 10028
TEL (212) 722-3536 FAX (212) 534-3612

Press Release

No.10
March 10, 1992

ARROGANT AND IMPUDENT ACT

Negotiations and agreement regarding the nuclear inspection problem are making a smooth progress between the Democratic People's Republic of Korea and the International Atomic Energy Agency (IAEA).

At this moment, some American Politicians are acting foolishly to mislead world opinion, spreading unfounded rumors about the DPRK's implementation of the Nuclear Safeguards Accord.

Among them is Solarz, Member of the U.S. House of Representatives.

He contended that it must be confirmed whether north Korea is going to "promote its nuclear program in secret" or not, after allowing the inspection of the IAEA to avoid the pressure of the world public and a measure must be taken as regards this. He cried that the United States must "apply to north Korea the lesson it learned in Iraq" when north Korea fails to solve the nuclear problem "satisfactorily".

His remarks were shameless words intended to distort fact and force his will upon the other by strength. They lash the people into fury.

We are compelled to avail ourselves of this opportunity to give some detailed accounts of the behavior of Solarz.

While staying in the Democratic People's Republic of Korea from December 17 to 19 last year, he agreed to our principled argument that the nuclear inspection problem must be solved fairly. But now he is even crying for the "need of the use of armed forces" against our country.

When he was visiting our country, he acted arrogantly and impudently from the position of big-powerism and would not see the problem fairly, captive to a partisan stand, bigoted view and political ambition.

240-3-2

0021

2

Solarz, truth to tell, visited Pyongyang, urged by his political desire to score points and distinguish himself by intervening in and coordinating the problem of our nuclear inspection which posed as a complicate problem in the international arena before the presidential election slated this year in the United States.

He behaved arrogantly from the position of big-powerism in our country and, back home, challenged the independent stand of our Republic, distorting fact. This shows his political and normal meanness in seeking to gratify his political desire at the sacrifice of the DPRK-U.S. relations.

We could not have a dialogue in good faith with the reckless and unreliable partner or open-heartedly explain to him our principles stand.

In the course of his dialogue with us, he revealed on the whole that he is a political illiterate lacking political ability and diplomatic knowledge to correctly understand and judge the point in question. Therefore, we had a direct contact with the U.S. authorities and held DPRK-U.S. talks, excluding Solarz who lacked the quality of a politician and with whom we could not have a dialogue in good faith.

The progress of the DPRK-U.S. relations toward a solution reflects the trend and demand of the times. However hard Solarz may try to reverse this trend, things will not go as he wishes.

The anachronistic mode of thinking of Solarz bent on spoiling the bright prospect for the settlement of the nuclear problem opened with much efforts and aggravating the tension deserves denunciation and criticism by world people.

Even though the like of Solarz talks trash, we do not give up what we should do or do what we should not. It is a consistent stand of our Republic to convert the Korean peninsula into a nuclear-free, peace zone.

We have neither the capacity nor the intention to develop nuclear weapons. Moreover, it is quite unthinkable for us to develop nuclear weapons which might exterminate the fellow countrymen.

Our Republic which has already signed the Nuclear Safeguards Accord will ratify and effectuate it at the earliest possible date and then accept inspection with dignity at a time agreed upon with the IAEA.

We will never tolerate such acts as Solarz did in bringing unilateral pressure upon us contrary to impartiality and equity of the international community or interfering in our internal affairs and insulting the sovereignty of our country and the dignity of our nation.

240-3-3

0022

원 본

외 무 부

종 별 :

번 호 : UNW-0767 일 시 : 92 0318 2100

수 신 : 장 관 (연일,정특,미이,기정)

발 신 : 주 유엔 대사

제 목 : 북한관계 기사

북한 핵문제 및 대 중동 미사일 수출관련 3.18.자 NYT 지 기사를 별첨 FAX 송부함.

끝

(대사대리 신기복-국장)

첨부: FAX (UNW(F)-277)

국기국 1차보 미주국 외정실 분석관 청와대 안기부

PAGE 1

92.03.19 13:23 WG

외신 1과 통제관

0023

UNW(F)-277 20318 2100 기안실 UNW-0767 총204

NYT March 18

How to Press North Korea

U.S. and Seoul Differ On A-Arms Prevention

By DAVID E. SANGER

Special to The New York Times

TOKYO, March 17 — Despite a flurry of pledges in recent weeks from North Korean leaders that they are nearly ready to allow nuclear inspections, officials in Seoul and Washington say they are mired in a game of diplomatic hide-and-seek, in which no one really knows how much time is left.

News Analysis

The officials say they are likely to let the negotiations play themselves out until June or a little beyond, the time North Korea and South Korea set Saturday for the first inspections to establish that neither side is developing or deploying nuclear weapons.

After that, they believe, enough evidence will have been assembled to argue to the United Nations Security Council that North Korea, much like Iraq, is dragging out negotiations in a play for time to build a bomb.

Because estimates vary widely on how much time North Korea needs to begin producing its own supplies of nuclear fuel, and then to make weapons, there are sharp differences of opinion over how long it is useful to keep the North Koreans talking.

No Attack Plan Now, but ...

Few believe that a full-scale crisis is imminent, and American military officials say there are no preparations under way for a military strike against nuclear plants. But that could change quickly, they say, if any evidence emerges that North Korea has begun to produce weapons-grade plutonium, a development many believe could take place this year.

"In the next few months we will know what it will be, a major crisis for Asia or a peaceful resolution," François Heisbourg, director of the International Institute for Strategic Studies in London, said recently. "And we will also see a major test of the relations between the U.S. and South Korea."

In recent weeks, Bush Administration officials have been in Seoul to try to defuse those tensions and to keep up the pressure on the North. But each new agreement, the latest of which creates a Joint Nuclear Control Commission between North and South to coordinate inspections, seems ridden with loopholes and chances for delay.

So does a separate agreement signed by North Korea in June to allow in the International Atomic Energy Agency. That still requires ratification by the North Korean Parliament, a step expected next month, and then the atomic energy agency will negotiate the sites and the nature of the inspections.

Providing a Way Out

"You must play a game with them," said James R. Lilley, Assistant Secretary of Defense for International Security, at a recent conference. "We are trying to create a series of clear incentives and disincentives and still leave them a face-saving way out."

The evidence is murky about how quickly the North Koreans are proceeding. In recent months, senior American officials say, reconnaissance satellites have detected "a changed picture" around Yongbyon, a secret research site north of Pyongyang.

Trucks have been sighted pulling up to the recently completed fuel-reprocessing plant, where the North Koreans are thought to be trying to make weapons-grade plutonium. But the reconnaissance photos, officials say, do not make it clear whether the trucks are loading or unloading.

If they are unloading, some theories go, the plant will soon be fully equipped and presumably ready to begin operations. If they are loading, the equipment is perhaps being moved elsewhere in anticipation of inspections.

Sanctions Against a Hermit?

Either way, American and South Korean officials concede that their leverage is limited. It is difficult to impose harsh economic sanctions on a nation with virtually no foreign trade. South Koreahas all but dismissed a military strike, because Seoul is situated only 35 miles from the 38th Parallel and its nuclear power plants would be vulnerable to retaliation.

North Korea has repeatedly denied that it is developing nuclear weapons.

Seoul and Washington have agreed on a basic objective: to force the North into a series of intrusive, short-notice inspections, both by the atomic energy agency and by South Korean teams to verify that the Communist Government has no nuclear intentions.

The two allies have coordinated their actions closely, especially in December, when the United States said it would allow North Korea to inspect its bases in the South to prove that nuclear weapons had been removed.

But recently, South Korean officials have said that the best strategy is to keep the two sides talking, meeting all the deadlines set under a reconciliation agreement reached in December. Last weekend, Seoul abandoned its long insistence on a clear set of dates and places for inspection before setting up a Joint Nuclear Control Commission.

The Pentagon has taken a generally harder line, urging the South to insist on specific inspection regimens rather than let the North win a propaganda battle by initialing vague agreements.

"We distrust the North's motives as much as the United States does," a South Korean negotiator said recently. "But as Koreans, we think we know more about how to negotiate effectively with the North."

277-2-1

0024

NORTH KOREA SHIP DELIVERS TO IRAN

Latest Vessel Thought by U.S. to Be Carrying Missiles Ignores Complaint

By ERIC SCHMITT
Special to The New York Times

NYT. March 18

WASHINGTON, March 17 — A second North Korean ship believed to be carrying Scud missiles or components delivered its cargo to Iran on Friday after United States officials concluded that they had no authority to stop it, Defense Department officials said today.

The Bush Administration threatened last week to board another North Korean freighter suspected of carrying Scud missiles to Iran, only to have the vessel elude Navy warships and successfully deliver its cargo to Bandar Abbas in Iran, just inside the Persian Gulf. American intelligence officials believe the missiles are ultimately bound for Syria.

In the case of the second North Korean ship, a senior Defense Department official said Navy ships in the region hailed the freighter, the Iran Salam, but acknowledged that there "was not much" Navy officials could do to prevent the ship from unloading its cargo at Char Bahar, an Iranian port near the Pakistan border.

The Administration's handling of the two incidents illustrates the limitations on Washington's ability to curb the sale and proliferation of advanced weaponry to potentially hostile nations.

Administration officials said they had hoped the public and diplomatic pressure might prevent delivery of the first shipment aboard the freighter Dae Hung Ho, although it did not violate international law. The saber-rattling strategy backfired.

"What we have lost by our failure to pick up that ship is we would have been able to alert our intelligence colleagues to determine more specifically what was there," Gen. Joseph P. Hoar, a marine who succeeded Gen. H. Norman Schwarzkopf as head of the United States Central Command, told a House committee last week.

Embarrassed by the failure to track the first ship after making such a fuss, the Administration quietly allowed the Iran Salam to dock and unload.

"The point of the matter is that we have no authority to stop those babies," a Defense Department official said today. "There are no international sanctions against Iran."

Under a United Nations naval blockade imposed on Iraq after it invaded Kuwait in August 1990, American military forces are authorized to board ships only if they enter the Persian Gulf or the Red Sea and are suspected of carrying cargo to Iraq.

277-2-2

0025

공　　란

공　　　란

공 란

공 란

공 란

공 란

공 란

공　　란

공 란

공　란

공　　　란

공 란

공　　란

공 란

원 본

외 무 부

종 별 :

번 호 : UNW-1104 일 시 : 92 0415 1600

수 신 : 장관 (정특,연일,해신,기정)

발 신 : 주유엔대사

제 목 : 유엔 사무총장 북한 핵문제 언급

4.15. 정보 브리핑에서 유엔 대변인은 ESCAP총회 참석차 북경 방문중인 BOUTROS-GHALI 유엔사무총장이 4.15. SHANGRI-LA HOTEL 에서 가진 기자회견중 북한의 핵문제 및 IAEA 조치 관련 질문에 '문제가 제기되면 그것은 안보리와 총회에서 논의될 일이다 (IT'S UP TO THE SECURITY COUNCIL AND THE GENERAL ASSEMBLY TO DISCUSS THE MATTER)'라 답하였다고 발표했는바 관련 PRESS RELEASE 별전 송부함. 끝

(대사 유종하-해공관장)

첨부: FAX (UNW(F)-389)

외정실 1차보 국기국 분석관 안기부 공보처

PAGE 1

92.04.16 07:16 DQ

외신 1과 통제관

0040

UNW(F)-389 20415 1600 | UNW-1104 | 20H

The following was received from
an information officer in Beijing

Secretary-General's visit to China

The Secretary-General held talks today with Chinese officials. This morning he met the Chinese Foreign Minister, Mr. Qian Qichen.

The discussions were qualified as positive and constructive. They centered on the following topics:

- Report of Summit-level meeting of Security Council of 31 January 1992 (peacekeeping, peacemaking and preventive diplomacy)
- Role of regional organizations in helping to resolve disputes, in accordance with Chapter VIII of the Charter (Yugoslavia, Somalia, Azerbaijan-Armenia on Nagorno Karbakh)
- Role of NGOs in helping the UN to carry out economic and social activities
- Rio Summit/UNCED
- Preparations for 50th UN annniversary and the Summit on Social Development
- Cambodia
- Myanmar-Bangladesh and Mr. Eliasson's mission to that region
- Libya
- African questions such as Western Sahara, Angola, Ethiopia/Eritrea, Sudan, Mozambique.

In the afternoon, at 12:30 hours, the Secretary-General attended a welcoming luncheon given by the Foreign Minister. And later on, at 15:45 hours, he had a meeting with the General Secretary of the Chinese Communist Party, Mr. Jiang Zemin. And then the Secretary-General gave a press conference at the Shangri-la Hotel.

In his opening statement, the Secretary-General summarized his talks with the Chinese leaders which centered on social, economic issues and cooperation. He praised the strong support China was giving to the Security Council on regional issues, and he also stressed the positive discussions he had with the Chinese officials on the new role of the United Nations in the field of peacekeeping, peacemaking and preventive diplomacy. Mr. Boutros-Ghali also mentioned the importance of the 48th ESCAP Commission session presently held in Beijing which in his view is to play a great and important role in promoting cooperation in the region. The Secretary-General briefly outlined his itinerary for the next days, Cambodia, Thailand, and India.

389-2-1

/...

0041

- 2 -

Highlights of the press conference:

During the question and answer session, the Secretary-General said about Libya that the role of the United Nations was a catalystic one and that resolution 731 was in effect since one hour, Beijing time. He also hoped, answering another question, that a peaceful solution to the issue would be found. As an oil embargo was suggested by another journalist, the Secretary-General replied that he would continue his diplomatic activities to help find a peaceful solution.

On Cambodia, the Secretary-General said that he had to wait to see by himself the prevailing situation before talking about the subject. Answering another question on the role of the world body in Cambodia, Mr. Boutros-Ghali said that the United Nations would interfer in its peacekeeping capacity and in helping set up local administration.

Regarding Yugoslavia he noted that there was a division of labour between the European Community and the United Nations, a concept he encouraged. He added that the United Nations was compelled to intervene in regional conflicts but could not do so unless all parties to the conflict agreed to that intervention.

On Azerbaijan, the Secretary-General stressed the fact that the dispute in this area could be solved through an active role by the regional organizations.

Asked about the role of the "Third World" in helping to solve regional conflicts, the Secretary-General said that there had to be a "political will" to enable the "South" and the "North" to get together and the United Nations should ensure an equilibrium in this exercise.

On the human rights issue, the Secretary-General said that to tackle the matter "you had to be two to tango". As the matter was not raised by the Chinese it was therefore not discussed.

Regarding the nuclear issue in North Korea and the IAEA mandate, the Secretary-General said that it was up to the Security Council and the General Assembly to discuss the matter, if it was raised.

On the restructuring of the Security Council, the Secretary-General said that his mandate was limited to the restructuring of the Secretariat and that the Security Council issue was the Security Council's members privilege.

15 April 1992

* * * * *

389-2-2

0042

공 란

공 란

공 란

공 란

공 란

공 란

공 란

공 란

공　　　란

5/7 신

관리번호	92-424

외 무 부

71

종 별 :

번 호 : UNW-1318　　　　일 시 : 92 0506 2030

수 신 : 장 관(연일,국기,정안)

발 신 : 주 유엔 대사

제 목 : 유엔 군축국장 접촉

1. 당지 UNDC 회의에 참석중인 금정호 심의관은 금 5.6. 유엔사무국의 PRVOSLAV DAVINIC 군축국장과 접촉(온찬, 박희원 서기관 동석) 북한의 핵개발 문제를 중심으로한 최근의 동향과 이에 대한 아측의 입장을 설명하여줌

2. 이에대해 동 국장은 군축국으로서도 북한의 핵개발 가능성에 매우 깊은 우려를 가지고 관련 동향을 주시하고 있다고 말하고 특히 자신은 HANS BLIX IAEA사무총장과의 오랜 친분으로 본건 관련 BLIX 총장과 수시 연락하고 있다고 하면서 어제(5.5) 에도 동인과 금번 북한방문이 자칫 북측에 의해 오용되는 일이 없도록 유의해야 할것이라는 요지의 의견을 나누었다고 말함

(대사 유종하-국장)

예고:92.12.31 일반

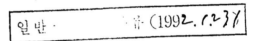

일반 문서로 재분류 (1992.12.31.)

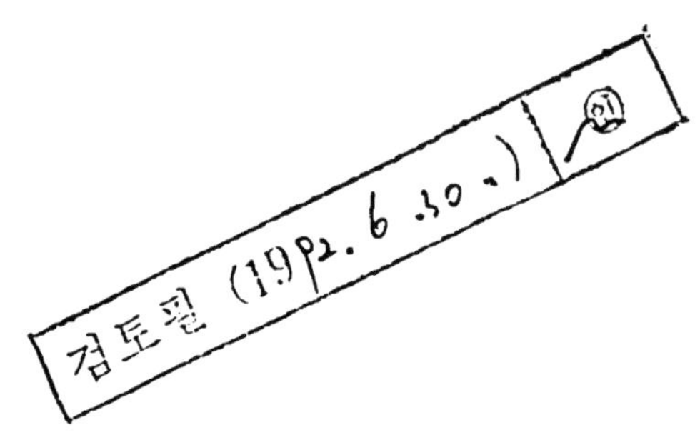

국기국 ~~장관~~ 차관 1차보 국기국 외정실 분석관 ~~청와대~~ 안기부

PAGE 1

92.05.07 10:05

외신 2과 통제관 BX

0052

공　　　란

공 란

공 란

공　　란

공 란

공　　란

공 란

2. Establish control over the use of special fissionable materials received by the Agency, in order to ensure that these materials are used only for peaceful purposes;

3. Allocate its resources in such a manner as to secure efficient utilization and the greatest possible general benefit in all areas of the world, bearing in mind the special needs of the under-developed areas of the world;

4. Submit reports on its activities annually to the General Assembly of the United Nations and, when appropriate, to the Security Council: if in connexion with the activities of the Agency there should arise questions that are within the competence of the Security Council, the Agency shall notify the Security Council, as the organ bearing the main responsibility for the maintenance of international peace and security, and may also take the measures open to it under this Statute, including those provided in paragraph C of article XII;

5. Submit reports to the Economic and Social Council and other organs of the United Nations on matters within the competence of these organs.

C. In carrying out its functions, the Agency shall not make assistance to members subject to any political, economic, military, or other conditions incompatible with the provisions of this Statute.

D. Subject to the provisions of this Statute and to the terms of agreements concluded between a State or a group of States

and the Agency which shall be in accordance with the provisions of the Statute, the activities of the Agency shall be carried out with due observance of the sovereign rights of States.

ARTICLE IV *Membership*

A. The initial members of the Agency shall be those States Members of the United Nations or of any of the specialized agencies which shall have signed this Statute within ninety days after it is opened for signature and shall have deposited an instrument of ratification.

B. Other members of the Agency shall be those States, whether or not Members of the United Nations or of any of the specialized agencies, which deposit an instrument of acceptance of this Statute after their memberhip has been approved by the General Conference upon the recommendation of the Board of Governors. In recommending and approving a State for membership, the Board of Governors and the General Conference shall determine that the State is able and willing to carry out the obligations of membership in the Agency, giving due consideration to its ability and willingness to act in accordance with the purposes and principles of the Charter of the United Nations.

C. The Agency is based on the principle of the sovereign equality of all its members, and all members, in order to

7. In the event of non-compliance and failure by the recipient State or States to take requested corrective steps within a reasonable time, to suspend or terminate assistance and withdraw any materials and equipment made available by the Agency or a member in furtherance of the project.

B. The Agency shall, as necessary, establish a staff of inspectors. The Staff of inspectors shall have the responsibility of examining all operations conducted by the Agency itself to determine whether the Agency is complying with the health and safety measures prescribed by it for application to projects subject to its approval, supervision or control, and whether the Agency is taking adequate measures to prevent the source and special fissionable materials in its custody or used or produced in its own operations from being used in furtherance of any military purpose. The Agency shall take remedial action forthwith to correct any non-compliance or failure to take adequate measures.

C. The staff of inspectors shall also have the responsibility of obtaining and verifying the accounting referred to in sub-paragraph A-6 of this article and of determining whether there is compliance with the undertaking referred to in sub-paragraph F-4 of article XI, with the measures referred to in sub-paragraph A-2 of this article, and with all other conditions of the project prescribed in the agreement between the Agency and the State or States concerned. The inspectors shall report any non-compliance to the Director General

who shall thereupon transmit the report to the Board of Governors. The Board shall call upon the recipient State or States to remedy forthwith any non-compliance which it finds to have occurred. The Board shall report the non-compliance to all members and to the Security Council and General Assembly of the United Nations. In the event of failure of the recipient State or States to take fully corrective action within a reasonable time, the Board may take one or both of the following measures: direct curtailment or suspension of assistance being provided by the Agency or by a member, and call for the return of materials and equipment made available to the recipient member or group of members. The Agency may also, in accordance with article XIX, suspend any non-complying member from the exercise of the privileges and rights of membership.

ARTICLE XIII *Reimbursement of members*

Unless otherwise agreed upon between the Board of Governors and the member furnishing to the Agency materials, services, equipment, or facilities, the Board shall enter into an agreement with such member providing for reimbursement for the items furnished.

ARTICLE XIV *Finance*

A. The Board of Governors shall submit to the General Conference the annual budget estimates for the expenses of

Abstaining: Albania, Argentina, Australia, Austria, Belarus, Bulgaria, Canada, Czechoslovakia, Denmark, Estonia, Finland, Greece, Hungary, Iceland, Ireland, Italy, Japan, Latvia, Liechtenstein, Lithuania, Luxembourg, Marshall Islands, New Zealand, Norway, Poland, Portugal, Republic of Korea, Romania, Spain, Sweden, Turkey, USSR.

Absent: Cambodia, Grenada, Rwanda.

RECORDED VOTE ON RESOLUTION 46/38 C:

In favour: Afghanistan, Algeria, Angola, Antigua and Barbuda, Australia, Austria, Bahamas, Bahrain, Bangladesh, Barbados, Belarus, Belize, Benin, Bhutan, Bolivia, Botswana, Brazil, Brunei Darussalam, Burkina Faso, Burundi, Cambodia, Cameroon, Cape Verde, Central African Republic, Chad, Chile, China, Colombia, Comoros, Congo, Costa Rica, Cote d'Ivoire, Cuba, Cyprus, Democratic People's Republic of Korea, Djibouti, Dominica, Dominican Republic, Ecuador, Egypt, El Salvador, Ethiopia, Federated States of Micronesia, Fiji, Gabon, Gambia, Ghana, Guatemala, Guinea, Guinea-Bissau, Guyana, Haiti, Honduras, India, Indonesia, Iran, Iraq, Ireland, Israel, Jamaica, Jordan, Kenya, Kuwait, Lao People's Democratic Republic, Lebanon, Lesotho, Liberia, Libya, Madagascar, Malawi, Malaysia, Maldives, Mali, Malta, Marshall Islands, Mauritania, Mauritius, Mexico, Mongolia, Morocco, Mozambique, Myanmar, Namibia, Nepal, New Zealand, Nicaragua, Niger, Nigeria, Oman, Pakistan, Panama, Papua New Guinea, Paraguay, Peru, Philippines, Qatar, Saint Kitts and Nevis, Saint Lucia, Saint Vincent and the Grenadines, Samoa, Sao Tome and Principe, Saudi Arabia, Senegal, Seychelles, Sierra Leone, Singapore, Solomon Islands, Somalia, Sri Lanka, Sudan, Suriname, Swaziland, Syria, Thailand, Togo, Trinidad and Tobago, Tunisia, Uganda, Ukraine, USSR, United Arab Emirates, United Republic of Tanzania, Uruguay, Vanuatu, Venezuela, Viet Nam, Yemen, Yugoslavia, Zaire, Zambia, Zimbabwe.

Against: Belgium, France, Germany, Italy, Luxembourg, Netherlands, United Kingdom, United States.

Abstaining: Albania, Argentina, Bulgaria, Canada, Czechoslovakia, Denmark, Estonia, Finland, Greece, Hungary, Iceland, Japan, Latvia, Liechtenstein, Lithuania, Norway, Poland, Portugal, Republic of Korea, Romania, Spain, Sweden, Turkey.

Absent: Grenada, Rwanda.

46/39. Israeli nuclear armament

Date: 6 December 1991 Meeting: 65
76-3-75 (recorded) Report: A/676

The General Assembly,

Bearing in mind its previous resolutions on Israeli nuclear armament, the latest of which is resolution 45/63 of 4 December 1990,

Recalling its resolution 44/108 of 15 December 1989, in which, inter alia, it called for placing all nuclear facilities in the region under International Atomic Energy Agency safeguards, pending the establishment of a nuclear-weapon-free zone in the Middle East,

Recalling also that the Security Council, in its resolution 487 (1981), called upon Israel urgently to place all its nuclear facilities under the Agency safeguards,

Noting with grave concern Israel's persistent refusal to commit itself not to manufacture or acquire nuclear weapons, despite repeated calls by the General Assembly, the Security Council and the International Atomic Energy Agency,

Taking note of resolution GC (XXXV) RES/570, adopted on 20 September 1991 by the General Conference of the International Atomic Energy Agency,

Taking into consideration the final document on international security and disarmament adopted by the Ninth Conference of Heads of State or Government of Non-Aligned Countries, held at Belgrade from 4 to 7 September 1989, 85/ and in particular its paragraph 12, which relates to Israel's nuclear capabilities,

---

85/ See A/44/551-S/20870, annex.

0062

Deeply alarmed by the information with regard to the continuing production, development and acquisition of nuclear weapons by Israel and its testing of their delivery systems in the Mediterranean and elsewhere, thus threatening the peace and security of the region, and equally alarmed by reports of Israel's placing on alert its nuclear arsenal during conflicts in the Middle East,

Aware of the grave consequences that endanger international peace and security as a result of Israel's development and acquisition of nuclear weapons and Israel's collaboration with South Africa in developing their delivery systems,

Deeply concerned that Israel has not committed itself to refrain from attacking or threatening to attack safeguarded nuclear facilities,

1. *Deplores* Israel's refusal to renounce possession of nuclear weapons;

2. *Expresses grave concern* at the cooperation between Israel and South Africa in the military nuclear fields;

3. *Expresses its deep concern* regarding the information on Israel's continuing production, development and acquisition of nuclear weapons and testing of their delivery systems;

4. *Reaffirms* that Israel should promptly apply Security Council resolution 487 (1981), in which the Council, *inter alia*, requested it to place all nuclear facilities under International Atomic Energy Agency safeguards and to refrain from attacking or threatening to attack nuclear facilities;

5. *Calls upon* all States and organizations that have not yet done so not to cooperate with or give assistance to Israel that could enhance its nuclear-weapons capability;

6. *Requests* the International Atomic Energy Agency to inform the Secretary-General of any steps Israel may take to place its nuclear facilities under Agency safeguards;

7. *Requests* the Secretary-General to follow closely Israeli nuclear activities and to report thereon to the General Assembly at its forty-seventh session;

8. *Decides* to include in the provisional agenda of its forty-seventh session the item entitled "Israeli nuclear armament".

RECORDED VOTE ON RESOLUTION 46/39:

In favour: Afghanistan, Algeria, Angola, Bahrain, Bangladesh, Barbados, Belize, Bhutan, Botswana, Brunei Darussalam, Burkina Faso, Burundi, Cambodia, Cameroon, Chad, China, Comoros, Cuba, Cyprus, Democratic People's Republic of Korea, Djibouti, Egypt, Gabon, Gambia, Ghana, Guinea, Guinea-Bissau, Guyana, India, Indonesia, Iran, Iraq, Jordan, Kuwait, Lao People's Democratic Republic, Lebanon, Libya, Madagascar, Malaysia, Maldives, Mali, Mauritania, Mauritius, Mexico, Morocco, Mozambique, Namibia, Nicaragua, Niger, Nigeria, Oman, Pakistan, Philippines, Qatar, Saudi Arabia, Senegal, Somalia, Sri Lanka, Sudan, Suriname, Swaziland, Syria, Thailand, Togo, Trinidad and Tobago, Tunisia, Turkey, Uganda, United Arab Emirates, United Republic of Tanzania, Vanuatu, Viet Nam, Yemen, Yugoslavia, Zambia, Zimbabwe.

Against: Israel, Romania, United States.

Abstaining: Albania, Antigua and Barbuda, Argentina, Australia, Austria, Bahamas, Belarus, Belgium, Benin, Bolivia, Brazil, Bulgaria, Canada, Central African Republic, Chile, Colombia, Costa Rica, Cote d'Ivoire, Czechoslovakia, Denmark, Dominica, Dominican Republic, Ecuador, El Salvador, Estonia, Federated States of Micronesia, Fiji, Finland, France, Germany, Greece, Guatemala, Haiti, Honduras, Hungary, Iceland, Ireland, Italy, Jamaica, Japan, Kenya, Latvia, Lesotho, Liberia, Liechtenstein, Lithuania, Luxembourg, Malawi, Malta, Marshall Islands, Mongolia, Netherlands, New Zealand, Norway, Panama, Papua New Guinea, Paraguay, Peru, Poland, Portugal, Republic of Korea, Saint Kitts and Nevis, Saint Lucia, Saint Vincent and the Grenadines, Samoa, Singapore, Solomon Islands, Spain, Sweden, Ukraine, USSR, United Kingdom, Uruguay, Venezuela, Zaire.

Absent: Cape Verde, Congo, Ethiopia, Grenada, Myanmar, Nepal, Rwanda, Sao Tome and Principe, Seychelles, Sierra Leone.

0063

At its 2282nd meeting, on 15 June 1981, the Council decided to invite the representatives of Bangladesh, Czechoslovakia, Egypt, Hungary, Mongolia, Sierra Leone and the Syrian Arab Republic to participate, without vote, in the discussion of the question.

At its 2283rd meeting, on 15 June 1981, the Council decided to invite the representatives of Indonesia, Italy, Morocco, Poland and Yemen to participate, without vote, in the discussion of the question.

At its 2284th meeting, on 16 June 1981, the Council decided to invite the representatives of Nicaragua and Sri Lanka to participate, without vote, in the discussion of the question.

At the same meeting, the Council also decided, at the request of the representative of Uganda,[52] to extend an invitation to Mr. Sigvard Eklund, Director-General of the International Atomic Energy Agency, under rule 39 of the provisional rules of procedure.

At its 2285th meeting, on 16 June 1981, the Council decided to invite the representative of Malaysia to participate, without vote, in the discussion of the question.

At its 2286th meeting, on 17 June 1981, the Council decided, at the request of the representative of Tunisia,[53] to extend an invitation to Mr. Clovis Maksoud under rule 39 of the provisional rules of procedure.

At its 2288th meeting, on 19 June 1981, the Council decided to invite the representative of the Libyan Arab Jamahiriya to participate, without vote, in the discussion of the question.

Resolution 487 (1981)

of 19 June 1981

The Security Council,

Having considered the agenda contained in document S/Agenda/2280,

Having noted the contents of the letter dated 8 June 1981 from the Minister for Foreign Affairs of Iraq,[54]

Having heard the statements made on the subject at its 2280th through 2288th meetings,

Taking note of the statement made by the Director-General of the International Atomic Energy Agency to the Agency's Board of Governors on the subject on 9 June 1981 and his statement to the Security Council at its 2288th meeting on 19 June 1981,

Taking note also of the resolution adopted by the Board of Governors of the Agency on 12 June 1981 on the "military attack on Iraqi nuclear research centre and its implications for the Agency",[55]

Fully aware of the fact that Iraq has been a party to the Treaty on the Non-Proliferation of Nuclear Weapons[56] since it came into force in 1970, that in accordance with that Treaty Iraq has accepted Agency safeguards on all its nuclear activities, and that the Agency has testified that these safeguards have been satisfactorily applied to date,

Noting furthermore that Israel has not adhered to the Treaty on the Non-Proliferation of Nuclear Weapons,

Deeply concerned about the danger to international peace and security created by the premeditated Israeli air attack on Iraqi nuclear installations on 7 June 1981, which could at any time explode the situation in the area, with grave consequences for the vital interests of all States,

Considering that, under the terms of Article 2, paragraph 4, of the Charter of the United Nations, "all members shall refrain in their international relations from the threat or use of force against the territorial integrity or political independence of any State, or in any other manner inconsistent with the purposes of the United Nations",

1. *Strongly condemns* the military attack by Israel in clear violation of the Charter of the United Nations and the norms of international conduct;

2. *Calls upon* Israel to refrain in the future from any such acts or threats thereof;

3. *Further considers* that the said attack constitutes a serious threat to the entire safeguards régime of the International Atomic Energy Agency, which is the foundation of the Treaty on the Non-Proliferation of Nuclear Weapons;

4. *Fully recognizes* the inalienable sovereign right of Iraq and all other States, especially the developing countries, to establish programmes of technological and nuclear development to develop their economy and industry for peaceful purposes in accordance with their present and future needs and consistent with the internationally accepted objectives of preventing nuclear-weapons proliferation;

5. *Calls upon* Israel urgently to place its nuclear facilities under the safeguards of the International Atomic Energy Agency;

6. *Considers* that Iraq is entitled to appropriate redress for the destruction it has suffered, responsibility for which has been acknowledged by Israel;

7. *Requests* the Secretary-General to keep the Security Council regularly informed of the implementation of the present resolution.

Adopted unanimously at the 2288th meeting.

---

[52] Document S/14540, incorporated in the record of the 2284th meeting.
[53] Document S/14545, incorporated in the record of the 2286th meeting.
[54] *Official Records of the Security Council, Thirty-sixth Year, Supplement for April, May and June 1981*, document S/14509.
[55] *Ibid.*, document S/14532.
[56] General Assembly resolution 2373 (XXII) of 12 June 1968.

관리 번호 92-1679

외 무 부

종 별 :

번 호 : UNW-1798 일 시 : 92 0626 1840

수 신 : 장 관(해외,미일,정특,연일,기정)사본:주미대사(직송필)

발 신 : 주 유엔 대사

제 목 : 북한대표부 기자회견

당지 북한 대표부 차석대사 허종은 6.29(월) 11:00(현지시간) WOLDORF-ASTORIA HOTEL 의 HILTON ROOM 에서 북한의 핵개발 관련하여 기자회견을 가질 예정이라고 하는바 관계자료 별전 송부하며 동기자 회견에 관련된 북한대표부의 동향및 회견내용은 추후 파악 보고예정임

(대사 유종하-해공관장)

예고:92.12.31 일반

일반문서로 재분류(1992.12.31.)

검토필(1992.6.30.)

공보처 장관 차관 미주국 국기국 외정실 분석관 청와대 안기부 안기부

PAGE 1

92.06.27 08:51

외신 2과 통제관 BZ

0065

JUN 26 '92 16:59 KOREAN MISSION P.1

UNW(작)-0565 20626 1840 #검토필

CAPITOL COMMUNICATIONS

Assignment to : Charles Kim Stanley page

URGENT ADVISORY

FOR IMMEDIATE RELEASE
JUNE 25, 1992

CONTACT: Jeff Harper
703-556-0242

NORTH KOREA ADDRESSES NUCLEAR ISSUE

NEW YORK.......In response to recent allegations and subsequent confusion surrounding North Korea's nuclear capabilities, intentions and site inspection availability and in an effort to further communicate North Korean state of affairs, North Korean Ambassador, Ho Jong will hold a press conference on MONDAY, JUNE 29TH.

Scheduled to begin at 11:00 a.m. in the Hilton Room (1st floor) of the Waldorf-Astoria, 301 Park Avenue, New York, the press conference will include a statement by Ambassador Jong followed by a question and answer period.

All interested participants should contact Jeff Harper at 703-556-0242 by close of Business on Friday, June 26th, in order to obtain proper security clearance.

Jeff Harper 703 556 0242

#

565-1-1

Capitol Communications/CAP-COM • 1235 Colonial Road, McLean, Virginia 22101
Tel. (703) 556-0241 • Fax: (703) 556-0379

0066

관리 번호	92-1103

원 본

외 무 부

종 별 :

번 호 : UNW-1808 일 시 : 92 0629 1700

수 신 : 장관 (미일,해외,정특,연일,기정) 사본:주미대사(직송필)

발 신 : 주 유엔 대사

제 목 : 북한대사 기자회견

연: UNW-1798

1. 연호 주유엔 북한차석대사 허종은 6.29. 당지 월도프 아스토리아 호텔 HILTON ROOM 에서 북한 핵문제, 미.북한 관계에 관한 기자회견을 실시함.

2. 동회견은 11:15-11:50 실시되었는바 허종은 북한의 핵문제와 관련, 6.26. 평양발 중앙통신 기사를 참고로 종래의 북한 주장을 장황히 되풀이함.

3. 허종은 이어 한국전쟁 발발 42 주년 및 7.4 공동성명 20 주년을 계기로 몇마디 하겠다고 전제한후 북한은 미국과의 관계개선이 한반도 문제 해결에 관건이 된다는 판단하에 대미관계 개선을 희망하고 있는바 미국으로 부터도 이에 상응하는 조치가 있기를 바란다고 수차 강조함. 이로 미루어 동회근은 핵 문제를 앞세워 왔으나 실질적으로는 미.북한 관계개선 필요성을 미국 여론에 반영시키기위한 것으로 분석됨.

4. 회견에서 NYT 의 ;FRED CONRAD 기자를 비롯 AP, AFP, WTN, NHK, VISNEWS, NBC 뉴스, US NEWS AND WORLD REPORT 및 아국 특파원, 교포언론등 20 여명이 참석함.

5. 동 회근은 북한의 경제난에 불구, 당지 최고급 호텔에서 실시됐다는 사실 및 버지니아주 MCLEAN 소재 광고대행 업소인 CAPITOL COMMUNICATIONS 가 회견예고 PRESS ADVISORY 를 배포한것이 특이사항으로 지적됨.

6. 회견 발표 요지 및 질의응답 요지 별전 보고 위계임. 끝

(대사 유종하-해공관장)

첨부: 동기자회견 영문요지 및 6.26. 중앙통신기사등 6 매 (UNW(F)-568)

예고:92.12.31. 일반

검 토 필 (1992.6.30.)	(인)

미주국 장관 차관 1차보 국기국 외정실 분석관 청와대 안기부
공보처

PAGE 1

92.06.30 08:08

외신 2과 통제관 BX

0067

UNW(功)-568 20629 1700 첨부물 홍604

Press Briefing: Ambassador Ho Jong
Waldorf Astoria: The Hilton Room
June 29, 1992

I would like to thank you all for coming. Today I would like to speak on the nuclear inspections on the Korean peninsula and also the anniversary of the Korean conflict and the Korean agreement of 1972.

As you are aware, the first IAEA inspections were held from 25 May until 6 June and the results were successfully discussed in a very satisfactory way at the IAEA Board of Governors meeting in June.

On this occasion, I would like to make it clear once again that DPRK is faithful to the duties of the safeguards focus under the NPT, and in the future, as in the past, accepts the IAEA safeguards inspection.

The government of the DPRK has carried out an anti-nuclear peace policy since the first days of its polity. The anti-nuclear peace policy is based on the basic principles of its external policy: independence, peace, and friendship. The DPRK has been making all sorts of sincere efforts to denuclearize the peninsula. The first round of IAEA inspections was successfully carried out in response to the agreement between the IAEA and the DPRK. During the inspections, we disclosed all nuclear facilities including even those which were not on the agenda for IAEA inspection in efforts to allow the IAEA to smoothly carried out its inspections. This shows the consistency and the purity of the DPRK's nuclear plan. Since the inspections were carried out with the cooperation of the DPRK, there are no longer grounds to doubt the will of the DPRK for the denuclearization of the Korean peninsula.

I would like to emphasize on this occasion that the DPRK's nuclear power policy for peaceful purposes is unchanged. The use of nuclear power only for peaceful purpose is the principled position of the government of the Republic, proceeding from the basic purpose of resolving the increasing demands for the national economy. A radio-chemical laboratory is under construction for nuclear power development, to effectively use and economize the nuclear field with a view to the future, and to conduct scientific research to separate necessary radio-active isotopes for various used for the national economy.

The role of nuclear power in our country clearly guarantees the active contribution of nuclear power to the development of the national economy.

The DPRK is carrying out exchanges of technical cooperation with other countries for the peaceful uses of nuclear power, and we are also expanding our cooperation with international agencies like the IAEA.

As far as North-South mutual inspections are concerned, we believe

568-6 -1-

0068

efforts should be made to verify the guarantees of a denuclearized Korean peninsula. It is known generally that the DPRK has initiated the introduction of the N-S Joint Declaration for the Denuclearization of the Korean peninsula, and it should be verified through mutual joint inspections. On this occasion, I would like to make it clear once again that the DPRK will make every effort for mutual inspections to be implemented as soon as possible in an effort to verify the denuclearization of the Korean peninsula.

The Joint Declaration should be put into practice through the joint and mutual efforts of the North and the South. The two countries have admitted that the relationship between the North and the South is not between...and therefore, have agreed to settle all the issues through consultations as well as through consultative efforts. It is not the South that should discuss the reasonable ways for implementing the Joint Declaration;

Accordingly, outside interference and pressure should not be allowed.

Secondly, North and South should consult each other in simultaneously removing the doubts for the denuclearization of the peninsula. The real nuclear threat results from the US nuclear military presence in the South. The purpose of inspections is to get rid of such doubts and concerns and to eliminate the nuclear threat on the Korean peninsula. The inspections should cover all suspicious sites, including the US nuclear bases in the South. The mutual inspections should be able to verify the complete denuclearization of the Korean peninsula. Therefore, the South Korean authorities are urged to accept our fair and reasonable position that mutual inspections should be carried out according to the principle of simultaneously dispelling doubts.

Third, United States is urged to allow the proper implementation of the Joint Declaration. The US is truly obligated to desist from being a threat to the territorial integrity of the North. The US policy is interpreted by many as proof of its nuclear presence in South Korea. The announcement of the Bush Administration in September last year on the elimination of tactical weapons, followed by South Korea's no nuclear announcement... The US and South Korea have accepted our proposal for mutual inspection, showed their willingness to allow the US bases in the South to be inspected.

The DPRK decided to sign the safeguards agreement with IAEA to show our flexibility for inspections, under the premise of inspections of US bases in South Korea. Those have not been allowed until today when the DPRK is fulfilling its international commitments under the nuclear safeguards agreement.

Inspection of the American bases in the South is the key to the denuclearization of the Korean peninsula. The DPRK has consistently held that if fair mutual inspections are to carried out, it must be allowed to inspect the US military bases in the

568-6-2-

0069

South. Now we are waiting for a clear response from the United States.

On the occasion of the 42nd anniversary of the breaking out of the Korean War, I call for the quick and real end to the cold war on the Korean peninsula. Nearly four decades have passed since the conclusion of the Korean War. During that period, the world situation has changed a great deal. The legacy of the cold war has not disappeared on the Korean peninsula and confrontation continues. It is high time for the United States to stop its cold war policies of strength, and it should respect the sovereignty of the DPRK, pull out all forces and do things beneficial for the inter-Korean peace process.

If the US discontinues its interference, then the DPRK will not look to the past, but rather forward to improve relations between the two countries.

4 July is the 20th Anniversary of the North-South Joint Statement, which holds that Korea should be reunified according to the three principles of independence, peaceful unification, and national unity. I call on the South Korean authorities to adhere to these three principles and to earnestly implement the Basic Agreement.

4 July is also important for American people who fought a long, hard struggle to achieve freedom and independence. On this historical occasion, I call on the US to respect the three principles for inter-Korean peace process and to take practical measures to ensure peace, prosperity, and national reunification of Korea.

Q&A

1)Is this press conference convened in any way because of the fear of North Korea that US is planning military action against your facilities?

I don't think so. I am aware that the threat has existed, but many Americans agree that such an action would be totally non-sensical. I don't believe such foolish action would be taken by the Bush Administration.

2) You say radioactive developments are for peaceful purposes only, but would it be possible, under different circumstances of tension, that these materials would be used for military purposes.

My government has clearly declared that these materials are to be used for peaceful uses only. The radio-chemical lab is conducting scientific research on isotopic materials for the national economy. Such developments are only for peaceful purposes.

3) You mentioned that DPRK wants to carry out mutual inspections,

568-6-3-

0070

and that it also wants to have better relations with the US. But North Korea has in the past been reluctant to accept mutual inspections, and also the US has preferred to have mutual inspections, but DPRK has demanded that South Korea first allow the North to inspect US bases in the South. What is the most important obstacle to mutual inspections.

I must point out that the idea of N-S mutual inspections were initiated by us, not by the US nor ROK. The reason why we initiated the idea was to get rid of the suspicions regarding the real existence of US nuclear facilities in the South. Therefore, before accepting IAEA inspections, we suggested to the IAEA and to the United States government that if we agree to mutual inspections, you will allow us to inspect the facilities which we find suspicious in the South. If you agree to allow us to inspect the places where we believe nuclear weapons are deployed, we will go along with IAEA inspections. The US and the South Korean governments agreed. So the main obstacle is the question of whether there are still US nuclear weapons in the South. In a few hours there will be a meeting of the North-South Joint Nuclear Committee in Panmunjom. First let's sit down on the procedural agreements on how to implement the Joint Declaration. Second, overall procedural matters, including whether or not they will allow us to go and inspect the US bases. If they say yes, they maybe in one or two weeks, we can have mutual bases.

4) ...

5) US sources have determined that a weapons program is being developed in Pyongyang. How do you explain that when North Korea denies it?

We are carrying out research on nuclear materials for economic uses to determine how to make use of nuclear field for peaceful uses. A minor amount of plutonium was obtained through such experiments. Our nuclear scientists have been involved in such activities. But I must emphasize that such activities are for peaceful purposes. Their activities and findings have ben clearly and fully reported to the IAEA. If the IAEA study is completed, you will have full information on it.

6) At the Tokyo news conference, the North Korean official said that North Korea wants to improve relations with the US. On what basis does it want better relations, and what process is going on to achieve that goal?

During his meeting with evangelist Billy Graham, President Kim said that DPRK is ready to improve US-DPRK relations because those relations are closely linked to the Korean question. The US is deeply involved in the unification issue. Kim Il-Sung exchanged verbal messages indicating that both governments want to improve relations. DPRK-US high level talks in January confirmed this. Since then more efficient contacts between US and DPRK in various economic, political, social, and academic areas have been promoted.

568-6-4-

0071

INSPECTION OF U.S. NUCLEAR WEAPONS AND BASES IN SOUTH KOREA URGED.

= STATEMENT OF DPRK FOREIGN MINISTRY SPOKESMAN=

PYONGYANG JUNE 26 (KCNA) -- A SPOKESMAN FOR THE FOREIGN MINISTRY OF THE DEMOCRATIC PEOPLE'S REPUBLIC OF KOREA ISSUED A STATEMENT TODAY, WHICH SAYS: INSPECTION OF THE U.S. NUCLEAR WEAPONS AND NUCLEAR BASES IN SOUTH KOREA HAS NOT BEEN ALLOWED TILL TODAY WHEN THE DPRK IS FULFILLING ITS INTERNATIONAL COMMITMENTS UNDER THE NUCLEAR SAFEGUARDS ACCORD AND, ACCORDINGLY, THE KOREAN PEOPLE'S CONCERN OVER THE THREAT OF THE U.S. NUCLEAR WEAPONS HAS NOT BEEN DISPELLED.

THE UPRIGHTNESS OF THE DPRK GOVERNMENT'S NUCLEAR POLICY AIMED AT USING NUCLEAR ENERGY ONLY FOR A PEACEFUL PURPOSE AND OUR CONSISTENT POSITION FOR DENUCLEARISING THE KOREAN PENINSULA HAVE BEEN CLEARLY PROVED ONCE MORE THROUGH AN IRREGULAR INSPECTION BY THE INTERNATIONAL ATOMIC ENERGY AGENCY SOME TIME AGO, THE STATEMENT SAYS, AND GOES ON:

WE WILL HONESTLY UNDERGO INSPECTION BY IAEA IN THE FUTURE, TOO, AND SHOW THE TRUTH OF OUR PEACEFUL NUCLEAR POLICY AT ANY TIME THROUGH THE AGENCY, IF ANYONE SUSPECTS THAT WE HAVE SOME NUCLEAR FACILITIES WHICH HAVE NOT BEEN OPENED TO THE PUBLIC.

IN FACT, THE NUCLEAR PROBLEM ON THE KOREAN PENINSULA TRACES ITS ORIGIN TO THE DAYS WHEN THE UNITED STATES ILLEGALLY SHIPPED AND DEPLOYED NUCLEAR WEAPONS IN SOUTH KOREA AND THREATENED THE KOREAN PEOPLE WITH THEM. AN INSPECTION OF THE U.S. NUCLEAR WEAPONS AND BASES IS A KEY TO THE DENUCLEARIZATION OF THE KOREAN PENINSULA TODAY.

THE DPRK GOVERNMENT HAS CONSISTENTLY HELD THAT, IF A FAIR NUCLEAR INSPECTION IS TO BE MADE, WE SHOULD BE ALLOWED TO MAKE AN INSPECTION OF THE U.S. NUCLEAR WEAPONS AND BASES IN SOUTH KOREA WHEN WE UNDERGO AN INSPECTION BY IAEA.

SINCE THE U.S. ADMINISTRATION COMMITTED ITSELF TO THE WITHDRAWAL OF ITS TACTICAL NUCLEAR WEAPONS LAST YEAR AND THE SOUTH KOREAN AUTHORITIES PUBLISHED "A DECLARATION ON NUCLEAR ABSENCE", WE SIGNED THE NSA AND SHOWED GOOD FAITH BY ACCEPTING THE IAEA'S INSPECTION FIRST ON THE PREMISE THAT WE WOULD MAKE AN INSPECTION OF THE U.S. NUCLEAR WEAPONS AND BASES IN SOUTH KOREA.

— r —

568-6-5

0072

BUT OUR INSPECTION OF THE U.S. NUCLEAR WEAPONS AND BASES HAS NOT BEEN ALLOWED TILL TODAY WHEN OUR COUNTRY IS FULFILLING ITS INTERNATIONAL COMMITMENTS UNDER THE NSA AND, ACCORDINGLY, THE KOREAN PEOPLE'S CONCERN OVER THE THREAT OF THE U.S. NUCLEAR WEAPONS HAS NOT BEEN DISPELLED.

NOW THAT THE DPRK HAS ACCEPTED INSPECTION BY IAEA, THE UNITED STATES MUST ALLOW INSPECTION OF ITS NUCLEAR WEAPONS AND BASES IN SOUTH KOREA ON THE PRINCIPLE OF EQUITY.

WHAT IS IMPORTANT IN CARRYING OUT THE JOINT DECLARATION ON THE DENUCLEARIZATION OF THE KOREAN PENINSULA IS TO MAKE AN INSPECTION OF THE U.S. NUCLEAR WEAPONS AND BASES IN SOUTH KOREA AND THUS REMOVE THE VERY CAUSE OF THE CONCERN OF OUR NATION OVER NUCLEAR THREAT.

AN OVERALL INSPECTION OF THE U.S. NUCLEAR WEAPONS AND BASES MUST BE MADE THROUGH INTER-KOREAN INSPECTION TO VERIFY DENUCLEARIZATION BECAUSE THE NUCLEAR THREAT IN KOREA WAS CAUSED BY THE U.S. NUCLEAR WEAPONS DEPLOYED IN SOUTH KOREA.

IT IS FOR THE EARLIEST POSSIBLE DENUCLEARIZATION OF THE KOREAN PENINSULA THAT THE DPRK GOVERNMENT INITIATED THE ADOPTION OF THE JOINT DECLARATION ON DENUCLEARIZATION AND IS UNDERGOING THE IAEA INSPECTION WITH SINCERITY.

THE MAIN HURDLE IN THE DENUCLEARIZATION OF THE KOREAN PENINSULA AT PRESENT IS THAT THE SOUTH KOREAN AUTHORITIES PROPOSE +INSPECTION OF THE SAME NUMBER+ ON THE PRINCIPLE OF +RECIPROCITY,+ +INSPECTION OF MILITARY BASES+ AND +SPECIAL INSPECTION+ WHICH CONTRADICT POINTS OF NORTH-SOUTH AGREEMENT AND THE REALITY OF THE KOREAN PENINSULA, NOT AGREEING TO AN OVERALL INSPECTION OF THE U.S. NUCLEAR WEAPONS AND BASES.

AS FOR THE +INSPECTION OF MILITARY BASES+ PROPOSED BY THE SOUTH KOREAN AUTHORITIES, IT IS NOT A MATTER TO BE DISCUSSED WITHIN THE FRAMEWORK OF THE JOINT DECLARATION ON THE DENUCLEARIZATION OF THE KOREAN PENINSULA. IT SHOULD BE DEALT WITH IN THE DISCUSSION OF DISARMAMENT AT THE NORTH-SOUTH JOINT MILITARY COMMITTEE.

THE SOUTH KOREAN AUTHORITIES MUST QUICKLY PRODUCE A DRAFT AGREEMENT ON THE IMPLEMENTATION OF THE JOINT DECLARATION ON DENUCLEARIZATION AS AGREED UPON BETWEEN THE NORTH AND THE SOUTH AND RESPOND TO THE ADOPTION OF THE RULES OF INTER-KOREAN INSPECTION SO THAT AN OVERALL INSPECTION OF THE U.S. NUCLEAR WEAPONS AND NUCLEAR BASES MAY BE MADE.

WE WILL MAKE EVERY POSSIBLE EFFORT IN THE FUTURE, TOO, TO ADOPT AT THE NORTH-SOUTH JOINT NUCLEAR CONTROL COMMITTEE DOCUMENTS NECESSARY FOR VERIFYING THE DENUCLEARIZATION OF THE KOREAN PENINSULA AND TO REALIZE NORTH-SOUTH INSPECTION AT AN EARLY DATE. -0-

-1-

568-6-6

0073

관리번호	92-1104

원 본

외 무 부

종 별 : 지 급

번 호 : UNW-1812 일 시 : 92 0629 1930

수 신 : 장관(미일,정특,연일,해외,기정) 사본:주미대사(직송필)

발 신 : 주 유엔 대사

제 목 : 북한대사 기자회견

연: UNW-1808

1. 연호 허종의 기자회견 내용중 핵관련 부분은 6.26. 북한 중앙통신이 보도한 북한외교부의 동일자 핵관련 성명과 대동소이하며 특별히 새로운것은 없으나 특히 아래와 같은 측면을 강조함.

가. 북한이 IAEA 의 임시사찰에 최대한 협조하였으며 앞으로도 협조 예정이므로 북한의 핵계획에 대한 의심의 여지가 없음.

나. 플루토늄 추출 및 방사화학 실험실 건설목적은 순수히 과학적 연구목적이며 이는 향후 원자력발전 수요에 대처하기 위한것이고 이것이 추후 IAEA 의 사찰로도 밝혀질것임.

다. 북한이 IAEA 안전협정 서명 비준 및 IAEA 임시사찰을 통해 국제적인 의무를 충실히 이행하고 있는 반면, 동협정 서명시 북측이 전제조건으로 요구했던 주한미군기지에 대한 사찰은 아직까지도 이루어지지 않고있음.

라. 한반도 비핵화 선언은 북한의 주도로 이루어 진것이며 상호사찰이 조속히 실시되어야 하나, 이는 의심동시해소 원칙에 따라 주한미군기지 사찰이 핵심이며 미국이 이에 협조해야함.

0 북한 외교부 성명에서는 아측의 동수주의, 특별사찰 주장은 비핵화 선언위반이며 양측 군사기지 동시사찰 (대칭주의)은 군사공동위에서 남북한 군축차원에서 다뤄져야 할 문제임을 보다 구체적으로 설명함.

마. 남북한 상호사찰은 남북한 당사자간에 협의될 문제로서 외부의 간섭이나 압력은 용납할수 없음.

0 최근 IAEA 이사회, 6.22. CARNEGIE COUNCIL 세미나 등에서의 남북한 상호사찰 수용 압력을 의식한 발언으로 보임.

미주국	장관	차관	1차보	국기국	외정실	분석관	청와대	안기부
공보처								

0074

PAGE 1 92.06.30 09:01

외신 2과 통제관 BX

검 토 필 (1992.6.30

바. 전체적으로 허종은 북한의 핵시설에 대하여는 IAEA 사찰을, 주한 미국기지에 대하여는 남북 상호사찰을 (북한의 사찰) 강조하는데 주안점을 두었으며 상호사찰에 입각한 아측의 북한 핵 및 군사시설 사찰문제에 대하여는 일체 언급하지 않음.

2. 상기 허종발언 및 북한외교부 성명에서 북한이 새삼스럽게 IAEA 의무이행과 주한미군기지 사찰문제를 연계시키고 있는점, 또한 외교부 성명에서 아측의동수주의, 상호주의 및 특별사찰 주장이 비핵화의 주된 장애라고 왜곡하고 군사기지 사찰문제는 군사공동위에서 남북군축 차원에서 다룰 문제라고 한점, 그리고 아측에 대해 비핵화 이행 합의서안을 조속 제시하라고 한점등 북측의 선전책동에 대하여는 가급적 본부에서 영문 TALKING POINTS 를 작성, 필요시 해당공관으로 하여금 조치토록 하는것이 좋을것으로 사료되어 건의함.

3. 북한 외교부의 6.26. 자 성명 관련 당지 추가동향 (PRESS RELEASE, 안보리문서등) 있을경우 추보 예정임. 끝

(대사 유종하-국장)

예고:92.12.31. 일반

관리번호	92-11523

원 본

외 무 부

종 별 :

번 호 : UNW-1814 일 시 : 92 0630 1130

수 신 : 장관 (미일,정특,연일,해외,기정)사본:주미대사(직송필)

발 신 : 주 유엔 대사

제 목 : 북한대표부 PRESS RELEASE

당지 북한대표부는 6.29. 아국내 핵시설에 대한 사찰을 주장하는 내용의 6.26. 자 북한 외교부 대변인 성명을 PRESS RELEASE 로 제작 배포한바 별전 송부함. 끝

(대사 유종하-국장)

첨부: UNW(F)-570

예고:92.9.30. 까지

미주국 국기국 외정실 안기부 공보처

PAGE 1

92.07.01 00:43

외신 2과 통제관 FK

0076

관리번호	92-1109

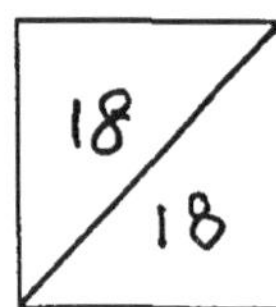

허종 駐유엔 北韓 次席大使 記者會見

1992.7. 1.

外 務 部

92.6.29. 허종 駐유엔 北韓 次席 大使는 뉴욕에서 北韓 核問題 및 美· 北韓 關係에 대해 記者會見을 實施한 바, 同 主要內容 및 評價等을 아래 報告드립니다.

1. 記者會見 概要

o 場　所 : 뉴욕所在 월돌프 아스토리아 호텔

o 參 席 者 : 뉴욕타임즈, NHK, NBC뉴스, AP통신 등 外國 言論社 및 我國 特派員 등 20여명

o 特記事項 : 美國 廣告代行 業所를 雇傭, 會見 豫告文 配布

2. 主要 言及 內容

【 北韓 核 問題 】

o 北韓은 IAEA의 臨時査察에 최대 協調하고 있으며, 北韓 核 問題에 대해 疑心할 소지가 없음.

- 플루토늄 抽出 및 放射化學 實驗室 建設은 純粹科學 研究 目的으로, IAEA査察時 確認 可能

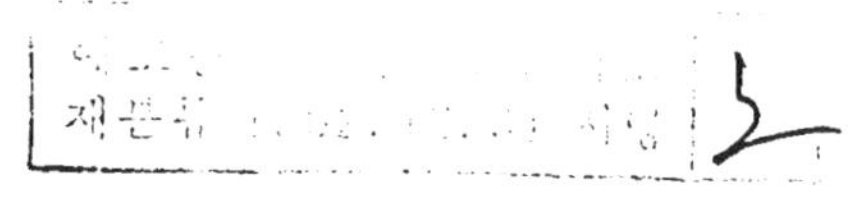

0077

o 北韓은 IAEA 臨時査察을 통해 國際的 義務를 충실히 履行하고 있으나, 駐韓美軍 基地에 대한 査察은 아직 實現되지 않고있음.

- 相互査察은 疑心 同時 解消 原則에 따라 早速 실시 되어야 하며 駐韓美軍 基地에 대한 査察은 韓半島 非核化의 核心 要素

o 南· 北韓 相互査察은 南· 北韓 當事者間에 協議될 문제로서 外部의 干涉이나 壓力은 용납될 수 없음.

【 美· 北韓 關係 】

o 韓半島에 冷戰時代의 殘在가 存在하고 있으며, 美國은 武力을 바탕으로 한 冷戰時代의 政策을 終熄시켜야 함.

- 北韓의 主權 尊重 및 駐韓美軍 撤收 必要

o 美國은 統一問題에 깊이 關與하고 있고, 美· 北韓 關係 改善은 統一과 直結되어 있는 바, 北韓은 美國과의 關係 改善을 希望하고 있음.

- 金日成은 빌리 그래함 牧師 接見時 美· 北韓 關係 改善을 希望하는 구두 메시지 交換

o 지난 1월 美· 北韓 高位接觸은 關係 改善을 希望하는 兩國 政府의 共通된 立場을 證明한 것임.

- 同 接觸 이후 經濟, 政治, 社會, 學術등 모든 분야에서 關係 增進中

0078

3. 分析 및 評價

o 北韓은 相互査察에 대한 國際的 壓力이 加重됨에 따라 이를 回避하기 위한 外交的 逆攻을 試圖하고 있는 것으로 分析됨.

- 그간 美· 北韓 北京 接觸 (6.1), 카네기 財團 學會에서의 發言(6.22), 호놀룰루 學會 發言(6.23) 등을 통해 '北韓式 槪念의 相互査察' 實施 强辯
- 6.26. 外交部 聲明을 통해 上記 立場 公式 表明

o 北韓은 上記 關聯, 美國의 壓力 및 美· 러간 協力等에 敏感한 反應을 보이고 있음.

- 당초 美側은 6.26. 北京 接觸을 통해 强力한 立場을 傳達코자 하였으나, 北韓側은 接觸을 6.30.로 延期 提議하면서, 外交部 聲明을 發表하고 同時에 허종과 駐中大使 주창준의 記者會見을 實施
- 同 問題에 대한 外部의 干涉 排擊을 강하게 主張

o 또한 核問題에 대한 我側과 國際社會의 壓力을 稀釋시키는 方法으로서 美· 北韓, 日· 北韓 關係를 歪曲 宣傳하는 戰術을 驅使함.

- 美· 北韓 關係가 큰 進展이 있는 듯이 宣傳
- 이삼로 (6.23), 현준극 (6.27)의 發言도 같은 脈絡

- 끝 -

豫 告 : 92.12.31. 一 般

0079

주 국 련 대 표 부

주국련(공) 35260- 730　　　　　　　　　　　　　1992. 7. 2

수 신 : 장 관

참 조 : 해외공보관장, 외교정책기획실장, 국제연합국장

제 목 : 북한 Press Release 송부

1. UNW-1814의 관련입니다.

2. 언호관련 북한 Press Release를 별첨 송부합니다.

첨 부 : 동 자료 1부. 끝.

주 국 련 대 사

선 결			결재(공람)		
접수일시	1992. 7. 6	38157			
처리과					

0080

Democratic People's Republic of Korea

PERMANENT MISSION TO THE UNITED NATIONS

225 East 86th Street, New York, N.Y. 10028

TEL (212) 722-3536 FAX (212) 534-3612

Press Release

No.20
June 29, 1992

INSPECTION OF U.S. NUCLEAR WEAPONS AND BASES IN SOUTH KOREA URGED
(STATEMENT OF DPRK FOREIGN MINISTRY SPOKESMAN)

A spokesman for the Foreign Ministry of the Democratic People's Republic of Korea issued a statement on June 26, which says: Inspection of the U.S. nuclear weapons and nuclear bases in south Korea has not been allowed till today when the DPRK is fulfilling its international commitments under the Nuclear Safeguards Accord and, accordingly, the Korean people's concern over the threat of the U.S. nuclear weapons has not been dispelled.

The uprightness of the DPRK Government's nuclear policy aimed at using nuclear energy only for a peaceful purposes and our consistent position for denuclearizing the Korean peninsula have been clearly proved once more through an irregular inspection by the International Atomic Energy Agency some time ago, the statement says, and goes on:

We will honestly undergo inspection by IAEA in the future, too, and show the truth of our peaceful nuclear policy at any time through the Agency, if anyone suspects that we have some nuclear facilities which have not been opened to the public.

In fact, the nuclear problem on the Korean peninsula traces its origin to the days when the United States illegally shipped and deployed nuclear weapons in south Korea and threatened the Korean people with them. An inspection of the U.S. nuclear weapons and bases is a key to the denuclearization of the Korean peninsula today.

The DPRK Government has consistently held that, if a fair nuclear inspection is to be made, we should be allowed to make an inspection of the U.S. nuclear weapons and bases in south Korea when we undergo an inspection by IAEA.

Since the U.S. administration committed itself to the withdrawal of its tactical nuclear weapons last year and the south Korea authorities published "a Declaration on Nuclear Absence", we signed the NSA and showed good faith by accepting the IAEA's inspection first

0081

on the premise that we would make an inspection of the U.S. nuclear weapons and bases in south Korea.

But our inspection of the U.S. nuclear weapons and bases has not been allowed till today when our country is fulfilling its international commitments under the NSA and, accordingly, the Korean people's concern over the threat of the U.S. nuclear weapons has not been dispelled.

Now that the DPRK has accepted inspection by IAEA, the United States must allow inspection of its nuclear weapons and bases in south Korea on the principle of equity.

What is important in carrying out the Joint Declaration on the Denuclearization of the Korean Peninsula is to make an inspection of the U.S. nuclear weapons and bases in south Korea and thus remove the very cause of the concern of our nation over nuclear threat.

An overall inspection of the U.S. nuclear weapons and bases must be made through inter-Korean inspection to verify denuclearization because the nuclear threat in Korea was caused by the U.S. nuclear weapons deployed in south Korea.

It is for the earliest possible denuclearization of the Korean peninsula that the DPRK Government initiated the adoption of the Joint Declaration on Denuclearization and is undergoing the IAEA inspection with sincerity.

The main hurdle in the denuclearization of the Korean peninsula at present is that the south Korean authorities propose "inspection of the same number" on the principle of "reciprocity", "inspection of military bases" and "special inspection" which contradict points of North-South Agreement and the reality of the Korean peninsula, not agreeing to an overall inspection of the U.S. nuclear weapons and bases.

As for the "inspection of military bases" proposed by the south Korean authorities, it is not a matter to be discussed within the framework of the Joint Declaration on the Denuclearization of the Korean Peninsula. It should be dealt within the discussion of disarmament at the North-South Joint Military Committee.

The south Korean authorities must quickly produce a draft agreement on the implementation of the Joint Declaration on Denuclearization as agreed upon between the north and the south and respond to the adoption of the rules of inter-Korean inspection so that an overall inspection of the U.S. nuclear weapons and nuclear bases may be made.

We will make every possible efforts in the future, too, to adopt at the North-South Joint Nuclear Control Committee documents necessary for verifying the denuclearization of the Korean peninsula and to realize north-south inspection at an early date.

0082

관리 번호	92-520

— 북한 보고서의 false part 시정 요시(?)

외 무 부

종 별 :

번 호 : UNW-2223 일 시 : 92 0817 2030

수 신 : 장관(연일,정안,미이,정특,기정)

발 신 : 주 유엔 대사

제 목 : 총회 결의 이행 (북한의 1위 문서)

연 : 주국련 20312-(1)273 (92.3.6), (2) 780 (7.16)

1. 연호 사무국측의 총회결의이행 보고서제출 요청에 따라 북한이 5.25 및 5.19 자로 각각 제출한 "지역차원의 재래식군축"결정 (46/412) 및 "군축주간"결의(44/119 G) 이행 보고가 총회문서 A/47/316 (7.28 자) 및 A/47/321 (7.30 자) 로 작성되어, 금일 배포된바, 별첨 FAX 송부함.

2. "재래식 군축" 관련 보고 부분중 특기사항은 아래와 같음.

포괄적 한반도 군축방안 기제시 및 일방적 감군조치 실시

남북한간 기본합의서 및 한반도 비핵화선언 발효

이에따라 군사공동위에서 "대량파괴무기" 제거를 포함한 군축문제를 협의중이며, 핵통제 공동위에서는 "북한핵시설과 주한 미군 핵무기"의 동시사찰 문제를 협의중임.

상기 2 개 공동위가 성공적으로 운영될 경우, "한반도의 비핵지대화" 및 재래식 무기 군축에 기여할것임.

역내 핵무기 배치국가들은 비핵국가 및 "비핵지대"에 대한 핵무기 사용 및 위협 금지

대규모 군사행동 자제 요망3. 상기 "재래식 군축" 결정 이행 보고서 제출국가는 현재 북한, 핀랜드 2 개국뿐이며, "군축주간" 결의의 경우 북한. 백러시아. 우크라이나. 몽고등 4 개국만이 의견서를 제출한 것으로 되어 있음.

4. 북한측이 원용한 상기 총회 결의 및 결정이 군축분야의 실질 의제에 관한것이 아니고 이에대해 회신하는 국가도 거의없을뿐만 아니라, 특히 "재래식 군축" 결정의 경우 핵무기등 대량 파괴무기 감축문제와 관련된 것이 아님에도 불구하고 북측으로서는 군축관련 결의 이행 보고를 최대한 활용, 한반도 군축문제 (핵문제

국기국 장관 차관 1차보 미주국 외정실 외정실 분석관 청와대
안기부

PAGE 1

92.08.18 13:23

외신 2과 통제관 BX

0083

포함)에 관한 입장을 선전코자하는 것으로 보임

(대사 유종하 - 국장)

예고:92.12.31 까지 예고문에 의거 일반문서로 재분류됨

첨부:UNW(F)-0674

PAGE 2

0084

AUG 17 '92 18:56 KOREAN MISSION P.1

UNITED NATIONS

General Assembly

Distr.
GENERAL

A/47/316
28 July 1992

ORIGINAL: ENGLISH

Forty-seventh session
Item 61 (m) of the provisional agenda*

GENERAL AND COMPLETE DISARMAMENT

Conventional disarmament on a regional scale

Report of the Secretary-General

CONTENTS

* A/47/150.

92-34605 3330f (E) 110892 140892

/...

0085

I. INTRODUCTION

1. On 6 December 1991, the General Assembly adpted decision 46/412, entitled "Conventional disarmament on a regional scale", in which the Assembly decided (a) to welcome the report of the Secretary-General on this question (A/46/333 and Corr.1 and Add.1); (b) to invite Member States that had not yet done so to convey to the Secretary-General their views on this matter; and (c) to include in the provisional agenda of its forty-seventh session the item entitled "Conventional disarmament on a regional scale".

2. Pursuant to paragraph (b) of the decision, the Secretary-General, in a note verbale dated 26 February 1992, requested all Member States to communicate to him their views on this matter. To date, the Secretary-General has recieved replies from the Democratic People's Republic of Korea and Finland. Other replies will be issued as addenda to the present report.

II. REPLIES RECEIVED FROM GOVERNMENTS

DEMOCRATIC PEOPLE'S REPUBLIC OF KOREA

[Original: English]

[25 May 1992]

1. The Government of the Democratic People's Republic of Korea, which regards independence, peace and friendship as the basic idea of its foreign policy, attaches a particular importance to the disarmament issue.

2. The achievement of disarmament is conducive to easing tension and ensuring peace and security. It is, accordingly, important to implement conventional disarmament along with nuclear disarmament at the regional and global level.

3. The Government of the Democratic People's Republic of Korea, with a view to removing the danger of war and ensuring peace on the Korean peninsula, put forward a comprehensive disarmament proposal, the main contents of which are confidence-building between the north and south, reduction of armed forces of the north and south, conversion of the Korean peninsula into a nuclear-free zone and withdrawal of foreign forces from the peninsula.

4. It took unilateral measures of reducing its 100,000 armed forces and mobilizing more than 150,000 forces in the peaceful socialist construction as part of its efforts to create favourable circumstances for disarmament in the Korean peninsula.

5. The Agreement on the Reconciliation, Non-aggression and Cooperation and Exchange between the North and South and the Joint Declaration on Denuclearization of the Korean Peninsula were adopted on 13 December 1991 and 20 January 1992, respectively, and both became effective on 19 February 1992.

/...

674-5-2

0086

6. The North-South Military Joint Committee was formed under the above north-south agreement and this Committee is now discussing disarmament issues, including the removal of weapons of mass destruction and the elimination of their offensive capacity, and practical verification measures to be followed.

7. The North-South Joint Nuclear Control Committee was organized following the Joint Declaration on Denuclearization of the Korean Peninsula, and this Committee is also now discussing the issue of simultaneous inspection of nuclear facilities in the north and the United States nuclear weapons and bases in the south.

8. The North-South Military Joint Committee and the North-South Joint Nuclear Control Committee, if they proceed successfully, will make it possible for the Korean peninsula to turn into a nuclear-free zone and promote the conventional disarmament on the Korean peninsula, which will contribute to peace and security in the Asia-Pacific region and the rest of the world.

9. In order to ensure peace and security in the Asia-Pacific region, nuclear and conventional disarmament should be achieved in the region.

10. States that have deployed nuclear weapons and maintained large-scale military armaments in this region should take the lead in the disarmament process by agreeing to the following points:

(a) A guarantee should be given that they will not use or threaten to use nuclear weapons against the non-nuclear weapon States and nuclear-free zones;

(b) Nuclear weapons deployed on the land and sea of this region should be withdrawn to their own territories;

(c) Bilateral military treaties concluded with the States in this region should be abolished, their troops stationed in the region should be pulled out and their military bases dismantled.

11. The States in the region should take unilateral, bilateral and regional disarmament measures according to their own specific conditions and characteristics:

(a) Bilateral or regional disarmament agreements should be reached and implemented in good faith;

(b) Large-scale military manoeuvres that may endanger other States or regions should be refrained from;

(c) Any arms build-up or arms race should be stopped.

/...

674-5-3

0087

UNITED NATIONS

General Assembly

Distr.
GENERAL

A/47/321
30 July 1992
ENGLISH
ORIGINAL: ENGLISH/RUSSIAN

Forty-seventh session
Item 63 (f) of the provisional agenda*

REVIEW OF THE IMPLEMENTATION OF THE RECOMMENDATIONS AND DECISIONS ADOPTED BY THE GENERAL ASSEMBLY AT ITS TENTH SPECIAL SESSION

Disarmament Week

Report of the Secretary-General

CONTENTS

---

* A/47/150.

92-35181 3623b (E) 130892 140892 /...

674-5-4

0088

16. Links with peace organizations in the United States of America were actively developed, that exchange of delegations, citizens and school children, residence by children in families in the other country and exchange of exhibitions of children's drawings. The traditionally strong links with proponents of peace in the United Kingdom of Great Britain and Northern Ireland continued, through an exchange of delegations, meetings with health-care experts, public education, ecology, and joint seminars of school children. On the initiative of the Minsk Committee for the Defence of Peace, the Byelorussian yacht Samanta sailed to the United Kingdom with a message to the English proponents of peace.

17. Contacts were developed with other countries (the German Democratic Republic, Bulgaria, Czechoslovakia, Poland and Japan), and steps were taken to establish new contacts with peace activists in Australia, Brazil, Argentina and Spain.

18. Republic and local information media gave regular broad coverage to public peace activities.

DEMOCRATIC PEOPLE'S REPUBLIC OF KOREA

[Original: English]

[19 May 1992]

On the occasion of Disarmament Week 1991, the following activities were organized at the national level:

(a) During the observance of Disarmament Week, the newspapers Rodong Sinmun, organ of the Central Committee of the Workers' Party of Korea, and Minju Choson, organ of the Government of the Democratic People's Republic of Korea, and other newspapers, including The Pyongyang Times, published a series of articles and commentaries regarding disarmament matters;

(b) Radio and television broadcasts were devoted to giving information about the situation and prospects of international disarmament efforts and explaining the disarmament proposals for peace on the Korean peninsula;

(c) On the occasion of Disarmament Week, the Institute for Disarmament and Peace organized a series of lectures under the titles of "Confidence-building between the North and the South and its contribution to the peace and security of the Asia-Pacific region" and "Denuclearization of the Korean peninsula", in which the following topics were discussed:

(i) Arms reduction in the North and the South;

(ii) Withdrawal of foreign forces;

(iii) Conversion of the Korean peninsula into a nuclear-free zone;

(iv) Verification through mutual inspections.

/...

614-5-5

67

연합 H1-061 S06 외신(567)

"유엔 안보리 불시핵사찰 결의해야"

핵 전문가, "북한 핵물질 은닉 가능성"

(워싱턴=聯合) 박정찬특파원=북한은 핵시설과 관련,기만적인 신고를 하고 무기급 핵연료를 은닉했을 가능성이 있으며 북한을 비롯한 일부국가의 핵개발을 저지하기 위해서는 유엔 安保理의 결의를 통해 불시사찰을 실시해야 한다고 레너드 스펙터 美카네기재단 수석연구원이 2일 주장했다.

스펙터 연구원은 이날 발매된 외교전문잡지 "포린 폴리시(외교정책)" 가을호에 실린 "회개하는 핵 개발국가"라는 제목의 기고문에서 남북한이 한반도 비핵화 선언을 통해 우라늄 농축및 플루토늄 분리 공장을 건설하지 않겠다는 약속을 했지만 북한은 이미 무기급핵연료를 은닉했을 가능성이 있다고 말했다.

핵 전문가인 스펙터 연구원은 아르헨티나와 브라질, 남북한이 핵 시설 건설을 포기하는 선언을 했지만 특히 북한은 국제원자력기구(IAEA)에 대한 핵시설 기만 신고를 하고 이미 무기급 핵연료를 은닉했을 가능성이 있다고 지적했다.

그는 북한등 핵개발국가의 노력을 억제하기 위해서는 이들 국가들의 약속을 검증하기가 어렵기 때문에 유엔 安保理가 일정한 횟수의 무조건, 불시, 강제사찰을 받도록 결의할 것을 주장했다.

그는 이같은 결의가 있을 경우 IAEA는 이라크에 대한 핵사찰을 실시한 근거규정이 된 제687호 결의의 경우처럼 안보리를 대신해 사찰을 실시할수 있을 것이라고 덧붙였다.(끝)

1

0090

서울신문

1992. 9. 13. 日, 2면

北, 韓·美에 군사훈련 중지 토록

【유엔본부聯合】北韓은 최근 韓美 양국에 美軍의 鎭海 해군기지 사용과 南韓내 모든 군사 훈련 중지를 촉구했다고 허종 駐유엔 北韓 차석대사가 11일 밝혔다.

北韓은 이와 함께 패트리어트 미사일의 對韓 판매 재고와 韓國내 모든 군사 기지를 포기하도록 美國에 촉구했다고 허 차석대사는 덧붙였다.

그는 이어 北韓의 이같은 요구가 받아들여지지 않을 경우 南北 대화가 타격받을 수 있음을 경고했다.

0091

韓國日報
1992. 9. 13. 日, 2면

"美, 남한에 核반입"

南北총리회담 霧散가능성

北韓 許鍾 UN대사

【東京AP聯合=特約】 북한의 許鍾 유엔대사는 12일 미국이 핵잠수함을 통해 수시로 남한내에 핵무기를 반입하고 있다고 비난하고 이를 중단하지 않을경우 오는 15일부터 예정된 제8차 남북총리회담이 무산될 가능성이 있다고 말한것으로 중국의 관영 신화통신이 보도했다.

이에앞서 북한反핵평화위원회는 이날상오 美해군잠수함들이 한국鎭海港口를통해 핵무기및 핵물질을 운반·반입함으로써 한반도非핵화선언을 스스로 위반 했다는 긴급 성명을 발표 했다고 북한관영 중앙통신이 밝혔다.

신화통신에 따르면 許대사는 이날 美뉴욕 유엔본부에서 가진 인터뷰에서 미국이 한반도에 핵무기를 들여와 극도의 긴장상태를 초래하고 있다고 밝히고 이러한 북한에대한 적대행위가 중지되지 않을 경우 평양에서 개최예정인 제8차 남북고위급회담은 무산될 지도 모른다고 언급했다.

0092

國民日報
1992. 9. 14. 月, 2면

美핵잠수함 鎭海기항
北, 총리회담지장경고

【東京·유엔본부=AP新華聯】北韓은 12일 한국의 비핵화 선언에도 불구, 核무기를 적재한 美잠수함들이 진해에 있는 美잠수함기지를 자주 들락거리고 있다고 비난하고 기지폐쇄가 이루어지지 않을 경우 남북대화에 지장을 초래하게 될 것이라고 경고했다.

북한 반핵평화위원회는 지난해 12월 盧泰愚대통령의 核부재선언에도 불구, 美核潛艦들이 진해기지에 정례적으로 기항하고 있다고 주장, 「한국과 미국 당국은 때늦은 감이 있지만 이같은 사실을 시인하고 범죄적 핵전준비행위를 중단하라」고 촉구했다고 조선중앙통신이 보도했다.

이와관련, 許鍾 유엔주재 북한 차석대사는 중국 신화통신과의 회견에서 韓·美양국에 대해 진해 美잠수함기지 사용및 군사훈련 전면중지를 강력히 촉구하고 이를 중단하지 않을 경우 15일로 예정된 제8차 남북총리회담이 곤경에 빠지게 될 것이라고 경고했다.

0093

朝鮮日報

1992. 9. 14. 月, 1면

北韓, 총리회담 무산경고

韓-美훈련 중단-진해潛艦기지 폐쇄 요구

【東京=宋熙永기자】 북한 反核평화위원회는 美잠수함들이 한반도의 비핵화 약속을위반한채 한국에 핵무기를 정기적으로 반입하고 있다고 비난했다고 북한관영 중앙통신이 12일 보도했다.

동경에서 수신된 중앙통신은 美잠수함들이 鎭海잠수함기지에 자주 기항하고 있다면서 북한 反核평화위원회가 미국과 한국당국은 핵잠수함의 진해기지 기항과 범죄적인 핵전쟁 준비행위를 시인할것을 촉구했다고 보도했다.

중앙통신은 그러나 비핵평화위원회라는 이색단체의 성격을 밝히지 않았다.

한편 許종 유엔주재 북한 대사는 美잠수함기지가 폐쇄되지 않고 韓-美군사훈련이 중단되지 않으면 다음주 열릴 남-북총리회담 개최가 위태롭게 될것이라고 경고했다고 중국 新華통신이 뉴욕발로 보도했다.

0094

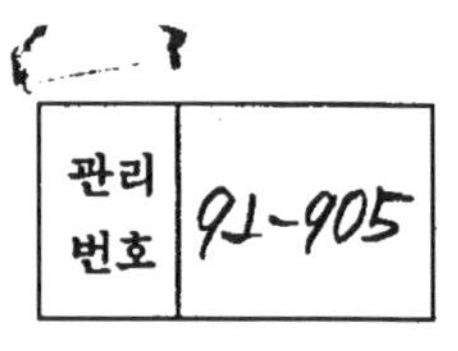

외 무 부

종 별 :

번 호 : UNW-2527 일 시 : 92 0914 1920

수 신 : 장관(해신,정특,연일,기정)

발 신 : 주 유엔 대사

제 목 : 북한 차석대사 인터뷰

1.진해항이 미국의 핵기지로 사용되고 있다는 북한 허종대사의 인터뷰내용에 관한 국내신문의 인용기사와 관련 동 기사의 출처인 당지 XINHUA 통신과9.14 접촉해본 결과,지난 9.11(금) 오후 동인이 XINHUA 통신 사무실로 찾아와 동사 지국장인 LIU QIZHONG 에게 인터뷰를 요청하여 이루어진 것이라고 설명했음. 2. 현재까지 북한 대표부가 인터뷰를 요청하였던 대상이 주로 구미계 통신사였던점과 지금까지 접촉이 없었던 XINHUA 통신을 통해 동 인터뷰를 했던 사실은 특기할만한 사실로서, 동 XINHUA 통신의 YANG YUEHUA 특파원등 유엔 외신기자들에의하면 한, 중 수교에 대한 역반응인것 같다고 하였음. 동 자료 별첨 송부함.

첨부:UNW(F)-0728

(대사 유종하-해공관장)

예고:92.12.31. 까지 고문에 의거 일반문서로 재분류 됨

공보처	장관	차관	1차보	국기국	외정실	분석관	청와대	안기부

0095

PAGE 1 92.09.15 09:06

* 원본수령부서 승인없이 복사 금지 외신 2과 통제관 BX

stf dpf024 9209112243 /aa (1642) nyz019 9209112243 uaa
wbny:p:n:liu qizhong:e:liu qizhong:92/09/11/22/57
060
united nations aaa0911050
eaed

dprk official urges to end operation of nuclear-sub base in south korea

united nations, september 11 (xinhua) -- a high-ranking envoy from the democratic people's republic of korea (dprk) told xinhua here today that his government strongly urged the authorities in south korea and the united states to stop the operation of the chin hae naval base and all the military exercises in south korea.

no jong, dprk ambassador to the united nations, also requested the united states to reconsider its sales of patriot missiles to south korea and give up all the military bases in the south.

otherwise, he said, the north-south dialogue may be spoiled.

at the same time, ho jong said, 'i'd like to emphasise the willingness and preparedness of my government to implement the inter-korean inspection to nuclear-related facilities on both sides of the korean peninsular as quickly as possible.'

all the suspicious nuclear-related facilities and military bases should be inspected, he said.

according to the dprk envoy, the chin hae nuclear-submarine base was finished in 1979 and has been in active operation ever since. recently, ho said, it has been called frequently by u.s. sub-marines.

'they blamed us for the delay of the mutual inspection,' ho said, 'but in fact it is they who have kept the nuclear-related naval bases intact and operated.'

so, ho said, the biggest obstacle to the mutual inspection is the position of south korea and the united states. enditem

nnnn

FROM XINHUA NYC 09/14/92 19:00 P. 1 TOTAL P. 1

028-1-1

0096

北韓,「鎭海核」쟁점 삼을듯

사실여부 확인위한 査察요구

高位級회담서 거론 시사

中央日報
1992. 9. 15. 화 2면

孫成弼駐러北韓대사

【모스크바·東京·平壤이타르타스·AFP·共同=聯】북한은 14일 한반도로부터 美핵무기가 완전히 철수했다는 한국정부의 공식발표에도 불구하고 미국이 여전히 남한지역을 核교두보로 이용하고 있다는 비난을 되풀이하면서 15일 시작되는 8차 남북고위급회담에서 이 문제를 제기할 의도가 있음을 재확인했다。

孫成弼 러시아주재 북한대사는 이날 모스크바에서 가진 뉴스 브리핑에서 한국의 월간『말』誌 9월호에 게재된 鎭海 기지에 근무한 前·現職 군무원들의 증언내용에 대해 언급, 鎭海에 美 核잠수함기지가 주둔·운영되고 있다고 주장하면서 북한측이 鎭海에 핵무기가 있는지 여부를 밝히기 위한 사찰문제를 남북고위급회담에서 제기할 것임을 시사했다。

북한 반핵평화위원회도 이날 조선중앙통신을 통해 보도된 성명을 통해 미국이 남한에 핵무기를 비축하고 있다는 사실이 관련업무를 맡고있던 군무원들의 증언에 의해 처음으로 확인됐다고 말했다。

東京에서 수신된 중앙통신은 이로써『지난해에 있었던 남한측의 核부재 선언과 남한으로부터 모든 핵무기를 철수했다는 미국대통령의 발표는 거짓이라는 것이 입증됐다』고 보도했다。

이와관련, 외교분석가들은 이같은 북한측의 일련의 입장표명으로 15일 열리는 남북고위급회담에서 성과를 거두기 어렵다는 우려를 가중시키고 있다고 말했다。

0097

진해에 핵잠수함 기지가 있다고 주장할 경우

▲ 우리측 지역에 핵잠수함 기지가 있다는 주장은 사실무근으로써 터무니없는 주장임. 귀측이 혹시 우리측에서 발행되고 있는 92년 9월호 '말'지에 게재된 기고문을 들어 그러한 터무니없는 주장을 한 것 같은데 그 기고문은 신빙성이 전혀 없는 것임.

▲ 우리는 91년 11월 8일 비핵화 선언과 12월 18일 핵부재 선언을 했는바, 우리의 관할구역안에 핵무기가 존재하지 않는다는 것을 언제라도 확인해 줄 수 있음. 우리 국방부 대변인은 9. 14자 성명에서 「대한민국 영토 내에는 하나의 핵탄두도 존재하지 않으며, 어떠한 핵잠수함 기지도 없다」고 확인한 바 있음.

▲ 귀측이 진정 의심을 가지고 있다면, 선전적 차원에서 말로만 우리측이 「공동선언」을 위반하고 있다고 주장할 것이 아니라 이를 직접 확인. 검증할 수 있는 남북상호사찰에 하루빨리 응해야 할 것임.

▲ 귀측이 가지고 있는 의심이나 우리측이 귀측에 가지고 있는 의혹을 철저히 해소시키기 위해서는, 민간.군사시설을 막론하고 「성역」없이 불시에 사찰할 수 있는 특별사찰제도가 필수적인 만큼, 특별사찰이 포함된 남북상호 사찰규정을 조속히 수락하여야 할 것임.

0098

(서울=聯合) 南北韓은 30일 판문점 중립국감독위 회의실에서 핵통제공동위 제8차회의 2차위원 접촉을 갖고 사찰규정안가운데 제2장 <사찰단의 구성.운영>에 관한 양측의 의견을 상호 제시하고 토의를 벌였다.

이날 접촉에서 남측은 사찰규정 발효후 10일 이내에 50명의 사찰관 명단을 서로 교환.유지하면서 이 가운데 20명 이내로 사찰단을 구성할 것을 제의했다.

그러나 북측은 핵무기및 핵기지에 대해서는 15명, 핵물질.핵시설에 대해서는 5명으로 각각 사찰단을 구성하되 자신들의 전면동시사찰 원칙에 입각,사찰대상 숫자만큼의 사찰단을 동시에 운영해야한다는 입장을 밝혔다.

북측은 또 사찰실시 10일전에 사찰단 명단을 교환하고 상대방이 인원교체를 요구하면 이를 받아들여야 한다는 조항도 삽입함으로써 남측이 주장하는 불시사찰 형식의 특별사찰에 대한 거부의사를 재확인했다.

북측은 사찰규정안 토의에 들어가기 앞서 盧泰愚대통령의 유엔연설,국제원자력기구(IAEA) 총회에서의 기조연설, 오는 10월7일 개최예정인 韓美연례안보협의회등을 지적, 남측이 南北韓간 문제를 국제무대로 끌고 나감으로써 핵통제공동위 회의에 난관을 조성하고 있다고 비난했다.

양측은 10월14일 제3차 위원접촉을 갖고 사찰규정토의를 재개키로 했다.(끝)

2020 ⑧ 0099

제46차 총회시 북한 핵문제 관련사항

1. 본회의 IAEA 연례보고서 (의제 14) 토의시

o 총 25개 발언국중 화란(EC), 오지리, 폴란드, 미국, 호주, 일본등 13개국이 북한의 핵 안전협정 조기서명 및 이행촉구

o 북한대표의 답변권 행사요지

- 남한내 핵무기 철수가 핵안전협정의 선결요건
- 최근 미국의 핵무기 철수발표에 주목, 남한내 핵무기 조속철수 희망

2. 제1위원회

가. 군축분야 일반토의

o 호주, 일본, 카나다, 뉴질랜드, 스웨덴등 다수국가가 북한의 핵안전협정 서명 촉구

나. 국제안보 일반토의

o 박길연 북한대사 한반도관련 발언

o 우리대표단은 발언예정이었으나, 북측 발언내용이 비교적 온건함에 따라 발언시 불필요하게 남북한 대결 자초가능성 감안 발언신청 철회

다. 남북한간 답변권 행사

o 계 기 : 남아공 핵능력 결의안 토의시 호주대표가 북한을 이유없이 거론

0100

o 북한 답변권 요지(김충국 외교부과장)

- 북한은 핵개발 하지 않으며 남한내 핵무기 때문에 한반도 긴장조성
- 북한은 하시라도 핵사찰 받을 용의가 있으나 이는 남한내 미핵무기와 동시에 해야 됨.

o 아국 답변권 요지(이량 심의관)

- 비핵화 선언요지 설명 및 북측이 핵무기 개발 또는 핵시설에 대한 국제사찰을 회피할 구실이 없어졌음을 강조

o 북한 2차 답변권 행사

- 남한측은 비핵지대화 선언거부
- 남한 대통령의 선언으로 한반도의 핵존재 공식 인정했는 바, 조속한 핵무기 철수

o 아국 2차 답변권 행사

- 북측의 근거없는 주장에 더이상 답할가치 무
- 북측 주장은 NPT 조약상의 의무 수행의사가 없음을 감추기 위한 술책

0101

r i BC-KOREA-UN 29-09 0419
BC-KOREA-UN
North Korea says Japan has no right to council seat

UNITED NATIONS, Sept 29, Reuter - North Korea's foreign minister on Tuesday appealed to the United Nations not to allow Japan to have a permanent seat on the Security Council and questioned the so-called "U.N. Command" on the Korean peninsula.

Without mentioning Japan by name, Kim Yong Nam told the General Assembly that special attention needed to be paid to the composition of the Security Council.

"We consider that a country which still fails to feel any responsibility for aggression and war crimes committed during World War Two is not qualified to become a permanent member of the Security Council, even if the number of its permanent member states is to be increased," Kim said.

Japan, one of the largest contributors to the United Nations, has been lobbying for a permanent seat and many other nations during this Assembly session called for expansion and reform of the council, dominated by World War Two victors.

North Korea has said previously that Japan should apologise and pay reparations to the government and the hundreds of Korean "comfort women" abducted by the Japanese military in World War Two.

Kim also renewed his criticism that American troops, once under a U.N. umbrella in Korea, were a legacy of the Cold War.

"It is indeed astonishing and suprising that these 'U.N. Forces' -- which do not obey the United Nations and over which the U.N. cannot exercise any authority -- still exist in this world."

Turning to agreements with South Korea, Kim advocated a unified nation "along the lines of conferation...based on one nation, one state, two systems and two governments."

Despite obstacles, he said "blood is thicker than water" and the "homogeneous nationhood of the Korean people surpasses the differences of the systems and ideas of the north and south."

He also repeated his government's contention that the deployment of U.S. nuclear weapons in south Korea needed to be included in any future agreement on denuclearising the Korean peninsula.

But he said South Korean authorities were "not in a position to exercise sovereign rights regarding the question of U.S. nuclear weapons and bases."

North and South Korea have ratified a pact banning nuclear arms but have failed to agree on a timetable for proposed mutual inspections, although they have concluded a non-agression accord and pacts on economic cooperation.

Seoul has insisted North Korea prove to the world it is not pressing ahead with weapons development.

REUTER EL GE
Reut20:16 29-09

0102

5 - 1

관리번호	92-1493

원 본

외 무 부

종 별 : 지 급

번 호 : UNW-2778 일 시 : 92 0929 1830

수 신 : 장 관(연일,정안,미일,정특,기정)사본:주미대사-직송필

발 신 : 주 유엔 대사

제 목 : 김영남 북한 외교부장의 유엔총회 기조연설

연:UNW-2758

1. 김영남 북한 외교부장은 금 9.29 오전 4 번째 연사로 등단, 약 40 분간에 걸쳐 우리말로 기조연설을 행한바 전문(영문) 별첨 FAX 송부함

2. 연설요지

(한반도 부분)

가. 최근 기본합의서 체결등으로 이제 연방제(CONFEDERATION) 통일은 단순한 가능성에서부터 현실적 목표로 다가왔으며 국제적 추세 및 한반도의 특수여건에 비추어 더이상 회피할수 없음

나. 기본합의서가 시행 과정에 많은 난관이 있으나 남북대화및 통일전망에 대해 낙관함

다. 비핵화 선언에 따른 사찰이 이루어지지 못하고 있는것은 주한 미핵무기및 기지에 대하여 남한당국이 주권을 행사하지 못하기 때문임. 남한내에 미국 핵무기가 비밀리에 저장되어 왔음을 진해 해군기지가 미군 핵잠수함기지로 사용되고 있음이 최근 밝혀진바, 이는 주한 핵무기 부재선언의 진실성을 의심스럽게함. 남한당국이 핵무기 존재도 철수도 확인하지 못하는 현실은 지극히 개탄스러움

라. 북한의 "핵개발"에 대한 의혹은 수차에 걸친 IAEA 임사사찰로 사라지고있으며, 이제 주한 핵무기 및 기지를 사찰할수 있도록 남한당국이 외세에 간섭받음이 없이 자주적인 입장을 취해야 될것임

마. 냉전이 끝나고 기본합의서에 따른 군사공동위가 발족한 이싯점에서 미국은 냉전적 사고에 근거한 "힘의 정책'을 중단하고 주한미군을 철수시켜야함

(유엔부분)

가. 일본의 핵연료과도 보유및 플루토늄의 행상운송계획 추진에 대해 우려를

국기국	장관	차관	1차보	미주국	외정실	외정실	분석관	청와대
안기부	장관중계(첨부운생략)							

PAGE 1 92.09.30 08:25

* 원본수령부서 승인없이 복사 금지 외신 2과 통제관 BX

0103

표명함

나. 핵, 생화학 무기및 기타 대량파괴 무기 폐기노력에 적극 동참예정

다. 남남협력이 강화되어야함

라. 지역분쟁의 평화적 해결이 필요하나, 국내문제에 간섭해서는 안되며, 인권문제를 정치적 압력수단으로 사용해서는 안됨

마. 유엔구조의 민주화가 필요한바, 수개국의 특권적 지위가 더이상 허용되어서는 안됨. 특히 안보리가 총회의 권능을 침해해서는 안됨

바. 일본을 지칭 2 차대전시 침략국으로서 여전히 책임을 회피하는 "한 국가"는 안보리 상임이사국 수가 증가되는 경우에도 상임이사국 자격이 없음

사. 주한 유엔사는 냉전시대의 유물인바 유엔이 불편 부당한 조치를 취하기바람

3. 분석

가. 김영남은 유엔의 주요관심사에 대하여는 거의 언급없이 전체 연설의 반이상을 한반도 문제에 할애하므로서 한반도 문제에 대한 북측입장 선전에 역점을둠

나. 연설내용은 92.9 비동맹 정상회의시 연형묵 총리연설과 작 9.28 김영남의 ASIA SOCIETY 연설내용을 상당부분 반복하고 있으며, 작년 연형묵의 총회 연설에 비하면 내용은 매우 빈약한 것으로 평가됨

다. 한반도 문제에 있어서는 연방제 통일방안을 강조하고 상호 핵사찰 지연책임을 아측(미측)에 전가하면서, 진해 핵기지 운운등 우리측의 핵정책이 대미의존적임을 부각시키는데 역점을 둠

라. 유엔문제에 있어서는 미국등 서방주도의 유엔운영이 시정되어야 함을 강력히 표명하면서, 일본의 플루토늄 구입.운송 계획과 상임이사국 진출 희망에 대한 강력한 반대의사를 공개적으로 천명한 것이 특징적임. 또한 지역 분쟁해결 내지 인권문제 차원에서의 유엔의 관여 가능성에 대한 우려를 간접적으로 표명함

마. 작년 연형묵의 기조연설에서와 마찬가지로 주한 유엔사의 해체가 유엔에서의 한반도 문제관련 우선적 현안이라고 부각시킴

PAGE 2 0104

공 란

UNW(万)-0777 20929 1830 #취부문

Democratic People's Republic of Korea
PERMANENT MISSION TO THE UNITED NATIONS
225 East 86th Street, New York, N.Y. 10028
TEL (212) 722-3536 FAX (212) 534-3612

Press Release

Please Check Against Delivery

STATEMENT

BY

HIS EXCELLENCY MR. KIM YONG NAM
VICE-PREMIER AND
MINISTER OF FOREIGN AFFAIRS
DEMOCRATIC PEOPLE'S REPUBLIC OF KOREA

AT THE 47TH SESSION OF THE
GENERAL ASSEMBLY OF THE UNITED NATIONS

SEPTEMBER 29,1992

NEW YORK

777-9-1

0106

1

Mr. President,

On behalf of the Delegation of the Democratic People's Republic of Korea, I would like to congratulate you, Mr. Stoyan Ganev, on your election to the Presidency of this General Assembly session. It is my conviction that under your able leadership this session of the General Assembly will come to a fruitful conclusion.

I would also like to take this opportunity to appreciate the efforts made by His Excellency Mr. Boutros Boutros-Ghali to discharge his heavy responsibilities as the UN Secretary-General over the past year to ensure world peace and security and strengthen the role of the United Nations in line with the changes in the international situation.

Mr. President,

The cessation of the Cold War which has persisted ever since the end of World War II has brought great changes in the recent international situation. In the vortex of such changes in the international situation, the phase of detente is also opening in the region of Northeast Asia.

The recent events taking place on the Korean peninsula are attracting world attention. Dialogue between the north and the south on many levels is underway to end the distrust and confrontation resulting from the prolonged national division. In particular, the North-South High-level Talks resulted in the adoption of the Agreement on Reconciliation, Non-aggression, Cooperation and Exchanges. This is a great victory achieved in the course of the nation-wide struggle to bring about the three principles of national reunification -- independence, peaceful reunification and great national unity -- and a new historic milestone in realizing national reunification. The North-South Agreement, along with the July 4 North-South Joint Statement, constitutes a program for national reunification that reflects the aspirations of the Korean nation for reunification and the current trends toward peace.

The north and the south have clarified in the North-South Agreement that relations between the two sides are not inter-state relations but rather the special relations formed provisionally in the process of moving toward reunification. In this Agreement, the north and the south have also pledged to recognize and respect each other's system and to refrain from interfering in each other's internal affairs.

This Agreement shows that both the north and the south want a single reunified state, not "two states," and look to achieve reunification along the lines of confederation. Reunification through confederation based on one nation, one state, two systems and two governments has become a realistic goal. It is an issue which can no longer be avoided both

7177-9-2

0107

in view of the present trend of the international situation which is moving toward rapprochement, detente, and the end of confrontation and in the light of the specific conditions on the Korean peninsula where two different ideas and systems exist.

The highlight of our proposal for reunification through confederation is that the north and south form a unified national government to be represented by the north and the south on an equal basis under which the north and the south exercise regional autonomy with equal rights and power. It will be the most peaceful and ideal method of reunification. It will form a single state by uniting the two autonomous governments, maintaining the two systems intact. And, it will be based on the principle of coexistence with neither side conquering or overpowering or being conquered or overpowered.

This proposal for confederation, acceptable to both sides during dialogue, is now turning from possibility to feasibility. The recent 8th North-South High Level Talks in Pyongyang have led to the functioning of joint committees for the implementation of the Agreement in different areas such as political, military, economic, social and cultural.

It is true that the north-south dialogue for inplementing the Agreement is confronted with a series of obstacles and difficulties because the feelings of distrust and confrontation conceived during the long period of the division still remain.

However, we are optimistic about the prospect of north-south dialogue and reunification. Blood is thicker than water. The homogeneous nationhood of the Korean people surpasses the differences of the systems and ideas of the north and south. Our people, with their strong sense of national independence, have good traditions and experiences of having achieved unity for the common cause of the nation, transcending the differences of ideas, political views and religious beliefs.

The Government of our Republic will exert all its efforts to follow through the already-begun reunification process to reach the final point of reunification by reviving such national traditions. We will also do our best to resolve the nuclear issue of the Korean peninsula at an early date in the interest of peace and reunification of Korea, as agreed upon by the north and the south in the Joint Declaration on the Denuclearization of the Korean Peninsula.

The nuclear issue on the Korean peninsula and the nuclear suspicion that remains unresolved stem from the deployment of US nuclear weapons in south Korea. Therefore, fundamental to resolving the nuclear issue on the Korean peninsula is the withdrawal of US nuclear weapons from south Korea and removal of the serious apprehension of our nation which has been under a nuclear threat during the last 30 years.

5117-9-3

0108

To this end, it is urgent to adopt an agreement and regulations of inspection under the Joint Declaration on the Denuclearization of the Korean Peninsula and to inspect the US nuclear weapons and bases in south Korea. The North-South Joint Nuclear Control Committee, although it has met several times, has not yet adopted the regulations of inspection to verify the denuclearization of the Korean peninsula nor has it carried out any inspection of the US nuclear weapons and bases in south Korea. This is due to the fact that the south Korean authorities are not in a position to exercise its sovereign right regarding the question of US nuclear weapons and bases.

This situation, we believe, has prevented the North-South Joint Nuclear Control Committee from arriving at an agreement to include the US nuclear weapons and bases in the scope of the parameters for inspection. Quite recently, it was revealed that US nuclear weapons have been stockpiled in the secret nuclear storage in south Korea and a naval base in Jinhae, south Korea, also serves as a US nuclear submarine base. This causes a great number of people to have suspicion about the sincerity of the announcement of the non-existence of US nuclear weapons in south Korea. It is most deplorable that the south Korean authorities do not have a say on the presence of nuclear weapons from other countries which are now on their own soil nor can they verify the withdrawal of these nuclear weapons.

As far as we are concerned, we have declared time and again that we have no nuclear weapons, nor intention nor capacity to make them. We have no need to produce them. It is our firm will, in line with our invariable anti-nuclear peace policy, to use nuclear energy only for peaceful purposes and not to develop nuclear weapons. The honesty of the peaceful nuclear policy of the Government of our Republic and the will for denuclearization have already been proved by several ad hoc inspections of IAEA. The so-called suspicion on our "nuclear development" is fading away. We do what we say and we never say empty words.

If the south Korean authorities are really concerned about the "future" of the Korean peninsula and interested in realizing its denuclearization, they should take an independent stand free from outside forces and respond as soon as possible to adopting the regulations of inspection, so that the overall inspection of US nuclear weapons and bases could be done as agreed upon by the north and the south.

Mr. President,

The reunification of the Korean peninsula presupposes the eradication of the legacy of the Cold War and the termination of foreign interference. The Korean question has been closely related to international relations historically.

 つかか-9-4

0109

4

The division of Korea was brought about not by the internal contradictions of our nation, but was imposed on it against its will, to serve only the interests of the foreign forces.

It is the foreign forces that impede the on-going north-south talks. Consequently, the key issue in realizing the reunification of the Korean peninsula today is to end foreign interference in the Korean question. The presence of US troops in south Korea is clear evidence of interference by a foreign force impeding the solution to the Korean question.

During the Cold War era the presence of foreign armed forces in other countries was "justified" under the pretext of preserving the so-called "balance of forces". However, this argument no longer holds today since the Cold War ended and power politics have become meaningless.

There is no justification whatsoever for the continued presence of US forces in south Korea. On the Korean peninsula, the north and the south have pledged themselves to non-aggression through the Agreement and have formed the joint military commission to deal with military affairs.

Nevertheless, the United States is still pursuing a policy of "power politics" based on the Cold War way of thinking. The United States continues to "justify" the stationing of its armed forces in south Korea with the new argument that "a power vacuum" could be created.

It is contradictory to claim, according to one's interest that on some occasion, peace has come to the world and, on other occasions to divide the world into friends and enemies, talking about "power vacuum." The United States must drop its policy of power toward the Korean peninsula and withdraw its troops from south Korea, thereby fulfilling its responsibility in helping achieve peace and the reunification of Korea.

In today's world - which stands on the crossroads of independence or domination, peace or war, cooperation or division - the peace, security and reunification of the Korean peninsula become one of the most urgent questions whose solution brooks no further delay.

The problem of Korea's reunification is a touchstone. Whether or not it is solved will clarify whether the international society is entering a stage of independent, peaceful and democratic development or still remains in the era of domination and subjugation, conflict and confrontation.

It is our hope that Korea's reunification will be realized through confederation on the basis of the three principles of independence, peaceful reunification and great national

0110

unity which the north and south have already announced with full commitment, thus showing one part of the genuine development of the international society.

Mr. President,

Humankind is now at a historical turning point for opposing domination and subjugation and building a new, free and peaceful world. Such aspirations of humankind, however, are still being gravely challenged by the old forces that pursue power politics. Despite the collapse of the Cold War structure characterized by confrontation between the superpowers, there are new open attempts to capitalize on this situation in order to establish world domination.

If such attempts were allowed to go unchecked, the world would change from the Cold-War structure of a bipolar system into the hegemonic structure of a uni-polar system, and the democratic development of the international society would suffer another setback.

Therefore, today's era can brook no further delay in establishing a new just international order to replace the old international order under which a few countries go unchallenged and freely dominate the destiny of humankind. There are big and small countries in the world, but there cannot be senior or junior countries; there are developed and less developed nations, but there cannot be dominating nations and nations destined to be dominated.

All countries and nations are entitled to independent and equal rights as equal members of the international society, regardless of the size of their territories and level of development. Neither privileges nor arbitrariness should be tolerated in international relations, and friendship and cooperation between countries should be developed positively on the principle of mutual respect, non-interference, equality and mutual benefits.

It is the expectation of the world's people that the United Nations, under the changed situation today, will play a pivotal role in securing peace and achieving the common prosperity of humankind by fulfilling its mission as the international organization to safeguard world peace and justice.

At the recent Tenth Summit Conference of Non-Aligned Countries, the Heads of State and Government were unanimous in their emphasis on the necessity of strengthening the role of the United Nations in safeguarding world peace and security and establishing an equitable international order.

0111

The United Nations should pay deep attention to effecting disarmament on the globe and dismantling the weapons of mass destruction, including nuclear weapons, in keeping with the present situation in which the cold war has come to an end.

Mankind can neither get rid of the danger of nuclear war, nor can it expect true peace, as long as the arms race continues unbridled and nuclear weapons remain. We hold that a comprehensive treaty banning nuclear tests should be concluded as soon as possible, testing and production of nuclear weapons should be stopped, and nuclear weapons should be abolished once and for all.

The prevention of the emergence of any new nuclear power is another important issue in settling the nuclear problem. In this connection, we could not but express our concern over the fact that, despite world condemnation, Japan is storing more nuclear fuel than it needs, and is even carrying out an adventurous plan involving the marine transportation of plutonium.

The Government of the Democratic People's Republic of Korea will in the future, as in the past, make positive efforts to abolish nuclear weapons, bio-chemical weapons and all other mass destruction weapons on the globe.

The United Nations should pay particular attention to the economic issue, one of the important problems in establishing a new international order at present, and endeavor to eliminate the ever-widening gap between the developed and developing countries. Peoples in many developing countries are undergoing bitter suffering from famine and disease. Anyone who feels responsibility for the survival and future of humankind will not turn aside such tragedy happening on the globe.

It is the most urgent common task of humankind at present to relieve the peoples of the developing countries from calamities of famine and disease. The developed countries should feel due responsibility for the economic poverty of the developing countries and refrain from hindering the economic development of the developing countries. In this regard, the Government of our Republic holds that dialogue between the developed and developing countries should be resumed at the earliest possible date, the present unequal international economic relations should be restructured, and constructive measures should be taken for the establishment of a new equitable international economic order.

Along with this, the developing countries should take practical measures to realize south-south cooperation, starting with the fields of food, agriculture and public health which will be indispensable in eradicating famine and disease.

0112

7

The United Nations should also continue to concentrate on the peaceful solution of regional disputes and the elimination of all kinds of interferences in internal affairs and unjust pressure. Today when the confrontational structure between the superpowers has collapsed and new many-sided international relations are emerging ethnic, national and racial contradictions which have long been obscured behind the cold war are rapidly surfacing with increasing intensity, thus triggering new regional conflicts. These constitute elements of instability which will complicate regional situations and cause serious damage to world peace and security.

Urgent measures should be taken to settle the problems of regional disputes peacefully through dialogue, negotiations and political coordination. All countries and nations are entitled to decide freely their own political and economic systems and development on the basis of respect for the principles of national sovereignty, the right to self-determination and non-interference in internal affairs.

We should not allow any attempts which could infringe upon the sovereignty of other countries, interfere in their internal affairs and impose unfair blockades and pressure. Human rights should no longer be used as leverage for political pressure and interference against the developing countries.

We take this opportunity to extend our unqualified support and solidarity for the struggle of the peoples in Asia, Africa, Latin America and the rest of the world for safeguarding national independence and sovereignty and achieving independent national development, particularly the struggle of the Cambodian people under the leadership of Prince Nordodom Sihanouk to restore peace and national unity and the status of a sovereign state; the struggle of the Palestinian and other Arab peoples for the fair solution of the Middle East question centered on the Palestinian question; the struggle of the South African people to end the policy of apartheid and attain their country's democratic development; and the struggle of the Cuban people to defend their sovereignty against all kinds of foreign pressure and interference.

The Government of our Republic recognizes that the United Nations should democratize itself as soon as possible in order to fulfil its responsibilities and roles in establishing a new international order. The United Nations should be restructured and reformed before anything else to develop international relations on a new democratic basis. The restructuring of the United Nations is indispensable as it will enable the world body to perform efficiently its main mission as an international organization safeguarding world peace and justice by dynamically coping with the changed reality and new challenges.

To this end, the United Nations should be democratized on the principle of ensuring independence, equality and justice of all member states and never tolerating privileges

077-8-8

0113

within the UN. Independence, equality and justice are, indeed, strong adhesive that enable more than a hundred countries on this planet to join in one community, the United Nations, irrespective of differences in ideologies and systems and the gap between the rich and the poor.

In order to realize the democratization of the United Nations and ensure its impartiality in line with the changing international situation at present, the privileged positions of a few countries should no longer be permitted at the United Nations. The relations among the Security Council, the General Assembly and the Secretary-General should be reorganized in favour of strengthening the United Nations. Particularly, the Security Council should not infringe on the supreme authority of the General Assembly.

In this regard, we believe that special attention should be paid to the problem of the composition of the Security Council. However, we consider that a country which still fails to feel any responsibility for aggression and war crimes committed during World War II is not qualified to become a permanent member of the Security Council, even if the number of its permanent member states is to be increased.

One of the important problems in democratizing the UN is to eliminate the leftovers of the past unequal cold war. The "UN Command", a legacy of the cold war era, still remains on the Korean peninsula at present. It is indeed astonishing and surprising that these "UN Forces" - which do not obey the United Nations and over which the UN cannot exercise any authority - still exist in this world.

The United Nations should no longer deeply disappoint the member states with the sense that its authority is applied selectively depending on what state is involved. The United Nations should live up to the expectations of the member states with its impartial and sincere image by eradicating all unjust and contradictory remnants of the cold war.

Mr. President,

Our delegation attaches great importance to the current 47th Session of the General Assembly and will make all efforts for its success. What is important in ensuring world peace and security and strengthening international cooperation is to further enhance the responsibility and role of the UN member states.

The Government of the Democratic People's Republic of Korea will actively contribute to building a prosperous, peaceful and free new world by faithfully fulfilling its obligations as one of the UN member states today, at this historic turning point in achieving a durable peace and security of the world.

Thank you.

0114

報 告 畢

報 告 事 項

1992. 9. 30.
國 際 機 構 局
國際聯合1課(34)

題 目 : 유엔總會參席 北韓代表團 動向

> 김영남 北韓 外交部長의 금차 유엔總會 基調演說(9.29) 및 아시아협회 招請 午餐演說(9.28) 要旨를 아래와 같이 報告드립니다.

1. **總會 基調演說**(9.29)

가. 韓半島問題

- o 연방제 통일은 회피할 수 없는 현실임을 강조
- o 남한당국의 미핵무기 및 군사기지에 대한 주권행사 불능과 대미 의존적 핵정책등을 거론, 상호 핵사찰 지연책임을 우리측에 전가
  - 진해 해군기지의 미핵잠수함기지화 주장
  - 수차의 IAEA 사찰로 북한의 핵개발 의혹 해소 주장
- o 남북한간 군사공동위 발족등 정세발전을 들어 주한미군 철수주장

나. 유엔關聯 問題

- o 일본의 핵연료 과다 보유 및 플루토늄 해상운송 추진에 대한 우려 표명
- o 생화학무기등 대량파괴무기 폐기 노력에 적극 동참예정
- o 유엔의 민주화 필요, 특히 안보리의 총회 권능 침해 반대
  - 일본의 안보리 상임이사국 진출 강력 반대
- o 냉전시대의 산물인 주한유엔사 해체 주장
- o 남남협력 강조 및 인권의 정치적 압력수단화 반대

안 고 제	92 . 9 . 30	담 당	과 장	심의관	국 장
		홍	김석		

0115

2. Asia Society 主催 午餐 演說(9.28)

가. 對美關係

ㅇ 냉전이 종식됨에 따라 미국 및 일본과의 관계개선은 시대적 조류

ㅇ IAEA 핵사찰 수용에도 불구, 미측은 남북 상호 핵사찰이라는 또다른 전제조건 제시

ㅇ IAEA 핵사찰로 북한내 핵개발 의혹이 해소된 반면, 남한내 핵문제 의혹 가중

- 진해 핵잠수함 기지 및 현대그룹 건설 원폭 저장소 예시

나. 聯邦制 統一 提案

ㅇ 연방제 통일방안이 가장 적절한 한반도 평화통일방안임.

ㅇ 남북 기본합의서는 남북한 공히 연방제하 단일 민족국가 수립을 염원하고 있음을 나타내는 것임.

- 남북한간 인적·물적 교류는 민족대단결 달성의 한 과정

~~3. 關聯措置~~

~~ㅇ 핵문제 및 미국 군사시설에 대한 우리의 주권문제 제기에 대한 대응문제 검토~~

4. 言論對策 : 별도조치 불요

- 끝 -

0116

報 告 畢
(signature)

報 告 事 項

1992. 9. 30.
國 際 機 構 局
國際聯合1課(34)

題 目 : 유엔總會參席 北韓代表團 動向

김영남 北韓 外交部長의 금차 유엔總會 基調演說(9.29) 및 아시아협회 招請 午餐演說(9.28) 要旨를 아래와 같이 報告드립니다.

1. **總會 基調演說**(9.29)

가. 韓半島問題

- o 연방제 통일은 회피할 수 없는 현실임을 강조
- o 남한당국의 미핵무기 및 군사기지에 대한 주권행사 불능과 대미 의존적 핵정책등을 거론, 상호 핵사찰 지연책임을 우리측에 전가
  - 진해 해군기지의 미핵잠수함기지화 주장
  - 수차의 IAEA 사찰로 북한의 핵개발 의혹 해소 주장
- o 남북한간 군사공동위 발족등 정세발전을 들어 주한미군 철수주장

나. 유엔關聯 問題

- o 일본의 핵연료 과다 보유 및 플루토늄 해상운송 추진에 대한 우려 표명
- o 생화학무기등 대량파괴무기 폐기 노력에 적극 동참예정
- o 유엔의 민주화 필요, 특히 안보리의 총회 권능 침해 반대
  - 일본의 안보리 상임이사국 진출 강력 반대
- o 냉전시대의 산물인 주한유엔사 해체 주장
- o 남남협력 강조 및 인권의 정치적 압력수단화 반대

0117

2. Asia Society 主催 午餐 演說(9.28)

가. 對美關係

ㅇ 냉전이 종식됨에 따라 미국 및 일본과의 관계개선은 시대적 조류

ㅇ IAEA 핵사찰 수용에도 불구, 미측은 남북 상호 핵사찰이라는 또다른 전제조건 제시

ㅇ IAEA 핵사찰로 북한내 핵개발 의혹이 해소된 반면, 남한내 핵문제 의혹 가중

- 진해 핵잠수함 기지 및 현대그룹 건설 원폭 저장소 예시

나. 聯邦制 統一 提案

ㅇ 연방제 통일방안이 가장 적절한 한반도 평화통일방안임.

ㅇ 남북 기본합의서는 남북한 공히 연방제하 단일 민족국가 수립을 염원하고 있음을 나타내는 것임.

- 남북한간 인적·물적 교류는 민족대단결 달성의 한 과정

3. 關聯措置

ㅇ 핵문제 및 미국 군사시설에 대한 우리의 주권문제 제기에 대해 금차 총회중 대응문제 검토

4. 言論對策 : 별도조치 불요

- 끝 -

0118

한겨레신문
1992. 10. 1. 木, 1면

"한반도 핵문제 해결 지연 남한 비자주적 입장 때문"

김영남, 유엔연설서 주장

【뉴욕=정연주 특파원】 북한의 김영남 외교부장은 29일 유엔 총회에서 행한 기조연설을 통해 "북한은 한반도의 평화와 통일을 위해 가능한 한 이른 시일 안에 한반도 핵문제를 해결하도록 최선을 다할 것"이라고 밝히고, 그러나 현재 한반도 핵문제가 제대로 풀리지 않는 이유는 "남한 정부가 핵문제와 관련하여 자주적인 권리를 행사할 수 있는 입장에 있지 않기 때문"이라고 말했다.

김영남 부장은 이날 연설의 상당부분을 한반도 핵문제에 대해 언급하면서 "한반도 핵문제 해결을 위해서는 남북 비핵화 공동선언에 명시된 협정과 규정을 채택하는 것이 시급하다"고 지적했다.

世界日報
1992. 10. 1. 木, 2면

"南北韓 효율적 査察절차 합의하면

美軍시설 사찰 허용"

美국무부 재확인

【워싱턴=金炳武특파원】 미국은 남북한이 신뢰할만하고 효율적인 핵사찰절차에 합의한다면 한국내 모든 미군시설에 대한 사찰을 허용하겠다는 점을 北韓과의 외교접촉경로는 물론 공개적으로·분명히 했다고 美국무부는 30일 재확인했다.

국무부의 한 관리는 이같이 밝히고 「미국의 방해때문에 南北韓 상호核사찰에 합의를 보지 못하고 있다」고 金永南 북한 외교부장이 29일 유엔총회에서 말한 것은 사실과 다르다고 반박했다.

이 관리는 核추진함정이 한국항구에 기항하기는 하지만 지난해 부시대통령의 선언에 따라 평화시 미국전함에 전술핵무기의 적재가 금지돼 있다고 말했다.

金永南외교부장은 워싱턴 포스트와의 회견에서 領海에 기항하는 미국전함에 核무기가 적재돼 있을 수도 있다는 점을 北韓은 특히 우려한다고 밝힌 바 있다.

金부장은 이어 워싱턴타임스와 70분에 걸친 회견을 갖고 북한의 오랜 맹방인 中國이 한국과 修交한 것이 북한에 영향을 미치지 않을 것이라고 전제, 「특별한 일」이 아니라고 애써 태연한 반응을 보였다.

金부장은 이어 北韓은 지난 1월 뉴욕에서 가진 것과 같은 수준의 고위회담을 미국에 요청했음을 확인했다. 미국은 북한이 남북한 상호核사찰에 호응하지 않고있어 이 제의를 거부해왔다.

Nuclear powered
N-Bomb loaded

0119

관리 번호	92 -1504

	분류번호	보존기간

발 신 전 보

번 호 : WUN-2751 921002 1629 WG 종별 :

WUS -4526

수 신 : 주 유엔 대사. ♣♣♣♣ (사본 : 주미대사)

발 신 : 장 관 (연일)

제 목 : 유엔총회대책 (북한 핵문제)

대 : UNW-2778, 2527

1. 대호 김영남(외교부장)의 진해 핵잠수함 기지화 주장에 대해서는 지난 9.19 핵통제 공동위 제8차 회의 1차 위원 접촉시 우리측의 아래 발언내용을 활용바람.

o 우리측 지역에 핵잠수함 기지가 있다는 주장은 사실무근으로써 터무니없는 주장임. 귀측이 혹시 우리측에서 발행되고 있는 92년 9월호 "말"지에 게재된 기고문을 들어 그러한 터무니없는 주장을 한것 같은데 그 기고문은 신빙성이 전혀 없는 것임.

o 우리는 91년 11월 8일 비핵화 선언과 12월 18일 핵부재 선언을 했는 바, 우리의 관할구역안의 핵무기가 존재하지 않는다는 것을 언제라도 확인해 줄 수 있음. 우리 국방부 대변인은 9.14자 성명에서「대한민국 영토내에는 하나의 핵탄두도 존재하지 않으며, 어떠한 핵잠수함 기지도 없다」고 확인한 바 있음.

/ 계속 /

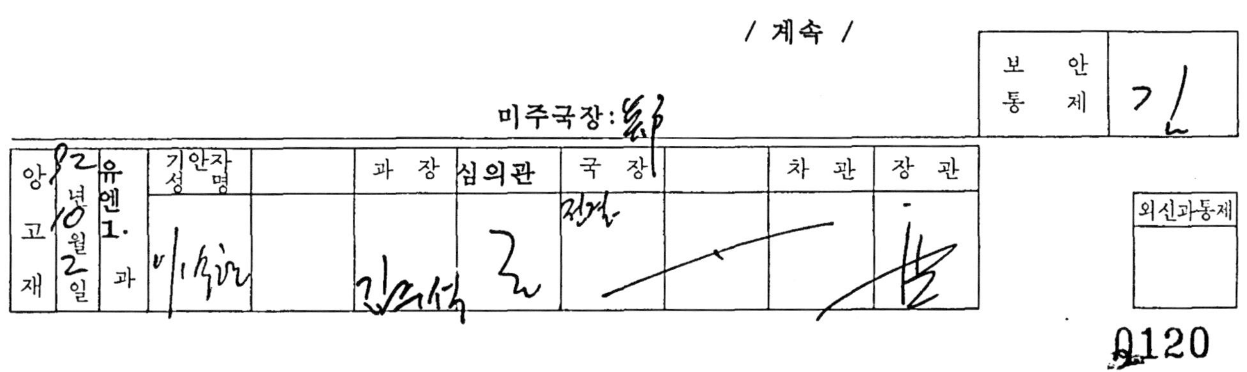

미주국장:

앙고재	92년 10월 2일	유엔1.과	기안자 성명		과 장	심의관	국 장		차 관	장 관
							전결			

보안 통제	71

외신과통제

0120

o 귀측이 진정 의심을 가지고 있다면, 선전적 차원에서 말로만 우리측이 「공동선언」을 위반하고 있다고 주장할 것이 아니라 이를 직접 확인·검증할 수 있는 남북 상호사찰에 하루빨리 응해야 할 것임.

o 귀측이 가지고 있는 의심이나 우리측이 귀측에 가지고 있는 의혹을 철저히 해소시키기 위해서는 민간·군사시설을 막론하고「성역」 없이 불시에 사찰할 수 있는 특별사찰제도가 필수적인 만큼, 특별사찰이 포함된 남북 상호사찰 규정을 조속히 수락하여야 할 것임.

2. 북한 핵문제관련 우방국 지원발언 교섭 및 미군기지 주권관련 ~~거론~~ 대응문제에 관한 우리입장은 추후 통보예정임. 끝.

(국제기구국장 김재섭)

예 고 : 1992. 12. 31에 일반문서로 재분류 됨

0121

공 란

공 란

공　　　란

공　란

공 란

공 란

공　　　란

공　　란

공　　란

공 란

EMBASSY OF THE REPUBLIC OF KOREA

Praterstrasse 31, Vienna
Austria 1020 (FAX : 2163438)

No : AVW(F) - 0274	Date : 2
To : 장 관 (연일. 국기. 미이. 중동일. 사본: 주독인대사 (FAX No :)	
Subject : 첨 부	

표지포함 2 매

Total Number of Page :

0132

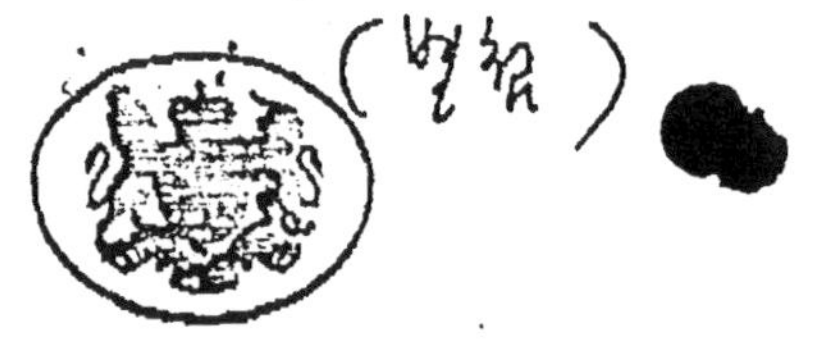

13 October 1992

HE Mr Fernando Arias-Salgado
Permanent Mission of Spain
Gonzagagasse 15/2
A-1010 Vienna

REPORT OF THE INTERNATIONAL ATOMIC ENERGY AGENCY

The Chairman of the Board, Ambassador Lamamra, circulated under copy of his letter of 9 October a "non paper" containing a draft Resolution for the UN General Assembly on the report of the International Atomic Energy Agency for 1991.

I am writing to you on behalf of the European Community and its twelve member states to inform you that this non-paper as it stands is unacceptable to us. There are two omissions in the substantive part of the draft which we would wish to see rectified before we could agree to such a text. There is no reference to the need for strengthening of safeguards, nor is there any appropriate reference to the Iraq question. In our view the following two substantive paragraphs should be added between substantive paragraphs 3 and 4 in the "non paper" presented by Ambassador Lamamra:

<u>Welcomes</u> the decisions taken by the Agency to strengthen its safeguards system;

<u>Commends</u> the Director General and his staff for their strenuous efforts in the implementation of Security Council resolutions 687, 707 and 715, in particular the detection and destruction or otherwise rendering harmless of equipment and material which could be used for nuclear weapons; and demands that Iraq immediately and fully comply with all of its obligations under its safeguards agreement with the Agency and under relevant Security Council resolutions.

G E Clark

cc: HE Mr Ramtane Lamamra
Permanent Mission of Algeria

0274-1

0133

관리번호 92-646

외 무 부

종 별 :

번 호 : AVW-1610 일 시 : 92 1016 1850

수 신 : 장 관(국기,연일,미이,중동일),사본:주유엔대사-본부중계필

발 신 : 주 오스트리아 대사

제 목 : 유엔총회 IAEA보고서 관련 결의안 동향

연:AVW-1603

1. 금 10.16 본직이 IAEA 이사회 부의장인 스페인대사로부터 파악한바에의하면 금일 오전 열린 이사회 의장단 회의에서는 알제리아 의장이 준비한 결의안 초안 (NON-PAPER)에 대형 콘센서스가 없음을 확인(WEOG 그룹의 수정안, G-77 의 콘센서스 부재등)하고 의장, 부의장국이 각각 자국의 주유엔대표부에 현상황 그대로 통보하기로하는데 그쳤다고함.

2. 이에따라 기 송부한 알제리아의 NON-PAPER 와 WEOG 그룹의 수정안및 작년 결의등을 참고로하여 관계국들간에 결의안 작성및 제출움직임이 진행될것으로보인다함. 끝

(대사 이시영-국장)

예고:1992.12.31 일반

예고문에 의거 재분류(19 . . .)
직위 성명

국기국 장관 차관 1차보 미주국 중아국 국기국 분석관 청와대
안기부 중계

0134

PAGE 1 92.10.17 08:09

* 원본수령부서 승인없이 복사 금지 외신 2과 통제관 FR

52

관리번호	92-1387

외 무 부

종 별 :

번 호 : UNW-3076 일 시 : 92 1020 2100

수 신 : 장 관 (연일,국기,정안,미이) 사본 : 주 오지리 대사

발 신 : 주 유엔 대사

제 목 : 총회 IAEA 보고서

연 : UNW-3064

대 : WUN-2991

1. IAEA 보고서 의제토의시 발언예정자 명단을 사무국으로 부터 파악한바에 의하면 금일 현재 아래 17 개국이 발언신청을 함

0 10.21(오후)

- BLIX 사무총장외에 호주, 헝가리, 중국, 오지리, 우크라이나, 파키스탄, 러시아, 불가리아, 핀랜드, 폴랜드, 영국, 벨라루스, 체코등 13 개국

0 10.22(오전)

- 나이제리아, 멕시코, 이락, 루마니아등 4 개국

2. 아국대표(주 오지리 대사)는 10.22 오전중 발언 예정(명일 신청예정)이며, 연설문안은 명일 보고예정임

(대사 유종하-국장)

예고 : 92.12.31 일반

예고문에 의거 재분류(1992.12.31)
직위 성명

국기국 장관 차관 1차보 미주국 국기국 외정실 분석관 청와대
안기부 중계

PAGE 1 92.10.21 10:29

0135

* 원본수령부서 승인없이 복사 금지 외신 2과 통제관 FS

UNW(5)-0 25 21020 2000 # 3월우울

Mr. Chairman,

On behalf of the delegation of the Republic of Korea, I would like to extend my sincere congratulations to you on your assumption of the chairmanship of this committee. We are confident that under your experienced and well-proven leadership, our deliberations will be effectively guided to their successful conclusion.

Before proceeding further, I would like to convey, on behalf of the Government and people of the Republic of Korea, my deepest condolences to the people of Egypt as they confront the aftermath of the devastating earthquake in their country. We earnestly hope that the families directly involved in the tragedy will overcome this period of hardship, and that a full recovery will soon be realized.

Mr. Chairman,

In recent years, we have witnessed significant developments around us with positive implications for global peace and security. The end of the cold war has undoubtedly contributed to a more benign international security environment. However, problems do remain. The Gulf War and the ongoing conflict in the former Yugoslavia are testimony to the persistence of threats to peace and security in this new era. Indeed, many of the present instabilities have surfaced as the cold war's rigid balance of power has receded.

As the Secretary-General pointed out in his "Agenda for Peace" report, we have entered a time of global transition marked by uniquely contradictory trends. International security has become an increasingly complex concept which goes beyond the traditional military dimension.

While the path to a safer and more peaceful world is still long and treacherous, there is a unique opportunity for the

10-1

0136

international community to seize the momentum created by the fundamental changes of the past years.

Of course, these changes have taken place on a variety of fronts, but few areas of international relations have seen as much progress as arms control and disarmament, where significant developments have been made at the global, regional, and bilateral levels.

My delegation welcomes the series of bold initiatives, taken by the United States and Russian Federation (and the ex-Soviet Union) to reduce or dismantle their nuclear arsenals. The INF Treaty and START, and the most recent agreement by the leaders of the two countries to drastically reduce their strategic nuclear armaments, mark a crucial turning point in the history of disarmament. Although we recognize the enormous difficulty in implementing such agreements, we wholeheartedly encourage both parties to persist in their welcomed "disarmament race".

Mr. Chairman,

Despite these achievements in nuclear arms control and disarmament, proliferation of weapons of mass destruction continues to be a serious threat to international security. The diffusion of nuclear and chemical weapons capability, as well as that of sophisticated missile technologies which will further facilitate weapons delivery, are truly disturbing trends which cause great concern to the international community as a whole.

In this connection, we fully endorse the statement made by the Security Council at the Summit meeting in January, which underlined the urgent need for all Member States to prevent the proliferation of weapons of mass destruction.

Under such circumstances, we cannot overemphasize the role of the nuclear non-proliferation regime, founded upon the nuclear Non-Proliferation Treaty (NPT) and the IAEA safeguards system. The NPT has significantly contributed to slowing the diffusion of nuclear capability over the past two decades, and thus warrants our full support for its extension beyond 1995. The recent accession to the Treaty of China and France, which will be followed by Ukraine, Belarus, and Kazakhstan, brings us one step closer to the goal of universal adherence to the NPT. By bringing all five declared nuclear powers into the NPT framework, the accession of China and France will contribute to accelerating nuclear disarmament and strengthening the global commitment to non-proliferation. We invite states which have yet to join the NPT to do so as soon as possible.

The other pillar that has supported the non-proliferation regime is the safeguards system of the International Atomic Energy Agency (IAEA). With only $70 million and 200 inspectors, the IAEA is charged with the inspection of approximately 1000 nuclear facilities worldwide, including the daunting responsibilities set down in Security Council Resolution 687 and other related resolutions.

Given the importance of the mandate of the IAEA and the limited resources at its disposal, my delegation believes it would be expedient to develop a more effective inspections system.

In this light, my government welcomes the Agency's recent reaffirmation of its right to undertake special inspections. One further way to bolster the IAEA's important role is for the Security Council to provide its backing. In this regard, we commend the Security Council for its decision to "take appropriate measures in the case of any violations notified to it by the IAEA" at the summit meeting last January. We look forward to seeing the Security Council play a more active part in this area in the future.

Another way to realize a more efficient inspection regime is to promote bilateral and regional arrangements with inspection-related objectives. The inspections regime envisioned by the Republic of Korea and the Democratic People's Republic of Korea in the Joint Declaration on the Denuclearization of the Korean Peninsula and the recent full-scope safeguards agreement between Brazil and Argentina, are good examples. In view of the importance of non-proliferation, my delegation supports the proposal made by Sweden at the UN Disarmament Commission this year that this issue be included as a new agenda item of the Commission for next year.

Mr. Chairman,

During the past few years, the world has seen a gradual reduction in the number of nuclear tests around the world. My delegation welcomes the announcement by Russia and France to temporarily suspend nuclear testing, as well as the decision by the United States to introduce a nine-month moratorium on nuclear testing. We sincerely hope that these positive developments will not only strengthen the non-proliferation regime, but will lead, on a step-by-step basis, to the ultimate realization of a comprehensive test ban.

We also hope to see the reestablishment of the Ad Hoc Committee on a Nuclear Test Ban, with a clear mandate agreeable to all States. In this regard, the Conference on Disarmament will have an important part in encouraging productive discussion of this issue in 1993.

Mr. Chairman,

The successful conclusion of the Convention on Chemical Weapons at the Conference on Disarmament represents a milestone in the global effort to eliminate weapons of mass destruction. It is all-the-more meaningful because it aims for a global, comprehensive, verifiable and non-discriminatory regime prohibiting a whole category of weapons of mass destruction. As a country with a sizable chemical industry, the Republic of Korea renews its pledge to become an original signatory of the Convention and wishes to actively participate in the process involving the Preparatory Commission.

My government's commitment in this regard has been evident in its repeated rejection of chemical weapons on the Korean peninsula. This firm policy was explicitly stated in the Presidential Declaration on policies concerning nuclear, chemical, and biological weapons.

My delegation, however, hopes that remaining concerns regarding a possibly negative impact on civilian chemical industries will be duly addressed during the implementation of the Convention.

As one of the co-sponsors of Draft Resolution L.1, we earnestly hope that this draft resolution will be adopted by consensus and that the Convention will be signed and ratified by all UN Member States, including those in our region.

Mr. Chairman,

Last year's General Assembly session took an important step forward in its promotion of transparency in military matters, adopting Resolution 46/36L on "Transparency in Armaments". We note with great satisfaction that the UN Register on Conventional Arms has now been established and that the Panel of Government Experts has produced a "consensus report", containing a standardized reporting form and some adjustments to the annex. The Register, if properly operated can prevent or reduce destabilizing arms transfers, thereby contributing greatly to confidence building throughout the world. As Ambassador Wagenmakers of the Netherlands rightly pointed out in his introduction of the consensus report on the Register of Conventional Arms, adequate developments of the Register and related efforts can only proceed successfully with the widest possible participation of States.

On the part of my government, we fully endorse the consensus report of the panel and will actively participate in the operation of the Register. We hope to see other aspects of Resolution 46/36L duly addressed at the 1993 Conference on Disarmament. Building on the experience of operating the register, the 1994 government expert group will also have ample opportunity to further elaborate on the details of the Resolution.

My delegation also welcomes the adoption through consensus of the Guidelines and Recommendations for Objective Information on Military Matters at the last session of the UNDC. Together with the existing CBM Guidelines adopted by the UNDC in 1988 and UN standardized system of reporting on military expenditures much earlier, the recent two achievements in military transparency underscore the increasing role of the UN in this area.

In this connection, my delegation would like to call attention to the annual White Paper on National Defense, which my Government has issued on an annual basis since 1988. The White Paper outlines in detail the budget, procurement policies, and capabilities in both material and personnel of my country's defense structure.

Mr. Chairman,

As bipolar confrontation at the global level recedes, growing attention is being focused on regional approaches to security and disarmament, especially in view of significant progress made in Europe. In this regard, we are pleased to note that emphasis is being placed on regional confidence-building measures, military and non-military, and on the importance of specific conditions and characteristics of the region in discussing regional approaches. This trend is evident in relevant resolutions of the General Assembly on this matter.

The emphasis on regional CBMs is particularly timely and warranted in the Asia-Pacific region, in view of its divergent security interests and diverse membership. Comprehensive and peaceful settlement of regional conflicts and disputes also constitute one essential element in the promotion of regional security and stability.

In this regard, it is encouraging to note that ASEAN and its dialogue partners, including my own country, have carefully initiated regional security dialogue on matters of common concern. Such dialogue will become increasingly necessary in the future. During the recent ASEAN post-Ministerial Conference, my foreign minister stated that "as regional exchanges intensify and become complex, the need for regional security consultations can no longer be neglected. We believe that it is time to study ways to develop security dialogue for the Asia-Pacific region as a measure to enhance confidence and dissipate possible tensions."

In the highly sensitive region of Northeast Asia, which has seen five major wars in the past century, an appropriate channel of dialogue and cooperation among the regional states is still lacking. Indeed, in Northeast Asia as well as others, such enhanced collaboration cannot be overemphasized as a means to cope with the various issues arising in the wake of the cold war. It is against this background that my President proposed, in his recent address before the General Assembly, a dialogue among all concerned parties in Northeast Asia to address issues of common concern.

0142

Mr. Chairman,

Since we met last year, South and North Korea have reached two important agreements which we hope will prove to be a break-through in their long-standing confrontation. Indeed, the "Agreement on Reconciliation, Non-Aggression, and Exchanges and Cooperation" commonly referred to as the "Basic Agreement" and the "Joint Declaration on the Denuclearization of the Korean Peninsula", have laid the foundation for future progress since their entry into force this past February.

The Basic Agreement governs a broad range of matters concerning inter-Korean relations, including confidence-building and arms-control measures. Under the agreement, a Joint Military Commission was set up to discuss ways and means to ease military tension and enhance security on the Korean peninsula. Both sides have been discussing operational details, but without meaningful progress so far. Thus, we will continue to make every effort to resolve our differences with patience.

The Joint Declaration follows President Roh's "Special Announcement of a Nuclear-free Korean Peninsula" of last December and its "Non-Nuclear Korean Peninsula Peace Initiative" of the preceding month. The Joint Declaration commits the two parts of Korea not to test, manufacture, produce, receive, possess, store, deploy, or use nuclear weapons. It also includes pledges of both parties to forego nuclear reprocessing and uranium-enrichment facilities which are not specifically prohibited under existing international law. The Republic of Korea is poor in natural energy resources and thus relies on nuclear power for over 50% of its electricity. Despite the vital importance of nuclear energy, to which nuclear fuel reprocessing and enrichment facilities contribute enormously, my government has waived our rights to such facilities for the broader aim of denuclearizing the Korean peninsula.

To verify Korean denuclearization, the South and the North agreed to conduct mutual inspections of nuclear facilities. As we witnessed in the case of Iraq, IAEA inspections alone cannot fully ensure that States determined to develop nuclear weapons will be prevented from doing so. For this reason, my government attaches great importance to a comprehensive and intrusive inspection regime between the two Koreas. It is our firm belief that allowing for special exceptions or sanctuaries would detract from the comprehensive nature of the mutual inspections. Therefore, we are of the view that both civilian facilities and military bases must be submitted to mutual inspections under the principle of reciprocity and subject to challenge inspections. Unfortunately however, North Korea is not fully receptive to our proposals on reciprocity and challenge inspections, thus impeding an early agreement on an inspections regime.

Whereas North Korea's submission of its nuclear facilities to IAEA inspection is welcomed, it is also a legal obligation explicitly demanded of all states parties to the international agreement, namely the NPT and the IAEA Safeguards Agreement. We wish to make clear that ongoing IAEA inspections do not exempt North Korea from cooperating with the South on the issue of mutual inspections, which is an obligation explicitly demanded of both parties in the Joint Declaration, a bilateral agreement.

With particular regard to inspections of US military facilities in the South, both my government and the US government have made clear on many occasions, that our proposal for challenge inspections includes all military bases in the South, including both South Korean and American, as part of a South-North agreement. Last year, my government announced that there were no nuclear weapons whatsoever, anywhere in the Republic of Korea. If North Korea harbours any doubts, the best way to resolve the issue would be to establish, without delay, a comprehensive and intrusive inspection regime which would include challenge inspections.

9 0144

Once IAEA and bilateral inspections have been fully implemented thereby dispelling any lingering doubts, a firm foundation for greater CBMs on the Korean peninsula will have been laid, and an important precedent for other regions under similar circumstances will have been set.

Mr. Chairman,

Building on many developments which have taken place around the world over the last few years, we must now carry the momentum forward to peace, security, and prosperity for all of mankind through not only arms control and disarmament, but also through preventive diplomacy, peace-making and peace-keeping.

In this regard, each and every Member State of the United Nations is expected to play its role in ensuring that this process evolves in a smooth and comprehensive manner. The Republic of Korea stands ready to join this endeavour with patience and resolve.

Thank you.

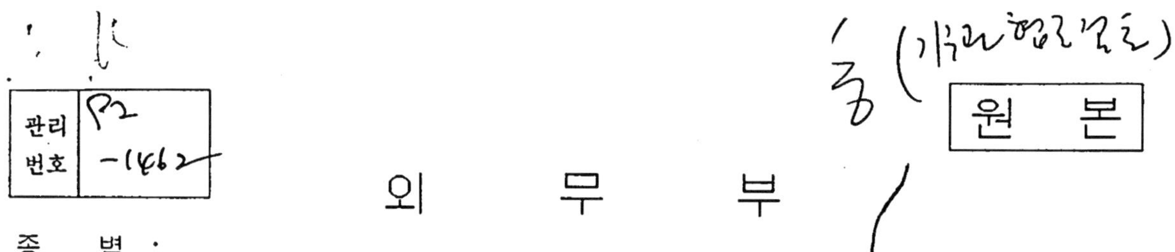

외 무 부

종 별 :

번 호 : UNW-3089 일 시 : 92 1021 2000

수 신 : 장 관(연일,국기,정안,기정) 사본:주오지리대사-중계필

발 신 : 주 유엔 대사

제 목 : 총회 IAEA 보고서 심의

연:UNW-3064

대;WUN-3036

1. 연, 주오지리 대사는 명 10.22 오후 발언 예정인바, 발언문안을 별첨 송부하오니, 본부지시 있을 경우 당지시간 명 10.22 09:00 까지 하시바람

2. 대호 지시에 따라 IAEA 보고서 관련 결의안에 공동제안국을 가담하였으며, 금일오후 현재 이락측의 수정안 제출 동향은 없으나, 서방측은 명일중 동수정안 제출 가능성을 배제하지 않고 있으며, 필요시 공동제안국 회의를 개최 예정이라고함.

3. 이란측 수정안 제출시 "NO ACTION MOTION" 계획에는 변동이 없으나, 이경우 공동 제안국 결의안을 명일중 표결에 회부할 것인지 아니면 작년과 같이 2 주정도 연기 시킬 것 인지에 관하여는 아직 방침이 확정되지 못하고 있음.

4. 대표단은 만약 이락 수정안 및 공동제안국 결의안이 명일 표결에 부쳐질 경우 공동 제안국과 공동보조를 취하고자 하니, 본부별도 의견있을 경우에는 하시바람.끝.

(대사 유종하-국장)

예고:92.12.31.일반 고문에 의거 일반문서로 재분류됨

첨부:UNW(F)-0891

국기국 중계	장관	차관	1차보	국기국	외정실	분석관	청와대	안기부

PAGE 1 0146

92.10.22 09:08

* 원본수령부서 승인없이 복사 금지

외신 2과 통제관 BS

OHW(R)-0[illegible]/ 21071 2000 # 국회보옹

(Check Against Delivery)

REMARKS

by

H.E. Mr. See-Young LEE

Ambassador and Permanent Representative

of the Republic of Korea

to IAEA and the United Nations in Vienna

on

Agenda Item 14

(Report of the IAEA)

at

the 47th Session

of the United Nations General Assembly

22 October 1992

New York

891-8-1

0147

Mr. President,

On behalf of the Government of the Republic of Korea, I would like to express my appreciation to Dr. Hans Blix, Director-General of the IAEA, for his important statement this morning introducing the 1991 Annual Report of the Agency.

My delegation would also like to congratulate the Director-General and the Secretariat of the IAEA on its 35th anniversary and commend their hard work and significant contribution in promoting the peaceful uses of nuclear energy, and in preventing its use for military purposes, for more than three decades.

We also welcome the admission of the Republics of Croatia, Slovenia and Uzbekistan into the IAEA at the 36th session of the IAEA General Conference last month.

Mr. President,

My delegation noted with satisfaction the accomplishments of the Agency over the last 12 months in both the promotional and regulatory aspects of its activities. One of the areas to which my government attaches great importance is non-proliferation of nuclear weapons and the role of the IAEA in implementing and strengthening the safeguards system.

Over the past year, significant developments have taken place in favor of non-proliferation and the strengthening of safeguards. In the non-proliferation field, the two declared nuclear weapon states have finally acceded to the NPT, a welcome and important step towards realizing a truly universal non-proliferation regime.

The newly independent states with significant nuclear activities which were part of the former Soviet Union, such as the Baltic States, Ukraine and Belarus Republics, are also expected to join the NPT as non-nuclear weapon states in the not-too-distant

991-8-2

0148

future.

The accession of more nuclear and non-nuclear states to the NPT augurs well for a successful conclusion of the Review Conference in 1995 to extend the NPT.

Furthermore, Argentina and Brazil have agreed to open up their nuclear activities to each other and to IAEA inspection. The Tlatelolco Treaty is also likely to enter into force in the near future.

Regarding South Africa, at long last, the General Conference last month decided to remove the item on South Africa's nuclear capabilities from its agenda for the next session, after examining the report of the Director-General on the result of IAEA's thorough inspection and verification of all of South Africa's nuclear installations over the last year.

The DPRK, after a delay of more than six years, finally concluded a safeguards agreement with the IAEA, which entered into force in April this year. Yet it seems still too early for the IAEA to make any judgment on the completeness and accuracy of the DPRK's initial inventory report. I shall come back to this issue later.

With respect to the strengthening of the safeguards system of the IAEA, my delegation welcomes the measures taken by the IAEA Board of Governors and endorsed later by the General Conference last month in Vienna to strengthen the safeguards system and to improve its effectiveness and cost efficiency.

We noted with particular satisfaction the reaffirmation of the Agency's existing right to undertake special inspections, which, in our view, has contributed to enhancing the Agency's capability and readiness in dealing with any clandestine nuclear activities. The endorsement of the Director-General's proposal for the earlier

SP1-8-3

0149

provision of design information was also a welcome achievement.

We also believe that the proposed system of universal reporting of exports and imports of nuclear material and sensitive equipment, which has yet to be finalized through further consultations, could contribute to increasing transparency and building confidence among states nuclear as well as non-nuclear. We encourage the Agency to soon devise new proposals accommodating the various concerns of the member states so as to enable an efficient and viable reporting regime based on the principles of non-discrimination and universality to be put into practice at an early date.

In view of the increasing requirements of the Agency's safeguards activities vis-a-vis states developing nuclear energy, and considering the Agency's continued financial difficulties, it has become all the more necessary and urgent to streamline and rationalize the safeguards system of the Agency. While fully supporting the Director-General's effort to explore desirable measures in this respect, my delegation believes that the streamlining or cost-saving measures should be considered without sacrificing the effectiveness of the safeguards system itself.

My government is willing to contribute through active participation in the process of consultation on this matter, including SAGSI.

Mr. President,

As Dr. Blix pointed out in his statement, we are moving into a post-cold war world where at long last, less resources will be used for military purposes, including nuclear arsenals - a

development that favours non-proliferation at the global level.

In this context, my delegation wishes to draw the attention of

3

811-8-4

0150

the General Assembly once again to the initiatives and commitment of the Government of the Republic of Korea with respect to non-proliferation in our part of the world.

After President Roh Tae Woo's Peace Initiative on a Non-Nuclear Korean Peninsula in November last year, the South and the North of Korea reached a historic agreement in December in the form of "The Joint Declaration on the Denuclearization of the Korean Peninsula". This inter-Korean agreement marked a first step forward in realizing non-proliferation of nuclear weapons on the peninsula and promoting a new order of peace and stability in Northeast Asia.

This encouraging development notwithstanding, suspicions and concerns surrounding North Korea's nuclear development program remain.( )

At the multilateral level, despite a visit by the Director-General to the DPRK and three IAEA inspections of North Korean nuclear installations and materials over the past five months, what has transpired so far has not provided sufficient evidence to clear suspicions about North Korea's nuclear program.

At the bilateral level, the mutual inspection regime based on the principles of reciprocity and challenge inspection was not agreed upon by the South and the North until last month at the 8th meeting of the Joint Nuclear Control Commission. Thus, the contention of the DPRK that it has neither the will nor the capability to build a nuclear weapon has yet to be verified at the multilateral and bilateral levels.

During both the Board of Governors meeting last month and the IAEA General Conference that followed, representatives of more than twenty member states expressed their serious concern over North Korea's still unverified nuclear program. They urged the DPRK

4

881-8-5

0151

authorities to continue to be cooperative with respect to IAEA inspections, and to agree to comprehensive reciprocal inspection measures with a view to implementing the North-South agreement on denuclearization as soon as possible.

In this connection, my delegation once again calls upon the DPRK to forego the construction or operation of reprocessing-related facilities in full compliance with the Joint Declaration on Denuclearization of the Korean peninsula.

Mr. President,

Allow me to turn to the question of nuclear safety and safe disposal of radioactive waste, which comprise one of the most important aspects in promoting peaceful uses of nuclear energy.

Although individual states are ultimately responsible for the safety of their nuclear facilities, international cooperation has become more important than ever in ensuring more effective and efficient nuclear safety.

While appreciating the various initiatives taken by the IAEA Secretariat in this regard, my delegation wishes to urge the Agency and the Member States currently engaged in negotiation on the draft International Convention on Nuclear Safety, to accelerate their efforts in reaching consensus on the Convention at the earliest date, and hopefully by the next session of the General Conference.

We also welcome the initiative of the Agency and the progress made thus far to work out a comprehensive series of internationally agreed Radioactive Waste Safety Standards, or RADWASS, and hope that phase I of the program will be completed by 1994 as envisaged.

In this connection, as recommended by the General Conference, all states with nuclear power development programs are called upon

891-8-6

0152

to avail themselves fully to the IAEA's services for advancing operational safety, including OSART and ASSET missions and the Incident Reporting system.

We are increasingly concerned about the safety of nuclear power reactors in Northeast Asia where the most extensive nuclear power programs are being developed and implemented. My Government has recently called upon the countries in the region to seriously consider setting up a regional cooperation program in the field of nuclear safety in close cooperation with the IAEA.

We urge the DPRK to join the RCA and other regional nuclear safety cooperation programs, and also to be receptive to the IAEA's services for upgrading the level of operational safety of its indigenously developed nuclear reactors presently operational or under construction, including such services offered by the IAEA as OSART or ASSET missions.

Mr. President,

With respect to the promotional aspect of the Agency's mandate, my delegation recognizes the recent initiatives and efforts of the IAEA and Member States in promoting the peaceful applications of nuclear science and technology for development in medicine, agriculture and industry, and in particular, in the field of food irradiation and potable water production. My delegation calls upon the Agency and other relevant specialized agencies, international organizations and NGOs to further expand joint efforts in this respect, with particular emphasis on technical assistance and cooperation to meet the growing needs of the developing world.

Mr. President,

In a constantly changing world, the IAEA and its Member States

6

0153

should be able to face the emerging needs and new challenges in promoting peaceful uses of nuclear energy.

One such need is that of controlling the growing quantity of weapons grade nuclear materials, namely plutonium and enriched uranium, separated from the nuclear cycle or recovered from dismantled nuclear weapons.

My delegation took note of the concerns expressed and the concepts put forward by the Director-General in his statement with respect to international measures to ensure the peaceful storage or use of fissionable material recovered from the dismantling of nuclear weapons or separated from spent fuel, and the role that the IAEA can play in the process.

We hope that the IAEA Secretariat would initiate in-depth studies on this important issue of growing international concern and come up with proposals and options for consideration by the IAEA and the General Assembly in the months to come.

In conclusion, my delegation wishes to reiterate the commitment of the Government of the Republic of Korea to the peaceful uses of nuclear energy and to its full support for and cooperation with the IAEA.

In this spirit, my delegation has co-sponsored the draft resolution contained in document A/47/L.9/Rev.1 and hopes that the resolution will be adopted by consensus.

Thank you.

7

0154

공 란

東亞
92.12.28.月, 1면

"상호査察 유엔에 제기"

金당선자 "내년 安保理 논의케"

金泳三대통령당선자는28일 南北韓 핵상호사찰문제와 관련,「새정부가 구성되면 이문제를 한반도주변 4强뿐만 아니라 유엔 안전보장이사회에 정식제의할 계획」이라고 밝혔다.

金당선자는 이날오전 汝矣島63빌딩에서 열린 한국기독교총연합회주최 대통령당선 축하 조찬기도회에서「남북한핵상호사찰이 이루어지지 않고서는 남북한간에 신뢰가 구축될 수 없다」면서 이같이 말했다.

金당선자는 또「금세기내에 통일을 실현시키기 위해서는 남북한간 신뢰조성이 전제돼야 한다」면서 북한이 핵상호사찰을 끝내 거부하고 있는 만큼 안보리의 힘을 통해서라도 상호사찰을 반드시 실현시켜야 한다는 게 나의 생각」이라고 덧붙였다.

0156

외교문서 비밀해제: 북한 핵 문제 10

북한 핵 문제 IAEA 핵안전조치협정 체결 6

초판인쇄 2024년 03월 15일
초판발행 2024년 03월 15일

지은이 한국학술정보(주)
펴낸이 채종준
펴낸곳 한국학술정보(주)
주 소 경기도 파주시 회동길 230(문발동)
전 화 031-908-3181(대표)
팩 스 031-908-3189
홈페이지 http://ebook.kstudy.com
E-mail 출판사업부 publish@kstudy.com
등 록 제일산-115호(2000. 6. 19)

ISBN 979-11-7217-083-7 94340
979-11-7217-073-8 94340 (set)